Back of beyond

Best wishes

Frances Brahes

Also by Frances Brand

Thorns
A study in human frailty
2018

Adam's Ark
A climate change catastrophe
2020

Back of beyond

By Frances Brand

Illustrated by Howard Waters

ISBN:978 1 9162708 4 8

Published by North Hill Publishing,
Shropshire England

Set in Times New Roman 11pt 1.2

Printed in Great Britain by Ingram Spark

The Earth is nobler
than the world
we built upon it

J B Priestly

Thistles

The kites are here often now, their high bubbling cry as they circle over the farm alerting me to their presence after waiting long years for them to cross the border into Shropshire, but when we first came here to see one was a rare event. The ravens too were absent then but they have bred and thrived each year along with the thistles which so entranced us in the glorious sunshine of a May afternoon. We lay in the grass and looked at their delicate purple heads against a deep blue sky and on that day they were beautiful. Much loved by goldfinches, their soft seeds float through the air to land and grow where they will. But back in Yorkshire Michael was scornful as we raved about the view and the magnificent thistles. He was the kind Somerset farmer who rented us land and stables but he had no time for thistles.

The pattern of the hawthorn blossom trimming the hedges is absent from the picture in my mind, it was probably too early. That was a joy to come later. Lounging on the sloping field we drank in the splendour of the landscape and fell in love with the place. A decision that was irrevocable. We had looked at it in February, in the bleak cold of winter, examining the land and the buildings, looking last of all at the house and then gone home to think about it.

We sat in the sun and drank in that view and knew we had to do it. Looking west the tall stone fingers of the Battlestones on Wilstone Hill are stark against the sky while the Wrekin looms on the eastern horizon. The panorama of hills enclosing this special little valley changes from craggy hilltops to pastures which at that season were green and thick with grass at its peak, ready for the first cut of silage. A warm May breeze was just enough to move the grass with a delicate tremor. The church tower completed the scene, prominent in a bowl of the hills — the same village which had so attracted us when we'd walked there by chance on our first visit. The lane junction still had its green triangle of grass and the sunny afternoon was tranquil, the only sound the faint drone of insects.

We found the place after two years of fruitless house hunting, one trip with my father who was to move with us. Frustration was setting in. Nothing was suitable. Usually the property had a decent house but useless land — like the single field rising nearly vertically from the back door — and most had just a small patch.

The view which sold it to us is still breathtaking, it never palls, even on a bitterly cold winter morning lugging hay to the horses, the land clad in a deep coat of snow. To the south east the sun which earlier had painted the dawn sky with scarlet hues is a watery imitation of itself struggling to probe the steel grey clouds. In the west that sky is dark, heavy with snow, presaging another fall. It could be rain but that particular ominous vaguely yellow tinge to the cloud curtain usually means snow. Snow on high ground, as the weather forecast says.

Back then we were overwhelmed by the whole idea, desperate to get it with no knowledge of any problems it might bring. The possibilities were endless for what we might make of it but for me its elevated position and that view were everything. A sensible person wouldn't buy a property just for the view but what the hell, that's what clinched it. I'd been in love with hill country since my early teens when a pony trekking trip to Dartmoor made a target for my dreams. Dartmoor, Exmoor, the Yorkshire dales and moors, all have one thing in common, high ground.

The thought of running a bed and breakfast never entered our heads, though the fact that the house was currently let as a holiday cottage should've given us a clue. The rest of the property, to me more interesting, the buildings and the land, was let to a neighbouring sheep farmer, a formidable woman who viewed our arrival with disgust.

We had no idea how much it had to offer, essentially a scruffy little hill farm for sale with only a portion of its land where over the years various families had scratched a living. Horses were what prompted the move, the search for somewhere with our own land.

Shropshire had been our choice for a three day honeymoon, a pharmacist and a journalist, an odd union but with jobs that will move because there is always a demand for locums. One thing that registered on our first visit to

Church Stretton was the two pharmacies in the main street. That a town of its size had two chemist shops told us a lot and something that ticked a box when we eventually decided to move.

Neither knew much about the county, put off by the ancient, brutal name Salop, brought back by local government change. When it reverted to Shropshire the old allure returned as somewhere that pops up in literature as a distant and desirable place, somehow unattainable, those blue remembered hills.

Having done the deal and our Yorkshire cottage sold we were homeless. Completion on the farm was put off until the autumn because the house itself was let for the summer but our cottage was gone. Beck, nicknamed for his middle name Beckett, had already sold the pharmacies in Bradford and was offered the management of the Ironbridge shop, a real tourist hotspot. That small shop was a mecca for Japanese tourists, crowding in to buy film for endless shots of the famous bridge. He sold so much film we won a posh dinner in a Fuji competition— digital cameras and smart phones were just a techie dream then.

He came south alone to lodge with our friends in Church Stretton, the riding centre owners who'd been responsible for finding the farm in the first place, pressing the rather dilatory agents to send the details to us in Yorkshire. Pat was mainly concerned with horses and not too bothered about indoors, including the mice in the larder, who one night consumed most of Beck's cornflakes. A kind woman she hosted an assorted group of horse riders, mostly singles, a sort of lonely hearts club, who came at weekends.

The horses and dogs and two newly acquired kittens, stayed with me, camping in a small cheap caravan in the paddock at Michael's. It seemed a good idea, a few sunny months, semi camping with the animals. Unfortunately it turned out to be the wettest July for years and much of my spare time was spent keeping the caravan clear of mud.

A job came up on the Shropshire Star and on interview day I had to cross the picket line of compositors protesting at the introduction of new technology. When we finally moved it was literally lock, stock and barrel. The barrels, old oil drums used for jumping practice which really should've been left behind, were stowed in our Bedford TK horsebox along with the furniture. At that point we still hadn't completed, the sale further delayed by the trust which actually owned the property and we spent several weeks in a farmer's field under Caer Caradoc. But eventually we got the okay to move the caravan into the yard and use the downstairs cloakroom.

An unusual arrangement which probably wouldn't be allowed today. But it was a glorious autumn, a true Indian summer and we were treated to spectacular sunsets each evening and a golden harvest moon rising in welcome over Wenlock Edge.

In the mornings just to wake up to that view across the valley was worth the inconvenience and discomfort. One of the loveliest things on an October morning then and now is crossing the fields with the dogs when the dew is heavy and the silver cobwebs spun across the grass glisten in the early sunlight.

The first visitor to check us out was an old tortoiseshell cat peering warily from the ugly block wall by the caravan, cautious at first about the dogs though she soon got the measure of them. She obviously liked the look of us and decided to adopt us — it was definitely that way round — making herself at home when we finally moved into the house.

We called her Fluffy for want of a better name because she was, though later we discovered her name was Chloe. She'd been living semi wild since the death of her owner who'd lived in the bungalow down the lane. His son, thinking she might be a nuisance, offered to shoot her but we assured him we were more than happy to have her around. She and the kittens got on well together.

Those three were just the first in a succession of cats who found us in one way or another. A place like this needs cats because however careful you are with feed and tidiness, mice and rats will appear sooner or later and some control is vital. Despite her considerable age she produced a litter of kittens and her son William stayed with us. He was a handsome fluffy ginger and white and proved to be a mighty warrior and star ratter like his mum. The wily old cat would wait patiently for hours watching a rat's nest in the wall, waiting to pounce and so account for the whole brood. She lived to be almost twenty-six.

We saw William one afternoon on the path in a fierce struggle with a huge rat, up on its hind legs fighting back. But the cat got the upper hand eventually. It's a shame about rats; one or two aren't a problem but you must never let them get out of hand.

One of the Yorkshire kittens, Caesar, grew up to be a dab hand with moles. He would wait beside a mole hill, listening to the subterranean movements until the little velvet creature appeared when he would pounce and despatch it with remarkable speed. He caught one which came up in the tiny space between the flag stones by the back door. Until his death he kept them more or less under control, much kinder than metal traps which are very cruel. Some seasons they seem to be scarce but in recent years they're everywhere, both in the fields and the garden and on the lane verge where as well as their hills they burrow near the surface, producing an odd quilted effect in the turf which is very difficult to mow.

Another happy portent was the early morning visits of a robin, russet breast throbbing, singing his passionate trills from a branch of the ancient hawthorn tree close to the caravan. The lusty performance was rewarded with crumbs from breakfast which became a daily ritual. Sometimes he – or maybe she – would move closer to sit on the wall by the window and one afternoon flew in through the open door, picked up some cake crumbs and left again before we needed to make the effort of catching it. Camping outside brought us close to the abundant and varied birdlife but robins have always been prominent, not afraid to get close to us. Every day one flits through the barn or perches in the hen pen waiting to share their food. It must roost in there with the poultry, along with a little brown dunnock. It's probably just fancy but it's good to think this robin may be descended from the one which first greeted us. When we began to take guests we realised how much the setting and the birds attracted people who appreciate the natural world.

On the first night we actually owned it all I stayed alone with the animals while Beck went to collect Dad. My apprehension at sleeping in a strange house was natural but the only vibes were warm and friendly. I slept in the single room, later christened Wagtail though to me it was always Dad's room.

Gradually we got to grips with the property and the responsibility of land. The farm is on a hillside with the upper land sloping down to where, in the 1840s, they dug out a flat area to build on. So everything is either uphill or down. The back field beyond the barn slopes steeply, fit only for grazing sheep. The previous owner had made it more useful by digging out a section to create a schooling area for his daughters' horses. The project was never completed but it made a good flat paddock. But on the steep bank below and much of the surrounding area the grass was submerged by a tide of weeds.

When we visited the second time the green growth of spring was just emerging and by autumn when we finally moved in the bracken was brown and beaten down by weather. It wasn't until our first summer in the high days of June and July that we were confronted by banks of bracken and other invasive weeds, strong patches of nettle and a host of thistles. Bracken climbed rampant to full height, pale green fronds reaching for the sky, decking the slope in a green forest well above head height. Sadly the beauty we'd seen in the thistles in our initial intoxication was overtaken by the necessity to make the most of the ground.

So Beck set to work to get rid of it. Strimming was pointless, if cut it would be back next year. It had to be sprayed, something which even then we disliked but it was the only option. The weapon of choice at that time was the brushwood killer Asulox, now rarely used and then only supposedly sold to farmers and other landowners.

A lingering image sees him working on the steep bank, dwarfed by bracken, spraying the waving fronds above his head with the vapour drifting over him. He should be wearing a mask and goggles, proper equipment for the job but my protestations are ignored as unnecessary in the hurry to get it done. The work went on for several sessions over the next few days till the entire slope was treated. The vegetation died back and the following spring only a few heads of bracken reappeared, to be hastily zapped. The other weeds were kept under control with cutting and less vicious chemicals but the bracken was gone. At the time we thought nothing of it but in light of future events the toxic drift may have played a sinister role.

Exploring the local pubs was fun and by the time we arrived new owners had bought the Royal Oak in the village, an interesting couple who we always thought weren't quite sure if they really wanted to be publicans. John was interested in painting and travel and always had a fixed smile with a certain grim quality about it.

We often recalled his attitude on the night of the 50th anniversary of VE Day when the pub was a heaving mass of people after the blazing beacon on the hill. It was a fight to get to the bar where he stood with his perpetual smile as if uncertain whether to be pleased with all the money he was taking or fed up with so many people needing attention.

And an amusing encounter marked our first visit to the Ragleth Inn at Little Stretton, in those days its interior still divided into various small rooms, dark and not very inviting. It was very different from the thriving place it is today, though just the same on the outside.

As we entered one of the tiny bars, an elderly couple watched with no hint of welcome or recognition, not even a nod. Presumably a farmer and his wife who had a decidedly downtrodden look as if not expecting much from life. They sat in silence, slightly apart, until eventually he got up and moved to the bar for another pint, plonking his glass down by way of request. As the publican drew his pint he nodded towards his partner with the terse words: 'Er'll 'ave 'alf.' A memorable cameo.

The yard we bought was bleak and ugly, concrete everywhere — probably acquired under the same grant which paid for the road — a row of rubble-like pigsties to one side and three 'loose boxes' which were actually three bits of block and brick sheds, badly put together and inadequate for the horses.

My gelding Byron who needed to stay fit for eventing, — another reason for the move —went into temporary livery in Church Stretton but his father Cloud Nine, who had been at stud in Yorkshire, was more tricky. In his prime and full of testosterone he needed careful handling and separate accommodation away from other horses. You couldn't stick him anywhere so the best of the boxes, though small was just about adequate as a makeshift.

But he settled in well. He was an amiable chap in himself and only difficult when his lust was roused, then every vein in his body was erect. A grey Anglo-Arab, he was a beautiful animal, born chestnut like most greys, then roan, then almost dappled for some years until as age took over he became a white horse.

The barn was a large empty space but it was fine for Beck's bay gelding Drummer when he wasn't grazing. It had a new section, good roof and sound walls but the corrugated iron roof of the old Dutch barn let in light and water through large gashes in the metal. We puzzled for years over this damage until a previous owner explained that another barn on the higher level had literally taken off one night, caught by the wind in a violent storm, most of it carried away downhill. In passing it dropped several large timbers on the lower roof.

That would've been a fearful sight. More recently Storm Arwen, blasting from the north, ripped several sheets off the lean-to, dumping them in the top field. Searching for them downhill, I was stunned to discover where they'd landed. Anyone in the path of this flying metal would be killed, riding the force of the wind it would slice off your head in passing.

By the time Cloud arrived in Shropshire he was well on the way to white. Which was what made it look so much worse when we found him one afternoon with his throat cut — or so it seemed. From just below the angle of his jaw on both sides the flesh was torn in a circular rip down his neck and across his upper chest, while below it a spreading tide of blood dripped onto his legs. We had missed a couple of rusty nails sticking out from the wood-work.

It's easy to panic in these situations but not much help. Should he be moved first or is it more important to call the vet? But he seemed calm so it was a dash inside to the phone — no mobile in a pocket then of course. He followed calmly into the barn and began munching hay, apparently unconcerned.

When Roger the vet arrived the bleeding had stopped and the blood was drying. After a cursory inspection Roger said with a smile: 'Don't worry it's not as bad as it looks, it's only skin deep.'

'Can you stitch it?' I asked.

'It doesn't need stitches, it should heal quite well; there may be a bit of scarring but probably not. We'll give him a tetanus booster but if there's any sign of infection get back to me.'

This same Roger had an earlier close encounter with Cloud's blood. We first met in the river outside the Bridges pub when we brought the horses down from Yorkshire for a few days holiday before we moved. After a stirring ride across the Mynd we called for lunch at the pub, next to the East Onny river, looking forward to the journey back by a different route.

The pub welcomed riders with tying up facilities provided. My boy being a stallion I took him across to secure him beside the river and went into the water to cool off and let him drink. As I sat on his back while he splashed in the flowing water I saw it turning red around us. He had a nasty gash on one rear fetlock — there must have been broken glass among the stones on the river bed.

The landlord called a vet and a round-faced cheerful man turned up surprisingly soon.Bending down under the horse to examine the wound he looked up and gasped: 'Christ, it's a stallion!' as he eyed Cloud's ample balls. He was gratifyingly surprised at the temperament, standing so sensibly while he was treated. Naturally when we made the move he was our first choice of veterinary surgeon and became a good friend.

It was the trip with the horses which made up our minds. Riding the Long Mynd was idyllic, the wide acres of heather moorland and grassy rides were delicious for galloping but more than the riding sensations it was the vista of valley and hills away towards the Stiperstones. On our initial visit we'd walked from Church Stretton through the Cwms, the track between Caer Caradoc and Wilstone Hill which became part of event training for Byron. That day we discovered Cardington, charmed by lunch in the pub nestled close to the church, meeting a few locals and thinking casually how lovely it would be to live there. Beck was entranced by the Malcolm Saville books as a boy, conjuring intriguing visions of the Mynd and its people and the whole county seemed almost another world.

Possibilities

The autumn was kind to us with the first Christmas to look forward to. In the line of old holly trees above the bank field several had heavy clusters of berry in early December and we anticipated the pleasure of cutting holly from our own land. Back in Yorkshire we raided the woods near Michael's farm but this would be much less effort. The weekend before the big day I went with the dogs and secateurs to collect the greenery. The bright glossy berries had mostly disappeared and we had to make do with some modest remnants clinging to the twigs. Only then did I appreciate the significance of the large flocks flying over recently, fieldfares and redwings which come south to feast on the abundance of berries in the English countryside. It doesn't take them long to strip the branches. After that lesson we collected what we wanted in early December, stored in buckets of water till needed. The birds were welcome to the rest.

From the start we were aware of a close proximity with the natural world, creatures of all kinds and the trees and hedges providing habitat and food. People often shy away from this intimacy with wild things, even a tendency to lash out and destroy, not accepting that all life has a right to exist.

We learned to be thankful for having moved in before the cold weather hit as that first winter revealed the realities of the place. Beck was busy outside in bitter, short November days laying foundations for a range of wooden stables ordered from Thrapston in Northamptonshire, flatter, milder country. Sod's law took hold, delaying the order, put off repeatedly with excuses until a date in February and by then the weather had really turned against us.

Winter here is a challenge and the early years brought a succession of bad ones. Stepping outside at dawn the harsh wind is biting but daylight often brings a period of calm before it rises again around mid morning to give the air a deeper chill. But properly clothed, with hands and ears protected, being outside can be fun as the sun glints brilliantly on the scene. The dogs love it, rolling in snow or crunching the ice from buckets or troughs with impunity. Cold air attacks the skin like knife cuts and it takes courage to remove gloves and break the ice so horses and sheep can drink. Lifting out chunks of ice is a painful business, no good leaving them to weld into a new freeze and make it harder the next time. Reluctant fingers grab a slippery edge before stinging hands are thrust into armpits to restore some feeling. The degree of cold is judged by the thickness of ice on the trough.

It's not called North Hill for nothing and when the sun is hidden by banks of dark cloud and the wind is howling round the house it's hard to venture out to tackle the chores. Facing due north the fields and garden are often snow covered while the valley is green or grey under a mere dusting. But the tops of Caradoc, Wilstone and the Lawley will be white. Often it works the other way. The village is a frost pocket, glistening in the grip of a real hoar frost, while up here the grass stays green and plants have escaped the ravages of the night.

Until we came here the impact of weather was insignificant, if you're in an office all day and it's raining outside, or snowing, it doesn't impinge on your work. But when you spend any amount of time outdoors it matters what the elements throw at you and being on a hill makes you more aware of the sky's mood and approaching storms. Often you catch moments of such beauty, maybe a new moon hanging fragile over Caradoc in the remains of the sunset, a pale sky edging towards darkness, the sky clearing after a cloud ridden day.

Up in the back field schooling Byron in the days when we were eventing a glance across the valley towards Ludlow revealed an ominous bank of dark clouds, a mass of cumulus tumbling in on each other. We carried on working till a rumble of thunder made me take more notice. The growing storm had gathered pace and was approaching rapidly. It's unwise to be caught in the open by a thunder storm so we headed down. By the time we reached the yard and the shelter of the barn the thunder had caught up and torrential rain battered the roof. The horse was remarkably calm as I sat, still mounted, shivering with the sudden cold. Around us the lightning flashed at short intervals and counting the seconds between flash and crash placed the thunder directly overhead. A loud bang announced a lightning strike on the pole by the sheep house, making me thankful we moved when we did. Lightning kills, especially in hill country.

We were still new to Shropshire when a walker died on Caer Caradoc, his upright body being the quickest route to earth.

Still waiting for our stables to arrive Beck got on with making the barn suitable to house Cloud and for stud work. In Yorkshire he attracted quite a number of mares but with our own facilities we were able to offer a better service and a safer one for handlers. Several clients who brought mares commented that the setup seemed calm and reassuring, which it was and we got good results and managed to handle difficult mares. We created sensible and nearly foolproof arrangements for handling visiting mares and foals.

That didn't stop me landing in hospital with concussion on two occasions, kicked on the head not by the stallion but by difficult mares. One evening Cloud was doing his duty and we were anxious to get the job done to watch a programme on TV about the Huddersfield paper where I'd worked. The mare lashed out and caught me on the side of the head — fortunately I was wearing a hat. Apparently we went indoors and I watched the programme but I have no recollection of anything after leaving the barn until we were nearly into Shrewsbury en route to the hospital when I asked why we were on the A49. I'd been talking gibberish for three hours which meant a night in hospital where they kept waking me up to ask my name.

A little 13 hands mare who came back to Cloud with his foal at foot was very eager and after a few minutes at the trying bar, suddenly took off and jumped into the pen with him. Another thoroughbred mare was less amenable and she was actually covered moving around the barn at a trot. But she produced a lovely filly foal which despite being only 15.2 became a frequent winner in the dressage arena.

February arrived with a definite date for the stables. We had been warned by our neighbour about the steep road — 'don't let them send an articulated lorry'. In several long conversations with the firm stressing the problem we were assured our stables would arrive on a smaller lorry. Obviously not recorded. By the delivery date the snow had set in hard, with a heavy fall the night before and winds which created drifts on the bottom bend and in the turning area. The cold was wicked. In the morning we called the firm but the lorry was loaded and scheduled for that day. Nothing we said would make them listen.   'Hope you haven't put it on an artic,' we said.

'Not sure about that but never mind, it'll be all right', said the voice on the phone.

We were anxious but relieved when the snow plough came up in late morning. Early afternoon we watched a long articulated lorry toiling up the hill. The road was still icy and we saw the wheels slipping as it got to the steep peak below the crabapple tree and stopped. The driver climbed out in his short sleeved T-shirt, shivering in the bitter air.

We had to say it. 'Didn't they tell you not to bring an artic?' He looked puzzled, shaking his head, muttering that nobody said anything about that. 'I can't get any further,' he said helplessly, eyeing the lorry with its heavy load of wooden sections.

Kind neighbour George had already arrived to see what was happening. He summed up the situation at once while we wondered what to do. 'We'll have to unload it all and lug it up here. I'll get my brother.'

His brother, a big strong chap built like an ox, pitched in and, watched by the driver, between them the three men carried each section piece by piece to be stacked against the house. Late in the afternoon the lorry was empty and ready to leave. They scattered grit under the wheels and got it moving carefully uphill to turn. The whole thing was worth recording if we'd had a mobile then. Difficult at any time for such a long vehicle the drifted snow and what had already been ploughed into a pile made the task impossible.

As the February afternoon dulled towards dusk and the temperature dropped, the driver said in near despair: 'I'll have to back down.' That meant all the way to the junction. Shivering in his thin denim jacket but armed with tea and sandwiches he put the thing into reverse and set off downhill.

It took ages, inching his way round the bends on our mile long icy road. The last bit on the level is straight and he must have drawn a sigh of relief but as the lorry backed round the junction it strained the brake lines which promptly snapped. The poor guy was almost in tears but another neighbour Geoff at the bottom house, had been watching with interest. Known locally as O-level because he thought he knew everything, he came up trumps that day, appearing from his shed flourishing the tool for the job. 'I can fix it,' he said. And he did.

It was dark before the driver eventually got away, probably vowing never to come near Shropshire again. What he said to his bosses we'll never know but they probably didn't learn from the experience.

Commercial drivers have their own agenda and tend to ignore advice, particularly from women. They may be better now but in those days they tended to assume you don't know what you're talking about. It means nothing that you know the place you live in and its issues. It almost happened again with building Red Kite Cottage and again it was February. The bulk of the building materials, blocks and all the sand and gravel for the new project had been ordered before the end of the previous year to avoid the increase in VAT.

As before the cold was intense, down to minus seven and the road still had a covering of ice, enough to make the hill a challenge, especially with a wagon. Again the turning area was blocked by piled snow. The phone rang early, Beck had already left for work in the Discovery, off to do a locum in mid-Wales. It was the driver from the builders' merchant saying he was setting off with our delivery .

Only half dressed I shouted in exasperation: 'You can't come this morning, you won't get up the hill, you'll get stuck.' As if I hadn't spoken he replied: 'It's all loaded, I've got to come now. It'll be fine, I'll be all right.' And put the phone down.

Swearing, I immediately rang the office and explained the situation. 'Don't let him come, he'll get stuck, he wouldn't listen but he won't make it.' They at least took notice and stopped him. A couple of weeks later in warmer weather he delivered the load and when it was all safely piled by the road he had the grace to say: 'I see what you mean.'

The mystery of spring creeps up almost unseen, a slight change in temperature, a flush of green on grass and hedgerow. The snowdrops have wilted but crocuses and primula are in bloom and all the approach lanes into the village are bright with crowds of Lent lilies — daffodils — planted over the years in a labour of love. They are much later here on the hill at nine hundred feet but twelve miles away in Shrewsbury they're fading before ours have broken free of the nodding buds.

Daffodils in Shropshire, like most of rural England come up each year in crowds dependent on the mind of the planter. Some like a regimented look, others prefer them scattered as nature would cast them. They come in all colours and variations, some hybrids, some more like the original wild daffy known to Wordsworth but all bring a taste of summer joy to come after long damp dark days

Pale primroses begin peering from the banks, their bright yellow centres catching the eye, less common now as the lane sides are increasingly riven away by ever bigger tractors and other machinery. Later, in summer, the purple harebells appear, always a patch of them on the dry bank beside the lane which is undisturbed. Bees love their nodding bells and the nectar keeps them going into autumn. We're thrilled to realise we have a resident pair of kestrels, most mornings one is perched on the electric wire across the field below the house. Silently it waits, watching for movement among the tussocks of long coarse grass and thistles, home for field voles, mice and shrews. Sometimes in the late afternoon towards dusk we're lucky enough to spot the ghostly shape of a barn owl quartering the land, hunting the same quarry.

But the first spring was a disappointment. The garden had been land-scaped by the Percy Thrower people who planted several unsuitable trees and a lot of shrubs but there was little to give colour in the early part of the year and no bulbs. In the autumn we put in snowdrop bulbs, indomitable little

flowers, shooting up in the depth of winter, breaking through grass or a covering of snow to bring pleasure at a gloomy time, a promise and reassurance that life goes on. The first herald of new life, we spread them widely in the border and under the hedge down the lane. Each year some are split and replanted in the green so now these un-pretentious flowers crowd together as a bright carpet of white. They're found in odd places all around the lanes.

Some are planted with purpose, others arrive by accident, perhaps in a clump of earth from somewhere; but on the steep banks near the farm at Wilstone they hang in profusion as flushes through the grass and are worth a walk just to see them.

The best thing planted by the experts was the crabapple tree in front of the house, its blossom a delicate mix of pink and white and in autumn glowing with glossy red apples. The obvious place to hang feeders it became a mecca for birds throughout the year.

The idea of bed and breakfast had been tossed around for some time, only half seriously. For a few months we had a lodger, complete with horse and dog — and a boyfriend who was butler to a duke — she needed a temporary home while a cottage was done up. It turned out to be a mixed blessing be-cause sometimes things are taken for granted. Returning from a break we were annoyed to find she'd decided to sort out the fridge, binning any cheese past its 'best before' date. A small crime since we like our cheese properly mature.

The house is a queer mixture of brick and stone, the original Shropshire 'hovel' — which is what they were called — a single storey, one width front to back built from the rubble stone available, with the cowshed at one end. An upper floor in strange thin bricks had been added during the war and the latest renovation was done to create a holiday let. That was fine for a family taking the whole place but with only one bathroom upstairs and a downstairs cloakroom, in retrospect our naivety was startling. But we did it.

The most basic lack in the place was a decent cooker, the kitchen cried out for some kind of range. Our first thought was a secondhand Rayburn but the difficulties of finding and fitting one were daunting. In the end we had a brand-new electric Aga and another lump on the mortgage. New on the market there were teething troubles but it turned out to be the best thing we ever bought, along with the press which came much later. It helped push us towards b&b, making cooking so easy, with ever-ready heat and the capacity to keep food and plates hot.

Having paying guests in your home is a strange concept, not for everyone and not worth considering in another setting. The old image, particularly at the seaside, is not appealing but the very nature of the place had so much to offer. It would probably be self regulating and unlikely to attract the sort of people we might not want. But we had a lot to learn.

Set on a hilltop, the approach is a steep concrete road with grass growing down the middle which tends to provoke comment from visitors. We are, in the words of a Shropshire councillor at the time of the water issue, 'at the back of beyond.' When the hills disappear into a winter fog it's hard for strangers to believe they exist. Hence the question posed by a disgruntled couple from the south coast in another February as they emerged from their car. Surveying the misty scene the woman asked: 'Are we anywhere near civilisation?'

Escorting them in I saw their eyes focus on a brace of pheasants hanging from a bracket on the wall and the lounge where I gave them a tray of tea and biscuits is adorned with country pictures; Victorian hunting scenes and a terrier emerging from a rabbit hole amongst others. Bad vibes. Asked about breakfast it turned out they were vegetarian, not mentioned when they booked.

They may have been house hunting and had a frustrating day or perhaps a row but while not exactly rude their attitude made it clear they were not comfortable. They drank their tea, went to the room, used two towels and then went out, supposedly to find a meal.

And that was the last we saw of them. New to the game, we didn't take cards so they hadn't paid a deposit but we were glad they didn't stay. Another lesson was the newlyweds who turned up for their first night. The bride had booked the room but it was obvious her new husband was expecting something grander so they too disappeared into the night. The girl offered a hundred pounds to compensate us but like a fool I didn't take it, concerned we might have spoiled their day. We wondered where they ended up so late in the day and if their wedding night was all it should have been. Soon after this two women who'd booked for one night arrived, looked at the rooms but made no attempt to bring in their luggage. They went off to visit Ludlow and rang later saying they were lost and weren't coming.

But what repelled the couple from the south is precisely what attracts people. As much as the landscape it's the isolation, the peace and stillness — most of the time —except when the wind thrashes the trees and rattles roof tiles or in autumn when the sheep and lambs are separated and the night air is filled with anguished bleating. Not that far from the beaten track this small valley tucked away in the hills evokes a feeling of remoteness. People from Liverpool and Birmingham seem amazed to find beautiful countryside so close, only an hour or so by car but a different world.

It began almost by default. In the early days we had a trickle of people along with friends and connections from Yorkshire who came mainly on a mates rates basis. But it was enough because father didn't have the right idea about holding back to allow guests first use of the bathroom. 'Don't worry,' he said: 'I'll make the beggers wait!' Which wasn't quite the attitude we wanted.

We tested the water with an advert in a country walking magazine — print media being the only way to advertise before the advent of the net. It taught us a lot. We also acquired a list of undesirables we wouldn't want to see again, difficult guests or those who took liberties, such as the couple who stayed a few days and set off for a long morning's hike after they'd checked out. Some time in the early afternoon we heard noises upstairs and found them using the bathroom. 'We didn't think you'd mind', was the excuse. Sighing we collected the pile of wet towels which had already been replaced ready for fresh arrivals.

Or another couple more recently staying in the cottage in wet weather who must have washed the dog in the bath which was left in a disgusting state with dog hair everywhere.

'We'll see you again,' they said. 'No you won't,' we thought.

A policeman with his wife and two young sons saw the ad and called to book, saying it sounded idyllic. They loved it and to our surprise kept coming back year after year as the boys grew up. They had the freedom to roam around the farm and the hills and play with the setters and spaniels. Their father, a National Trust volunteer, was in his element tidying up and moving fallen trees and anything else that needed doing. To him it was fun but a great help to us. Despite the shared facilities they all loved it, particularly breakfast served in the kitchen. The boys' excitement was a joy to watch one time when they arrived to find a litter of Gordon setters in a box by the Aga. The puppies were irresistible and their parents struggled to drag them away. The exercise was mutually useful as the boys were also very good for the puppies — wonderful socialisation.

But one family's holiday turned into near disaster. A woman with two children, her mother and a dog wanted an overnight stop on the way from eastern England to Wales. They arrived at teatime just as I came in from the horses. They all seemed pleased with their rooms but within half an hour the young daughter came down to say her mother wouldn't be able to stay because she was having an allergic reaction. Thinking it must be the dogs I said I'd get them out of the house but the child shook her head explaining that the horses were the problem, or rather traces of their dander on me. Hastily I made some calls and found a room for her in the village, while granny and the children would stay with us as planned. My friend was a nurse and quickly became very worried about her guest who suffered badly from asthma.

During the course of the evening her condition deteriorated, a doctor was called who immediately summoned an ambulance to rush her to Shrewsbury hospital with anaphylactic shock. Had she not been treated so quickly the attack could have been fatal. She was in hospital for three nights while her children and their granny amused themselves about the farm. Eventually they set off again for Wales to catch up with their holiday.

Small visitors

Initially guests had breakfast in the kitchen at the old oak table we bought with the house — a relic from the 17th century with a modern slab of oak on top. Visitors so far had found it part of the charm but to carry on seriously it wouldn't be acceptable, many people would find it too informal. We needed to make bigger changes. By now the internet was having a major impact on ordinary people, though it still came down the phone line very slowly. The garage, full of clutter from Dad's home, was an untapped resource. Originally the cowshed, it had a tiny door for feeding grain and standings down the sides for the animals. It had been turned into a garage with wooden doors and a pit in the floor, complete with a forty gallon drum of waste oil.

A couple who stayed recently had holidayed at North Hill a couple of years before we bought it. They'd come across it online and remembered their visit, with their parents and young children. When they arrived they asked if the garage was still there.

'Yes but it's now the dining room.' They explained the exhaust pipe had come off their car and they'd been very grateful to use the pit to repair it. We had looked down into that pit, sighed and covered it up again, before filling the space with junk. When we eventually began the conversion it took a fireman friend to remove the oil drum from the pit, using a classic fireman's lift.

So it remained for more than ten years. We considered going up another storey to make a self-contained flat for Beck's mother. But her dementia had gone too far to make that feasible and it remained closed up, useful for storage or hanging pheasants after a shoot, a habit which provided a gruesome incident. While we were away in France one summer a friend arrived with a dozen wood pigeons. Lucy, in charge, rather than drop them, feathers and all in the freezer, hung them on a nail in the garage. By the time we came home not much was left but the maggots on the floor would've been a fisherman's delight.

Things often seemed to have a nasty habit of happening in our absence. Dad was now in his nineties, still pretty fit but inclined to emotional blackmail if we mentioned holidays, saying things like 'Don't you know I'm dying?' when looking remarkably fit for his years. I remember my reply: 'We all are; it's just a question of when.'

Planning a quick break in Morocco before Bonnie's puppies were due we checked with the doctor who said Dad would be fine but for everyone's peace of mind he was booked into a local nursing home for the week.

Perhaps it was just imagination but all that week I was ill at ease, uncomfortable that we'd left him. On the flight home my thoughts were so full of foreboding that when we landed at Gatwick it was no surprise to hear us called on the tannoy. My sister telling us Dad had died on the Tuesday after we left. Fortunately she was with him at the end. To this day I'm convinced he did it on purpose. He'd been in good health for the fourteen years after he left Berkshire and never looked his age but at ninety-four his heart and kidneys finally let him down.

The pregnant spaniel had been left in Sussex with Beck's daughter who met us at the airport equally anxious, saying Bonnie had been hanging on to her puppies till we got back though she wasn't due for another five days. Rushing back to Shropshire at around four thirty am she began scrabbling on the back seat. As I leaned over to see what was happening blue lights began flashing behind us and Beck stopped for the stern policeman at the window.

'You're behaving very oddly and driving too fast, what's going on?' he demanded.

'Take a look, our spaniel is about to give birth!'

He leaned into the car to look. 'Ah! You'd better get on your way then.'

Half an hour later we parked and opened the rear door. Bonnie climbed out with a pup hanging from her which promptly slid out onto the icy concrete. I scooped it up and dashed to the house as Beck opened the front door and found a blanket. She settled by the Aga watching me dry the puppy which began to suckle lustily as mum stretched out with new contractions. Number two was quickly on the scene followed by another three, all born safe and well.

With Dad gone we decided to do something with the garage and much of his furniture from my childhood home ended up on a bonfire. The outer wall was already bulging dangerously in the obvious place for a large window looking over the valley. The wall was demolished to ground level revealing the simple building technique with rough stone and rubble from what was locally available.

Cavity walls and insulation were unknown in the 1840s and the loose inner wall was home to a family of newts — thankfully just the common variety which were gathered up safely and moved to a suitable spot. Their presence was worrying as these small amphibians tend to like damp areas. The feed door begged to be another window and glass topped double doors opposite gave access to the terrace.

Modern architecture often seems designed to keep nature at bay — some people rarely open a window — 'insects might come in'. While the dining room was still unfurnished but newly carpeted we found a small toad in there one evening at dusk when we went to close the terrace doors. He sat In the middle of the floor blinking in the sudden light. He'd come in from the damp flagstones outside and stared at me, confused by the strange feel of the carpet under his feet. I moved him to safety behind the stone trough against the wall.

Toads are common here, thriving among cold stone and dank places, usually only seen at night. But one time I raked one up unseen among leaves piled around the bins, a refuge in hot weather, cool and damp under the overhanging cotoneaster. Sometimes especially in winter when the dogs go out last thing a toad will be caught out by the yard light, hopping away to hide behind the water trough. The dogs sniff at them, sometimes touching with a tentative paw but these little reptiles have a toxin in the skin, bufotoxin, which repels the dogs and makes them sick if they lick or bite one.

Thoughtless people ask how they can get rid of or kill them. Their little rough-skinned bodies are charming and they're totally harmless and actually do a good job in the garden, controlling snails and slugs and other insects. One lived for a time in the shed where we keep the recycling, often caught out in the sudden light as the door opens. The weather-boarded gable end and the old garage doors were replaced in stone with a second large window and high in the apex a small one with an unusual stone frame which from outside created an impression of age. It was very old but Beck had found it on a rubbish tip in Yorkshire, probably the relic of some chapel. It had looked good as a planter full of flowers but fitted beautifully into that space and attracts interest from intrigued guests, looking as if it's been there for ever. The downside on bright sunny mornings is the sunbeams it directs into the room which show up any cobwebs.

Old properties are a magnet for spiders who share the house with us. One large specimen which Beck named Winsy lived in the sitting room. It would emerge in an evening from under a chair or the curtain and make a dash across the floor to disappear again. It amused us to see him — or her — though some might cringe at the thought. But spiders have their role in the world and human fear of the little creatures always seems illogical. For years we waited for a shriek in the night from a guest disturbed by a spider. It hasn't happened yet — but there's time. We're always careful to remove these unwanted visitors but they have a habit of returning. At certain times of year, especially in summer, the cobwebs proliferate, spun incredibly fast by a busy spider.

But maybe I should be more cautious. The subject of spiders came up at breakfast with a couple who related their experience of arachnids sharing the sitting room. The husband grinned as his wife described trying to evict one from the room, bravely putting her hand beneath a chair to grab it. She was bitten on a finger which subsequently swelled quite badly. The culprit was the increasingly common noble false widow which has a venomous bite — only used when molested.

Knocking through the yard wide wall from the sitting room into this new space was a messy task. While they were still cladding and plastering the walls I set to work on the beams. Grey with dirt and cobwebs, whose owners disappeared into cracks, and full of old nails, the triangular shaped trusses supporting the roof were intimidating to tackle. But an electric sander and a wire brush made it easier than it looked.

It was hard and time consuming work but the timber beneath was worth the effort. A mellow golden wood with fine grain which was transformed by oil. We couldn't decide if it was pitch pine or hemlock but on each section of the truss the carpenter's marks in Roman numerals are clearly seen and for me the dining room is the best part of the house.

The pitched ceiling makes it light and airy. A sexy room, someone once said, wonderful for entertaining and ideal for breakfast, its red sofa invoking erotic memories. Soft lights or perhaps just candles at Christmas create a magical, cosy effect. The bright clustered holly berries on the beams catch the light with another twinkling bough in the corner. By new year the holly has dried to brittle twigs which burn fiercely on the open fire. Ancient beliefs and superstition dictate that once taken indoors holly should not go out again or it will bring bad luck.

Bringing strangers into your home means handling a cross-section of human nature and relationships between guests can be intriguing and sometimes embarrassing. To date we've had no noticeably abusive partnerships but several cases of what we call 'under the thumb' liaisons.

'Poor Godfrey' and his wife came when we were installing a new kitchen. In retrospect we shouldn't have taken the booking but though we explained the situation when she called to book two nights she said it would be fine and not a problem. My special fluted sink hadn't arrived and the dishwasher wasn't plumbed in so washing up for several days was in a bowl outside on the wall with hot water from the kettle and the downstairs cloakroom.

In the warm late spring evening we were relaxing on the terrace, drinking in the soul-cleansing aspect of the valley, the hawthorn by the summerhouse at the peak of its blossom, hanging in creamy scented curds, bees buzzing dreamily as they fed. On the opposite slopes the hedges too were trimmed in white. On his second glass of fizz Beck raised a welcoming hand as Godfrey appeared at the gate.

He came in hesitantly and made straight for the hawthorn to stare at the bees and cradle a cluster of flowers in his hand. He accepted with alacrity the offered glass of wine and sat down cheerfully to chat. Before long his other half appeared, complete with disapproving frown.

She hovered behind us before reluctantly taking a chair but declined a drink. Godfrey's happy chatter dried up under the baleful gaze of his beloved but he carried on sipping his wine with obvious pleasure. We made conversation but it became stilted as she waited in silence and growing impatience. Godfrey emptied his glass and put it down with a smile. 'I really enjoyed that,' he said.

Beck stood up, bottle in hand, poised to top him up: 'A little more?' Godfrey smiled and nodded but before the wine could be poured a hand shot out to cover his glass .

'That's quite enough,' she said. 'Come along Godfrey, we need to go.'

Unwillingly, he got up, thanked us profusely and trooped off behind the woman whose body language did not bode well.

Laughing we looked at each. 'Poor guy,' Beck said ruefully. 'He'll get it in the neck now. What a miserable woman.'

Next morning Godfrey sat silent at the table as if not daring to speak but consumed his breakfast with relish. I reminded the guests to be sure to take their keys in case they wished to return during the day, at which Mrs Godfrey piped up: 'Oh, Godfrey was going to speak to you about that.'

Godfrey met my eye with sad embarrassment and mumbled something.

'Tell her Godfrey!' came the command at which he said: 'We've decided not to stay another night. Sorry.'

'Change of plan?' I asked.

'Well,' he began, hesitating before his wife took over. 'There's a smell of dogs which I don't like, as soon as you come out of the room. We can't stay.'

'Right,' I murmured, gathering their dirty plates.

As she marched out he whispered: 'I'm so sorry, I'd love to stay.'

Meanwhile the young man at the end of the table crunched his toast, maintaining a straight face. 'That's unfortunate,' I remarked to him, embarrassed. 'Have you noticed a smell?'

'Well, I suppose it does smell a little of dogs but it doesn't bother me.'

He'd come on his own from Brighton for a week. The previous Saturday when it was time to check out he'd looked at me with a tentative smile before asking if there was any chance he could stay another week. It was comforting to know he at least was enjoying the place

When Saturday came round again he lingered about the farm till late morning, seeming very reluctant to leave before finally say goodbye — which was a welcome boost for morale. On each of his fourteen days he demolished a full English breakfast. Asked if he fancied a change he shook his head, all he wanted was the traditional start to his day.

Hawthorn blossom is a spring highlight and an American couple and his mother came at just the right time to see it at its best. They were mesmerised by the view from the kitchen window of green countryside, lush, long grass and the hedges all in white. It was something totally unknown to them, accustomed to the arid landscape of Arizona and New Mexico. The blackthorn blossom comes earlier, its flowering often coincides with a spell of bitter cold in April, a Blackthorn Winter.

They were even more delighted to find Saffron, our lovely Gordon bitch in the act of giving birth in the kitchen. Mother and wife had to get almost cross with the man to drag him away for supper at the pub.

We met another American having lunch at the bar there, loudly extolling the ambience and antiquity of the pub and telling us how wonderful he found the area, its countryside and historic towns and villages. Pausing for a moment in his excitement he said: 'I've always wanted to visit the Cotswolds and now I'm here.'

We looked at each other and the landlord but said nothing, just hoping that before he left he realised he was actually in Shropshire.

Visitors from across the pond find their way in a steady trickle up the narrow lanes to our door but they and Australians tend to struggle with the roads, so different from the wide straight highways they're used to. They don't understand the etiquette of passing places and pulling in or backing up. They complain about meeting farm vehicles, especially at silage, hay making and harvest times and most don't know what those terms mean. Some think they can argue with a combine harvester but it's all part of the ethos they come to find.

The Global Positioning System seems more accurate now but sat nav has often proved to be a pain. Our wide postcode covers several square miles and it frequently takes people to the wrong house. When our neighbours were away in South Africa one couple arrived at their gate and despite it being marked clearly with a different name spent ten minutes banging on the doors. They eventually continued the hundred yards up the lane to arrive at our door, disgruntled, apparently unable to accept that the sat nav had got it wrong.

Wild hawthorn is usually white but sometimes tinged with pink, especially in ageing trees and Shropshire boasts many ancient trees. Cultivated varieties can be dark pink or crimson, beautiful against the pale green leaves like the Paul's Scarlett we planted on the lane side. Those there now are a second attempt as both older trees were destroyed in a vicious storm which ripped them out by the roots.

The trees give much besides their spring beauty, nesting cover among the dense thorny foliage and the autumn feast of haws provides food for insects and birds.

A pagan symbol of fertility, the ancestor of the maypole, the blossom marks the change into summer and its leaves and flowers were the source of May Day garlands and the Green Man's wreath.

One spring I was tempted to use the gorgeous blossom as a posy for the table but a neighbour warned me against it. According to folklore bringing its branches indoors can presage illness and death. I thought I was well up on superstition but that was a new one. In our age of technology the old ways linger in the imagination and maybe the mere thought of bringing the May indoors was enough to cause ill luck, while the sight of a single magpie always makes me whisper foolishly, 'How's your wife?'

But I left the blossom on the tree and brought in a sprig of flowering rosemary and the pretty white tipped pink leaves of the actinidia which grows close to the dining room door. For most of the year it's plain green but in spring it's worth its place. Its rampant, long tendrils grow vigorously over the roof and reach inside if not pruned back hard.

The views of the valley and hills are a constant attraction but sometimes in the darker months the grey pall of fog obscures everything beyond the hedge and sometimes even that is hidden. One late February morning we hosted a charming couple from Wisconsin, where the Great Lakes have a big impact on the climate. From the dining room window all they could see in the mist was the crabapple tree, its twigs and branches encased in ice, gripped by a deep hoar frost. The dismal prospect made me begin apologising for the weather. They both laughed: 'Don't worry about that, we've left three feet of snow at home.

We and our guests are just one aspect of life here; there's a constant interaction with the creatures of the hillside, where the wild things are. Sometimes they could be intrusive like the mice in the kitchen in the early years who outstayed their welcome, coming in through a hole in the rough brickwork behind the sink. When we disappeared to France for a fortnight we came back to find their droppings in a bedroom chest of drawers. They had been having a high old time in our absence. Reluctantly we resorted to using a trap and caught eighteen in one day. It was surprising that the cats weren't on top of the job but the small invaders were probably hard to get at. We kept them at bay by blocking the holes until major work when the new kitchen went in.

Fortunately rats have never been a major problem though we have had incidents from time to time, including an invasion in the garage before we converted it when we realised they were in the pit and travelling under the house through the loose foundations. And after the death of our widowed neighbour at Fluffy's old home down the lane, her rats decamped up the hill. Her husband died suddenly from a heart attack, almost literally as farmer Ken arrived to present them with a basket of mushrooms, an odd conjunction of fate.

On an autumn morning we'd looked down on the borehole field in the valley to see it white over with an incredible crop of mushrooms, never seen in that field before or since. Some accident of climate will have triggered the sudden growth but there must have been a massive maze of mycelium beneath the turf to launch such bounty.

Ken who owned the field was amazed. He picked as many as he could and took some to the couple who lived in the new house on the site of his father's bungalow, only to find Gordon dead in his chair. One of his widow's remaining pleasures was feeding the birds and when she saw rats climbing up the bird table she put food for them on the ground. Within a couple of weeks of her death we began to notice damage in the feed room and one morning I discovered two almost full grown rats in the big corn bin. They had found a way in but couldn't manage the smooth metal sides to escape. They are great jumpers and bounced up and down in agitation as I peered warily in at them, considering the options.

It's likely they were two young males driven away by an older one. Of course Beck was away on a locum somewhere so it was down to me. I could have bashed them with a heavy lump of wood but that seemed a nasty thing to do and being very quick on the uptake they could have used it to escape or jump at me.

I've nothing against rats personally — we all have to live — and felt sorry for them. But you don't want too many of them around, though in themselves they can be quite endearing. It's the speed and the suddenness of their movements that scares people.

We visited a rat temple in Rajasthan, in the Thar desert where the rats are considered to be a reincarnation of departed souls and therefore sacred. It must be one of the few places in the world where corn is delivered specially for the rats. True to Hindu custom it was necessary to remove our shoes to enter. It was fascinating to watch them, totally unconcerned by human presence, continuing their usual daily life, eating, drinking, copulating — enjoying all the privilege of their existence. It was forbidden to hurt them and we were wary of treading on one as the penalty for killing one of these holy creatures was to provide a silver substitute.

27

Still contemplating the captive pair I decided to give them a sporting chance by placing a handy broom handle in the bin and standing well back while they scuttled up it in a flash and scarpered. With luck old Fluffy or young William would detect their presence and deal with them.

Several times we tried to keep guinea fowl. Intended mainly as a delicacy for the table their small pointed hard-shelled eggs are delicious but we never succeeded in rearing any. We bought in a broody hen with a clutch of ten two day old gleany chicks. Installed in a loose box she seemed comfortable and safe, the chicks growing nicely. After about a week we found the poor hen with only two chicks.

A hole in the brick base gave me a clue and when we investigated the tack room next door, down behind the big wooden tack box was the pile of dead chicks neatly stored for later consumption. It can only have been a rat, or two.

Before we created the dining room the rats in the pit had literally made a rat run and we could hear them moving around at night in the chimney above our bedroom, not a good experience. Jackdaws had been nesting there before we came but were frightened away. We preferred the jackdaws as guests and they returned once the pit was filled in.

The cats generally kept them at bay and a couple of small ones in the feed room one evening who shot away up the wall didn't trouble me too much. Foolishly I thought two of them wouldn't matter. Until I discovered the end loose box seemed suddenly very damp. By then it was used as a store and home for a chest freezer. Thinking there might be a fault in the freezer causing condensation I started to investigate, moving things about and uncovering the alkathene pipe which fed the stable drinkers. From a pinprick hole a fine spray of water was soaking everything — unwanted visitors had nibbled the plastic.

Along with the rats we also inherited our neighbour's cats, two female tabbies quirkily called Hinge, which we changed to Hinny and Bracket. It took them a long time to decide it was a good bet to move in with us. Bracket was never friendly but Hinny made herself very much at home and lived well into her twenties, dying at last on the bottom of our bed. Most of the cats here have made a good age, almost always at least twenty, hunting and enjoying life until the end.

Out in the cold

Shropshire is a mesh of footpaths and bridleways, an entrancing lure for walkers and riders but how much better they could have been if our planners had shown some foresight. What a golden opportunity they missed in the fifties and sixties when rural rail lines were axed. Wonderful long distance routes, ready-made for public pleasure were sold off piecemeal to adjacent landowners and an inestimable gift to the future was lost for ever. Imagine riding the line from Craven Arms to Wellington under the brow of Wenlock Edge.

But the paths we have — many from the days when agricultural workers trudged daily to work over fields and hills — are a marvellous introduction to the great outdoors and a popular choice for Duke of Edinburgh award scheme hopefuls. Small parties of teenagers with very large rucksacks on their backs are part of the scene from spring to autumn trudging up and down the lane, maps in hand, seeking the right path. Often doing the gold award, many look miserable and exhausted, especially when the summer weather is unkind. We are the first house they find coming down after negotiating Hope Bowdler and Wilstone hills. A knock on the door announces an anxious teenager, map in hand with a puzzled expression or asking to use the toilet. Young urban girls often have a problem with the countryside, reluctant to find a rock or gorse bush to squat behind — so much easier for the boys.

We let them use the outside loo while it was still there beside the lane, wickedly amused at the screams of alarm from behind the door. More than one girl rushed out doing up her trousers after a very brief visit, unwilling to share the space with the chunky spiders which lived in there. Several departed unrelieved to seek alternative arrangements. Perhaps unkindly we thought it defeated the object of the exercise which is largely to learn and improvise.

It's not only teenagers in trouble who find their way to our door; plenty of adults have arrived, needing water or a cup of tea having overdone the walking or hurt themselves. All kinds of situations arise. Before the advent of smart phones we frequently had to call someone, or ferry them to Church Stretton when they were lost and landed at the wrong spot on the map. During a January cold snap, with the concrete a treacherous sheet of ice from water running off the fields and across the lane, I was disturbed by the dogs' commotion downstairs, barking at a worried looking guy outside.

'Sorry to disturb you,' he began 'but my friend has fallen on the ice and I think his arm is broken.'

Grabbing my outdoor fleece I followed him to find a pale-faced man sitting in the muddy grass supporting his right arm with the other hand, obviously in pain. He'd slipped on the ice and landed where a careless lorry driver had churned up the verge, causing the water to spread. We got him up and led him well clear of the ice across to the house and the chairs by Chaffinch. Still clutching his arm he refused offers of pain relief and tea. 'It's definitely broken,' he said. 'I've broken a lot of bones in my time so I know how it feels.'

Fortunately they hadn't come far, just north of Shrewsbury and knew the hills well; all they needed was a lift back to their car in Church Stretton and away to hospital.

The poor guy was plastered with mud but we protected the seats with dog towels and got him comfortably settled. He was much brighter at the sight of his own car, confident at the thought of imminent treatment. Several weeks later a carrier bag appeared hanging from the front door handle holding a thank you card, with an unreadable name and a large box of chocolates.

These hills may not have the vast expanses of the Lake District, Scotland or the Welsh mountains but they deserve respect and can lead the unwary into difficulty and even danger. In warm weather the sandy slopes and heathlands attract adders, Britain's only venomous snake, which love to bask in the sun, a hidden threat to walkers and their dogs. These endangered creatures with their striking black zigzag markings are not aggressive and a bite is usually the result of a careless footstep.

We had first hand experience of this peril when grazing mares and foals on our bottom land in the valley which had a large area of rough bramble strewn ground. These were visiting mares staying for Cloud's services and the lovely bay Welsh cob cross mare Susie had his grey foal at foot which seemed to be lying down too much in the July sunshine.

When Roger's locum vet came out to her he found nothing amiss apart from a strange swelling on the fetlock. A young vet from Zimbabwe, in Britain to widen his experience, he stood back puzzled, stared at the recumbent foal and said: 'If this was back home I'd say it could be snake bite but you don't have poisonous snakes here, do you?'

'Yes, we have adders,' I told him, 'they're poisonous'.

He gave baby a local anaesthetic and began to debride the flesh which was already putrefying. As he scraped two tiny marks emerged, exactly right for the fangs of a snake. The reaction of the flesh was another tell-tale sign. The poison had caused the flesh to rot and he said nothing could stop that, all the surrounding flesh would go. We were horrified when he said if it stops at the coronary band she should recover but if it carries on into the hoof she will lose the foot and have to be put down.

For the next few days we watched and worried, removing the dead flesh each day. When the band round the top of the hoof was reached we realised the flesh was regrowing. And growing surprisingly fast. Because she was so

young it was healing in line with her general growth rate. But along with the healing came proud flesh. Horses are very prone to this phenomenon which happens during healing when the granulation tissue continues to grow, mush-rooming over the skin surrounding the wound. It has to be removed but the process isn't painful as there are no nerves in the new tissue.

The wound needed dressing every day and Beck took over the job, slicing away the proud flesh with a scalpel, rather like salami, and bandaging the foot, while the mare stood behind him, watching every move. One evening as he knelt by the foal she raised a front hoof and placed it gently on his back as if to say: 'I'm watching what you're doing to my baby'.

Recovery took time and patience but the filly grew into a fine little mare though the scabby scar on her fetlock remained.

Several other horses in the county have been snake victims. One, stretched out in a field in the valley below the Long Mynd at Little Stretton was bitten in the belly as she lay in the sun. She was lucky, treated and survived but in another instance at a horse show near Brown Clee Hill a horse was bitten in the throat as it grazed by the trailer and choked on the swelling before the vet could do anything for it.

Human deaths from adder bites are very rare but they can be dangerous for children.

Dogs are more frequent victims and one summer a golden retriever arrived with his owner for a week's recuperation. The dog had been bitten and it was touch and go before he recovered. Each evening they walked together down to the village for supper in the pub. He was perplexed that each time he reappeared with his dog the landlord showed no sign of recognition. At that time the menu relied heavily on the freezer and our guest related in the morning how he had asked for the mixed grill, to be told after a long delay 'we can't find one'. 'One' was found at last but proved to be a poor choice

The open ground of the uplands is deceptive and away from the well-trodden paths there is enough open country to get thoroughly lost, especially in bad weather when rain or fog hide the familiar landmarks needed to find your bearings.

Sheep make their own ways through the grass in single file following close behind the one in front in a wavering line across the land. It was such a trail to nowhere which fooled the guest who spent a very wet August night under a gorse bush on Hope Bowdler Hill. He had taken his son back to school near Shrewsbury and came alone, though with his wife he had been a few times before and knew the area well. Early in the evening he came down saying he was going for a walk on the hill. Beck called to him, 'Don't forget your key' as the front door closed.

It had rained all day in heavy driving blasts and by evening the clouds were hanging low on the hills, giving very poor visibility. The top of Caradoc and the Battlestones were hidden in a combination of mist and cloud. Warm indoors and busy with chores and TV, at one point later in the evening Beck asked: 'Has that guy come back?'

'I expect so,' I said casually. 'Shouldn't think he went far in this.'

The problem is you can't go opening the door of a room to check the guests are in bed, they won't thank you if they're fast asleep. That was it and at around ten thirty we locked up for the night..

Downstairs making early morning tea Beck was startled to see our guest outside at the door. The poor man didn't say much but drank the mug of tea thrust into his hand before retiring to his unused room for a hot shower.

He was very hungry and enjoyed a full breakfast with a lot of tea as we apologised for not realising he was still out. Afterwards with rueful embarrassment he explained what had happened. Despite the weather he was enjoying his walk and decided to go a bit further across Hope Bowdler Hill, following a track away from the top of Wilstone in the direction of Church Stretton. He had picked up a sheep path which eventually petered out into the heather. Surrounded by open land in the gathering dusk and thick cloud he realised he was lost.

On a clear night however dark, the outline of the hills is sharp against the sky, easily indicating direction and the red light on the Wrekin and lights in the valley are visible. But lost in mist and cloud it's a different story. He had huddled down under a gorse bush until first light revealed the way back. But with no key to get into the house he had waited in his car for signs of activity. He didn't want to bang on the door and disturb us so early. The following year came a guest we knew. As we were chatting I found myself recounting the unfortunate story of the night on the hill. A wry smile hovered as she listened, before saying: 'Sounds like my husband, he never told me about that.'

We had already extended the house at one end and created the dining room but as North Hill became known we needed better facilities. The major lack was bathrooms. We had puzzled to find some way to build onto our bedroom at the front of the house without a ground floor, on the existing extension. In fact we had been here ten years before we realised it had been done without planning permission. Fortunately it was out of time but it seemed that was the way things were done round here and council officers in far away Shrewsbury didn't often bother to venture as far as our rural backwater. Much of the property around had been tinkered with without benefit of official sanction. Those were the days. Small developments which didn't affect anybody else frequently slipped under the net.

Locals told us gleefully that had we seen the road before it was made up we would never have bought the place. A rough and rutted track with ridges of underlying rock and enormous potholes, plus the gradient, made it a nightmare mile. Over the years many lorry loads of hard-core had been brought to fill the holes, a pointless exercise as every time it rained heavily the road became a torrent which washed it all away. At least now the water we watch rushing by runs off the concrete and into the fields

The new road had been a joint effort between the owner and his neighbour George, nearly a mile away round the hill, who with his brother had actually laid the wet concrete, the same valiant pair who helped when the stables came. Poor George, so many times we heard the same refrain, bewailing the decision not to concrete the track all the way to Middle Hill. That road remains rough and unmade but at least it is more or less flat.

The first heavy snowfall after we moved in brought him to the door to remonstrate with us over the amount of salt we applied to keep the road open. He reckoned too much would damage the concrete and shorten its effective lifespan. We duly took note and have aways been sparing with the salty grit although others have advised that the concrete would have provision to cope with the salt.

Probably seventy-five per cent of our guests ask the same question, usually when having breakfast, watching the birds on the crabapple tree outside with the slope of the road beyond. 'Do you often get snowed in?'

In fact not that often; most of the bad snows were in the early days but usually we managed to get off the hill, sometimes leaving a car at the bottom and walking up.

We had to be somewhere on a certain Sunday in January when it had snowed and thawed and then rained and finally frozen into a bright glaze on the concrete. Beck, myself and Dad, had to plough through rough snow on the bank, clinging to the wire fence. The concrete was lethal, impossible to keep a footing for even a moment.

There were several years of bad snow but it comes less frequently now. On one memorable occasion all the roads out of the village were blocked because someone left his car stuck in the middle of the road, locked and immovable so the snowplough couldn't get through to clear the way. Given this excuse everyone adjourned to the pub for a wonderful morning and lunchtime, unable to do anything except enjoy the opportunity.

Another time heavy snow brought the phone line down — mobiles then were something hanging from the ceiling — Beck walked to the village to make a call while I stayed by the fire, listening to the howling wind. When the door opened I assumed he was back but he didn't appear and eventually I discovered the force of the wind had opened the door and the blizzard was filling the hall with snow. That time I got chilblains on my thighs from digging out the drifts on the corner to get the road open.

When we were both working it mattered to get out to shop or office, worrying if we would make it. Sometimes at the office in Telford or Shrewsbury disbelieving faces greeted me as I explained the snow problems. There is a line across the A49 at Leebotwood, as clear as a designated barrier — to the north it would be green and free of snow but to the south a white out.

Now the work comes to us in the form of people and with no necessity to go anywhere if the weather is bad it's simple, just wait till it improves. As long as the freezer is full and there's enough wine to drink there's no point in worrying.

Concrete was prominent on the farm, probably done at the same time as the road which was built with the benefit of a then EEC grant for rural roads. The yard was a mess of tatty block and concrete and the 'lawn' just about covered the rubble they'd dumped from the renovation.

At the rear of the house the yard was stark with concrete and Beck set out to build stone walls to soften the effect and create a terrace, making the most of the view. The horrid block walls which weren't even tied together lie buried between two thicknesses of stone, now mellowed and draped with sedum. This hard local stone was tough to cut and temper but strong arms and muscles coped with it, a fact which made it so difficult to understand what was to come. He would come home from the shop and change into scruff to push on with the latest scheme.

The house we bought was an odd combination of old and new. The current owners had added an extension at the back and we built on again. With the addition of the dining room the interior of the house has over time prompted the comment from guests that it was 'just like the Tardis' — seeming much bigger than it appeared from outside.

The same remark once referred to the car after a trip to France. Five guys were staying here for some event, out on the terrace enjoying a few beers in the sun. They watched with bemused expressions as the car was unloaded.

That time we brought back a new table and chairs for the terrace, sun loungers, several plants, all our luggage and of course a considerable quantity of wine. They congratulated us on what one of them called a miracle of packing.

What we planned was a prominent and obvious addition so an application to the council was essential. My architect nephew designed a clever scheme on stone pillars which transformed the master bedroom into a light-filled en suite room with windows on three sides. The scheme also provided an extra bathroom for one of the other rooms with the bonus of a cloakroom near the front door.

At ground level an extended porch area made a useful space with outdoor but under cover seating, handy for friends who stick with the tobacco habit. Willow baskets for logs and kindling add a rustic tone and make guests feel they really are in the countryside. Despite urgings from others with wood burning stoves we retained the open fire, a comfort for the cold months. Fire has a life of its own and there's a fascination in watching it blaze into life, catching the wood and licking the logs like a hot tongue as the heat rises and begins to warm the room. Best when its ferocity has settled into the red depth of intense heat, enough to turn bread into toast or crumpets. In some mysterious way toast created on the end of a fork against such heat has a more intense flavour than anything done in an electric toaster.

People say it's a lot of work, messy with ashes to clear and logs to lug; all true but we love it. It's something real, another link with nature, the gift of fire, so vital through all our genesis. It sounds primitive but then primitive can be good.

Kindling sticks are never in short supply as the farm is generous with its bounty, especially the ancient stalwarts on the lane side which, battered by the wind, will fling small boughs to the earth and sometimes larger ones. A mighty limb ripped away leaves a raw scar on the trunk but good ash logs for the winter fire.

Some of them must be several hundred years old, gnarled and bent with holes in the trunk where the woodpeckers nest until the holes are big enough and they are ousted by the jackdaws. Twisted and dangerous in a gale these old timers go on spring after spring while I watch and check their leaves but still so far they come green again. They seem unaffected by the encroaching ash dieback and seedlings pop up all over the land, in a border, next to the summer house and not long ago one grew unnoticed right against the barn wall and reached almost seven feet before it was spotted — not the site of choice for an ash tree sapling.

The project was traumatic from the start since we unwittingly picked another cowboy. It's hard to find reliable builders when new to an area with no knowledge of local tradesmen. Work had not long begun when I came home and glanced at the brick bases for the pillars and knew immediately something was wrong. They would be almost in line with the kitchen window. The builders were just packing up for the day as I emerged with my steel tape. Sure enough they were several feet out.

'How have you managed that?' I asked.

'Don't know.'

'Did you look at the plans?'

'Sort of.'

He pulled out the plans from where they had been stuffed under a brick and I pointed out the measurements of the pillars and the space between.

'We didn't include that bit,' he said, pointing at my nephew's meticulous work. 'These architects don't know much about building, we don't usually bother with plans.'

They had added up the figures incorrectly and carried on regardless. Struggling to control my temper I said through gritted teeth: 'You'll have to start again.' In the morning I didn't leave until they were attacking the new brickwork with sledgehammers. That was just the beginning.

The work was supposed to be finished by the end of the year but they were behind schedule so the new room wasn't ready. We had a pushy vicar wanting an en suite room for New Year. I explained it wasn't ready, therefore not available but he seemed to think that by some act of the Almighty the work might be completed. Despite my protestations he insisted on booking. We were still very green about handling potential guests.

With us still camping in the double room while ours was transformed, the only one available was the twin. We explained the situation but they booked anyway. That room is nearest the stables, though well away, popular with guests who like horses which they can see from the window. In the morning he came down coughing, complaining that proximity to the horses had brought on his allergy, so the room was unsuitable and they would leave. That was good news but we said all the right things in commiseration, though doubtful with the windows shut that anything could really have travelled that distance to affect him. His discomfort didn't stop him enjoying a large full English breakfast with several rounds of toast.

It was full moon the first night we were back in our own room and long before dawn we were roused by its brilliance. The view from the new window showed the gleaming golden disc prominent in a clear sky to the west, above the rugged bulk of Caer Caradoc. And from there with binoculars you can spot the ravens on their nest in the tallest of the four Scots pine.

But the room brought a new dilemma — as the only en suite it would command a premium price. Now with these improvements in what we could offer we decided to be more adventurous. Few local guest houses would accept dogs and a magazine pitched at pet owners had been our main source of business. Now we decided to go for a wider clientele and test the exciting new worldwide web. It had to be worth a try. Beck was dubious about the idea and his words are etched in my memory: 'I can't see that bringing much business.' Such innocence before the tsunami of technology that changed the world and it's difficult now to imagine how tentative people were when the net first appeared. But advertising on a local independent website proved effective and the enquiries began to flow.

Before TripAdvisor made inspection redundant you needed some official accreditation in order to advertise on local websites. The best bet at the time was the AA and I soon discovered how little I knew when their inspector told me all the things we were doing wrong. This was helpful but embarrassing, such as bars of Imperial Leather soap in the bathrooms which of course was unhygienic — and expensive — and no locks on the rooms. But that was easily remedied with trips to the cash and carry for packs of individual soaps and a hardware shop for locks.

Keys are something you have to get to grips with running a b&b, for bedroom doors and the main entrance. This in turn means remembering to ask all guests on leaving: 'Have you left your key?'

Many guests don't think about it and go off with keys in their pockets or handbags or sometimes dropped accidentally into the luggage, occasionally along with the TV remote. It's very aggravating if you don't get them back. More common are the guests who, despite being reminded — go out for the day's adventures with the key left in the room door.

The inspector asked what star grading we were after and I looked blank, not realising we were supposed to apply for a certain level. He said when things were sorted we should be fine at four star, which was pleasing. Asked about the requirements for five star he advised me to stick with four. His opinion on that was enlightening. 'Five star often puts people off,' he said. 'Prissy, pricey and pretentious, that's what I call them.'

Despite the omissions he gave us a good write-up in the AA guidebook — still going strong then — making a point of the ambience and the open fire.

But he turned up his nose at the dining room with its handsome oak table, made specially for the room, where the guests all eat together.

'My idea of a nightmare,' he said, adding he preferred a small private table. 'People always want to know what I do and when I say I'm a hotel inspector it leads to all sorts of complications.'

'You could always lie,' I whispered.

Feathers fly

The little crabapple tree grew to be a twice yearly joy, beautiful in spring with its delicate pink and white blossom and in autumn when the small bright scarlet apples make a feast for birds of all kinds. Its branches protect the small ones against attack from marauding sparrowhawks. They also have to live but we don't want them snatched away in front of guests watching the greedy antics of a greater spotted woodpecker or a nuthatch hogging the peanuts. Decked in attractive blue-grey and chestnut plumage with a dashing black stripe on the head the nuthatch pair scurry up and down the bark to grab a whole peanut and away to the hedge to eat it before coming back for another. A sudden shaft of sunlight highlights the roseate breast of a male chaffinch clutching a wind tossed branch among the new leaves and the flash of bright yellow is a yellowhammer, more wary of human activity.

On a mild and sunny morning the ubiquitous robin is singing for sheer joy, darting through the buildings. He's up near the barn roof trilling loudly, short verses in trickles and splashes like an upland stream. He and his mate have chosen the shed to build a nest among the garden tools. They watch our every move waiting to dash in with a beak full of moss or feathers.

The farm's comparative isolation encourages a wide variety of birds, just two properties alone on the hillside surrounded by grazing land, with the next nearly a mile away. Trees and hedges, open buildings and patches of wild ground provide cover for everything from blue tits to thrushes. The kitchen acts as a hide, from its wide window the activities of feathered friends make it hard not to pause and watch them.

Small birds shelter in the large round conifer opposite, using it as a launchpad for the peanut hanger on the wall. They fly in and out of its protective branches, the tiny heads of blue tits peering from cover to check the coast is clear, unaware they are being watched. People ask why we don't get rid of it, thinking it spoils the view. But it is in itself a view.

This bush is probably what attracts the goldcrests whose presence we discovered with a mixture of sadness and delight after finding a small dead female below the window. They like to peck around window panes, hunting insects which are their main diet. This one must have hit the glass. But the tiny corpse was an alert to keep eyes open to spot our smallest British bird.

The mounting block is another handy surface for feeding, close to a window and chaffinches, sparrows and the cheeky robins will carry on eating despite a human face peering at them. They and the wood pigeons have a confidence in human proximity, shared by the jackdaws which will hop a short distance away but are not deterred. But the crows and magpies are wary and if waiting on a pole or the birch tree for a chance of food they will immediately take flight. Maybe it's guilty conscience, given their predatory habits, or just greater intelligence and a strong instinct for self preservation. The corvids as a clan are very bright and family orientated though vicious to other creatures.

We watched this in action when fixing a new gate in the yard, interrupted abruptly by screeching and shrieks of terror so violent we rushed towards the racket. Out on the lane a carrion crow had a jackdaw helpless on its back, riving savagely at its throat. A few seconds more and the hapless bird would've been a meal for the three half-grown crows watching intently from the hedge.

In spring and summer crows raid the hen shed to steal eggs and when big enough the young are taught by the parents to help themselves. The hens stay in till late morning so we can collect the eggs, hopefully avoiding the flying thieves who will also grab any laid away in the hay. Sometimes a hen lays late and returns to deposit her offering, another temptation for the crows. The sound of raucous cawing caught my attention to the shed where several young crows were inside. I was just in time to slam the door and trap one.

The youngster thrust its head thorough the wire mesh in an effort to escape and with the metal corn scoop in my hand I could have killed it, lashing out immediately. But its black eyes peered at me in fear while its frantic parents' distraction antics overhead made me pause. She who hesitates is lost and I thought about it too long. In cold blood I couldn't bring myself to aim at its defenceless head. I watched it watching me and my hesitation gave its struggles a chance for a final push to squeeze through the wire and fly away with its parents. But the incident had some benefit, keeping the black raiders away for several weeks.

We had a few chickens in Yorkshire but here on our own patch there was more time to take notice of the small lives around us, precious moments to stand and stare. Hens are much brighter than humans realise. Like sheep they are considered stupid but it's just they have their own way of doing things. When you clean out their shed they watch the procedure in alarm but given fresh bedding they're eager to see what might be found.

Easily trained they quickly learn what listening to a human voice can do for them. Call it intelligence or learned behaviour but they are both intriguing and entertaining, especially the cackle of exultation as a hen tells the world she's laid an egg. There is a special pleasure in collecting new laid eggs still warm from the hen.

They are always alive to the main chance, watching for any opportunity to grab something edible, their quick eyes catching any movement around them. We've always kept a cockerel though they don't need a male around, they lay their eggs regardless but the hens seem happier with a man about. A good rooster is usually very solicitous to his wives, calling in a particular voice to tell them he's found something good to eat such as dandelion leaves, soft thistles or lettuce trimmings or he's scratched up a good patch of insects or worms. He will also do his best to defend them, flying with hard, sharp spurs thrust out at a marauding dog or maybe a fox.

Such courage cost the poor Light Sussex cockerel his life in the polecat attack. That was a dreadful morning, confronted by a horrible mess of blood, mud and feathers.

The shed was a scene of slaughter, dead and dying birds, and several missing, dragged away by the culprit, including the feisty guinea fowl. The hefty cockerel had been attacked. He must've put up a valiant fight, bloodied and torn, bitten viciously about the neck, which is typical of the tactics of the mustelid clan. We hoped he would recover but his injuries were too severe and after a couple of days he had to be put out of his pain. The surviving birds were left traumatised and began roosting away. At the time we thought it might have been a roaming mink but the polecat is the more likely culprit since they have recovered from near extinction and moved across from mid Wales

Various small birds roost with the hens, sharing their feed, pecking on the floor around the trough. A tiny wren is often there too, close to the ground and harder to spot, just a quick flash of something brown darting away.

The seasons have a marked impact on poultry. Birds kept in a natural fashion, more or less free range will follow the pattern of the seasons. They go into autumn perky and full of life but as the weather changes to short cold days they begin to moult, their combs and wattles turn pale and dry and most striking is the feather loss, turning them into ragged bundles of dejection.

A Light Sussex hen went into dramatic moult in bitter weather just before Christmas. She lost almost all her feathers down to her pink skin, effectively naked. I feared she wouldn't survive the cold but she cuddled up to the cockerel, her brother and by mid January had blossomed again with a new coat of radiant smooth white feathers. Sometimes one bird will carry on laying through the winter, one lonely egg every few days.

But as the days lighten towards the end of January they smarten up with new feathers and a reddening around the head. The process accelerates as their combs suddenly grow into scarlet health, blooming like a flower as they turn again into laying machines. By early spring they are doing what all birds do, laying eggs as if their life depended on it, which of course it does. For wild birds procreation is the raison d'etre and perpetuation of the species rests on a few short months.

Sometimes if a hen goes broody we give her a clutch of eggs to hatch. The only problem is you can end up with more males than females and boy chicks don't lay eggs. One brood produced five pullets, four cockerels and a puzzle — a chick which didn't know what it was.

At birth it looked like all the others but gradually it became less clear which sex it was. It looked a bit like a male but acted like a pullet and the other young cockerels began to attack it. It became more odd as it grew but one morning we found it dead. It's not only humans who can be born in the wrong body. We kept the four cockerels, which meant sparring and fights as they grew up until time and nature sorted them out.

Thinking to rear some birds for the table we bought a few broiler eggs from a local farm which supplied them to commercial rearers. The elderly Brown Leghorn sat them faithfully for twenty-one days and five chunky chicks pecked their way out of the shells. Prepared with a few pounds of chick crumbs to last a week I watched the little ones tuck in almost at once. Their appetites were prodigious and it was obvious the crumbs would last barely two days. These babies weren't as cute and fluffy as those we'd hatched before and their feathers came through earlier. They put on flesh at an incredible rate and by four weeks were already struggling to keep up with their agile mother who watched them with surprise. They trailed after her around the yard and barn, constantly squatting to rest. We knew that broilers, commercial poultry bred to eat, live short and uncomfortable lives but watching these chicks was a salutary lesson.

Put simply their legs couldn't support the rapidly fattening bodies. By seven weeks they were nearly ready to kill but we left it longer and by then they could hardly walk. One afternoon the hen flew onto the low wall, calling her brood to follow. They gazed at her with pathetic eyes, no more able to fly up to her than me. The experiment, not repeated, was a sad insight into the production of the cheap chicken meat which consumers have come to expect.

If you keep poultry you meet foxes, one way or another. These beautiful russet creatures arouse mixed feelings in a love hate relationship. We catch glimpses of them trotting unconcernedly across the field below or ambling over our own land in the distance or sometimes close. The hens or guinea fowl are most at risk in spring and early summer when the cubs are growing fast in the dens. Almost past the suckling stage their mother will be out hunting to find them meat. You can't blame a vixen for seeking easy pickings and if her family is down the steep bank below us in a hole among the growing bracken she is bound to come calling.

One year when we still had guinea fowl we were woken at dawn by the cacophony of an anxious bird shouting a warning. Rushing down we arrived in the yard in time to see a vixen trotting through the barn. We must have been a shock for her as she shot off over the yard wall and away through the grass while one of the guinea fowl roosting outside screamed from the roof ridge. Another year a vixen must have come in early evening. On a bright summer night it's good to leave the hens out as long as possible. At ten o'clock they were all safely inside watching me close the door. Next evening, going earlier, they were already huddled on the perches, nervous and unsettled. A head count revealed one missing and a closer look revealed tell-tale signs where an unwary bird had been taken. Clumps of feathers were scattered near the shed, brown tipped shading into white in a trail across the paddock with a large cluster where she'd been dragged through the fence — one of the best layers of course.

Incidents like these are down to the 'local' foxes but sometimes outsiders appear which break all the rules. The locals generally look well fed and glossy in coat but the intruders usually appear almost grey and bedraggled, lost in a country environment they don't understand. There is little doubt that these foxes have been brought here and dumped. One Sunday afternoon we went into the barn in time to see a fox at the small wicket gate with a hen in its mouth. My bellowed yell startled it into dropping the bird which shook itself and rushed back squawking, scared but unharmed. We watched the thief disappear across the hill.

We summoned the aid of the local foot pack to bring the hounds when another fox took several birds in just a few days. We suspected it must be injured and lying up somewhere nearby to be so brazen about taking regular meals. They found it on the slope below in a sorry state, one of its back legs totally useless. Because it couldn't hunt properly our birds were an easy supper option. Incidents like these, frustrating at the time, don't happen that often and are part of country life.

Walking up to Wilstone one day Beck was saddened to find a large handsome dog fox hanging in the wire fence. It must have tried jumping and was caught between two strands of barbed wire. Unhappy to simply leave it there he brought it down and was going to bury it. But we'd recently got to know a teacher in the village who did taxidermy and was eager for subjects to practise on. It was larger than anything he'd yet tackled but he took on Mr Fox. His dramatic portrayal of the poor animal was very effective, standing upright for many years outside his house, topped by a cloth cap, with a pipe in its mouth.

During one vicious spell of bitter weather we found a sparrowhawk dead in the field, succumbed to the cold. We put it in the freezer thinking we might get it stuffed until I mentioned it to someone and discovered we were breaking the law by even keeping it. Taxidermy is disliked these days. People often call it sick but it's useful for studying animals and the charge of cruelty is unfounded. It's an interesting skill but not for the fainthearted.

One small visitor appeared literally out of the blue. Suddenly one sunny summer afternoon Pidge appeared on the stable roof ridge, happily surveying the scene. A sleek racing pigeon in shining pale grey plumage we thought he'd stopped for a rest and would soon be gone. But he showed no sign of leaving. Obviously lost, he seemed happy to be here, specially when food was offered. He quickly grew quite tame and eventually we were able to catch him and read the number on his leg.

We contacted the owner in Wiltshire who asked us to take him somewhere south and throw him up into the sky. On the side of a hill twenty miles away we opened the wicker basket and away he went.

He was home before us, back on the ridge. We left him alone after that. He lived here happily for a couple of months until one day he was gone, leaving us to wonder sadly about his fate

A small bay tree languished for years in a terracotta pot, barely growing, until it was shoved into a hole behind the wall at the back of the house and left to flourish or die. It decided to flourish. Now shaved each autumn into a dense oval, it blocks the view from the office window, its evergreen cover loved by nesting wood pigeons along with roosting sparrows and starlings. The window looks directly at a nest and the sitting bird is never sure whether to sit tight and ignore me or rush away in a splutter of feathers. The cream bay flowers with tiny orange stamens and a delicate scent are so small they go unnoticed.

Flocks of cheeky house sparrows nest under the eaves and in the hedges. They love the dense yellow line of conifer which acts as a high-rise block for birds. In winter some roost in the bay tree where at dusk their raucous chattering is incredibly noisy as they settle for the night, arguing over space on a twig. Sometimes just for fun I call: 'Quiet you lot!' The startled hush lasts a few seconds before they start again, gradually subsiding into peace.

House sparrows are less common but we have plenty though we never see the rare tree sparrows. The thick hedge on the lane, mostly hawthorn, gives them cover and it's wide enough to protect them from the savage beaks of marauding crows.

The tit family are prominent with the bold little blues most common, sometimes perched on the sill peering into the house. A commotion in the tree usually means the long tailed gang has landed. Cheeky ruffians, chunky and beautifully dressed in pink and grey, we see them more in winter, arriving mob handed in groups of up to ten to plunder the nuts. The others can only watch helpless from higher branches till their thuggish cousins have moved on.

Given the bird life it seemed natural to name the rooms for them, Nuthatch, Blue Tit, Wagtail and Woodpecker and eventually Chaffinch and then the cottage, Red Kite. On a trip to Whitby, redolent of kippers and jet, in one of the intriguing alleys in the old town we found a small pottery which made pretty painted terracotta signs. We ordered one for each room. The bird signs are attractive and appeal strongly to children.

Maybe we should've called one room Jackdaw. These pushy but endearing smaller corvids with their silvery necks and light eyes are always here, especially in spring when the insistent chattering of the fledgling babies sounds loudly from the unused chimney above the kitchen. They build every year, constantly busy as the parents fly back and forth with food for gaping beaks.

Sometimes they try at the other end. Clattering noises overhead didn't register until we spotted a large hawthorn twig in the grate. But smoke from a new-lit fire quickly makes the point that building there isn't a good idea. That chimney was a nuisance in the early days. It smoked horribly, billowing into the room if the wind was in the wrong direction. We tried various cowls and

Beck dropped a brick when fitting one of them. He hadn't warned me so we'd taken no precautions such as covering furniture — in case. The resulting cloud of soot covered everything in a thin film of black dust. He seemed surprised by my fury.

In the end the solution was a higher grate which made the fire draw properly. It drew particularly well on a New Year's Eve when the central heating packed up and we had friends for supper. Beck's mother was also staying. Asleep in an armchair by the fire she was oblivious to the fierce blaze which set the whole chimney alight. For ten minutes it was chaos as we struggled to control it, rushing around her chair in near panic. As we calmed down in relief she woke up and looked at the fire with approval: 'Ee, you've got a grand fire going now.'

This communing with nature is all very well but sometimes you have to take a stand. From their station on the roofs the jackdaws watch with complaining eyes since we shut them out of their nests in the roof space above the office and our bathroom. They got in by invitation you could say, via holes left in the hope of attracting a barn owl. We were stupid not to realise how quickly these intelligent guests would capitalise on the new building and they must've been doing it for years.

Twiggy detritus began appearing, dropped because the nest top was now level with the hole. We were horrified by the size of the pile they'd created, thorny twigs and small branches, horse hair, wool and moss. These tangled nests were difficult to clear, it had to be done from inside, doubled up under the beams, shoved into plastic bags and out through the hatch into the bathroom beneath. An unpleasant dirty job, half crouched in warm, stuffy air — and a mask was essential.

In early spring the fields are pockmarked by hooves from the weeks of wet weather and strewn with remnants of hay. The land is desperate for harrowing but very forgiving and in a few weeks will look very different, the poaching smoothed as the grass grows. Two pairs of jackdaws are scratching at droppings and under the hay seeking beetles and worms and other tasty morsels. They waddle away unhurried, just far enough to retain a distance but not really concerned. The galloping dogs send them winging a low flight over the ground to settle again and continue their search. They have seen it all before, used to our presence, part of the familiar scene.

As the horses lose their thick winter coats the jackdaws perch on their rumps as they graze, pulling out thick clumps of hair. When we cleared the roof nests the contents were fascinating including bright chestnut hair from the mare Vale. You have to admire the work they put in to create such comfortable nests. On the grass in the field and on the lawn sphagnum moss is loose and tumbled by the wind where the birds have pulled it free for nesting. The strong beaks and claws of the jackdaws have done much of it though the long tailed tits and other species make great use of this soft and malleable material.

They are determined and mischievous birds, their nonchalant activity reassuring. But they don't miss much. Beck was always rushing first thing, driving down the hill, mug of coffee in one hand and a bacon sandwich on the seat beside him. Later than usual one day he went out, plate in hand but no coffee. Without thinking he put the sandwiches on the car roof and came back. Off he went again in time to see the jackdaw pair flying back to the chimney with his breakfast in their beaks. In two sharp dives they had snatched the lot. He was furious, cursing loudly, made worse because I was convulsed with laughter. It was just so funny. He was more cross with me than the birds.

We found ourselves frequently moving out of our new room because it brought in more cash. A succession of couples enjoyed staying there, especially for the views but it became increasingly inconvenient.

The small window towards the hills was usually open on warm nights and its easy access from the adjacent roof proved too tempting for the enterprising Black Sam in his younger days. More than once he made himself comfortable between sleeping guests. We had to warn people not to open the window if they were allergic to cats, or didn't like them.

One couple were especially heavy sleepers. Parliament at the time was arguing over the rights and wrongs of hunting with the prospect of a law to ban it. Country people descended several times on London to demonstrate support for the sport and to explain the issues of liberty and livelihood.

For some reason Beck went alone on one of the Shropshire buses for the big march which drew around 400,000 people to central London from all over the British Isles. Two lots of guests were tucked up in their respective rooms while I made do in the twin. They had spent some of the evening out together on the terrace enjoying a drink and the long fiery sunset.

Some time after midnight, a loud rumbling roused me to feel the whole house shaking. The glass on the bedside table fell to the floor and the dogs began barking furiously. The tremor lasted maybe a minute — just the latest in a succession of small earthquakes which have disturbed Shropshire during our time here.

The first was when we were house hunting with my father, staying in a b&b by the railway line. Beck slept through it all, assuming it was a train. By British standards this one was big, 4.8 on the Richter scale, enough to crack walls and knock stuff off supermarket shelves. Centred on Dudley in the Black Country the tremor was felt over a hundred mile radius, right across to the Welsh coast.

At breakfast the Nuthatch couple were up early discussing their disturbed night. The Woodpecker guests arrived and began telling the others how they had pulled back the bathroom curtains to see two crows on the top of the Victoria plum tree making a hearty breakfast from the best plums, always the most difficult to reach.

They laughed about the greedy birds but looked totally mystified when I asked: 'You weren't bothered by the earthquake?'

'What earthquake?'

So the earth hadn't moved for them and they slept untroubled through all the excitement. But the concrete block walls in the barn still show evidence of that night, long cracks in the pointing where the walls were shaken, made worse later by the angry hooves of horses.

To be caught in a major quake must be terrifying. My closest encounter was in the big open plan news room at the Shropshire Star with its mass of desks and computers. Just before first deadline time in late morning suddenly all the lights went out and everything stopped as the whole floor rippled beneath our feet. There was hardly enough time to be scared but it was a weird sensation to feel solid ground moving like waves. The generator kicked in and after a few gasps and exclamations we got on with getting the paper out. That building was on the site of a former coalfield, supposedly above an old mine shaft.

Lessons learned

In late spring the lane banks stand tall with red campion and cow parsley, the white haze set with flowers like jewels in platinum and the air is filled with the scent of wild garlic, thick banks of it in bloom beside the paths on Wenlock Edge.

The road from Church Preen to Chatwall provides a stunning view to the south west, a different aspect of the hills. The drive to Cardington is through an arch of tender green where the overhanging branches of oaks on either side are bright with shafts of sunlight on foliage fresh from the bud.

This is the time to watch lambs dance, in the evenings when the approach of night fills them with excitement, runnIng in small gangs about the fields, delighting in a mound or sloping ground. They race for pure fun, butting heads together, prancing stiff legged in sheer joy.

The land across the valley is suddenly pale, stripped almost to the root for the first cut of silage, stark against the deep green in the adjoining fields where cattle graze, a patchwork of shadowed gold crossed by dark hedgerows. Within days the first emerald blush creeps over as new grass emerges towards the sun.

A kestrel hovers over the paddock — Windhover, the ancient name so apt for what they do, hanging on the wind. One moment it's there in front of me and then away to the east hovering again further on, waiting for some tiny creature to emerge from cover before plunging to earth. Often one of a pair waits on the wire in the field below the house watching for movement among the tussocks of long coarse grass, home for field voles, mice and shrews.

This field used to attract barn owls, a ghostly shape quartering the land in the late afternoon approaching dusk but it's grazed much tighter now with less cover for small mammals.

Sheep always had a fascination for me and seeing the lambs close by prompted the thought of putting the vision into practice and learning more about them with a small flock of our own. They're good to run with horses, helping keep the land in good order.

It began with a few cade ewe lambs, those who for whatever reason had no mum and needed to be hand fed with a bottle. Gradually we built up to about sixty ewes, hiring tups each year from farmer friends, usually Texels, which produced a good shaped butcher's lamb from our mixed bag. It was all one big learning curve from lambing to slaughter.

Endearing creatures they are much brighter than people give them credit for. They do have a habit of following each other but that doesn't make them stupid and many show great intelligence. Trying to keep the sheep away from the horses whose food they will steal if they can, I thought all the gates were closed but one determined old ewe set off across the paddock to go the long way round.

Lambing time is hard work whether it's sixty or six hundred — watching for those about to lamb, helping another, dabbing the navels with iodine, ensuring baby is sucking properly, feeding the cades, banding tails and testicles and keeping an eye on everything.

We lambed our little flock in the barn, better for newborns if the weather is unkind and easier for humans sleepy from bed in the middle of the night. And good to have light on the job, not wandering around a cold, dark field to find a struggling ewe. A weak lamb born in the open has little chance if left unspotted by the shepherd, especially if it's a twin and the mother has her attention elsewhere. Carrion crows are quickly on the scene, going first for the eyes of helpless ewes or their lambs. Getting a lamb safely into the world is enormously satisfying. But we had a lot to learn.

Proportionately we had more than our share of triplets and with a small flock there isn't always the chance to foster one onto another ewe so we often ended up bottle feeding. One season we had quads, which was a problem, but being a big ewe she managed to rear them all with a bit of help from us.

T.S. Eliott's famous line about the cruelty of April can be horribly true. Sometimes a late covering of snow is enough to ball the horses' feet and we've had Easter guests forced to brave icy winds and biting cold in their pursuit of hilltop walks.

Farmers who plan to lamb their flock in the open fields often put the tups in later to bring an April crop. This can mean fresh grass for the newborns to play on, with sunshine on their backs, filling the ewes' udders with milk. But it can be a wickedly deceptive month with vicious weather to greet a weak wet creature as it slithers free from the warmth of the womb.

We never forgot our first spring when the neighbour who still rented the remainder land had planned a later lambing. Cold winds and driving, icy rain swept the field where the ewes were giving birth. In the morning she collected more than eighty dead lambs from the sodden grass.

We had offered her the use of the buildings which she'd used before we arrived but some kind of awkward pride made her refuse and the price was very high. But she was persuaded to bring the rest under cover in the sheep house until they'd finished and the weather improved.

We are the first house coming down off the hill and spring frequently brings a walker to the door bearing a lamb. Usually it's not abandoned, just sleeping, as its mother grazes further away.

I don't buy spring lamb. Small carcasses in the shops for Easter haven't known the joy of sunshine and young grass and their meat has little flavour. At least the later lambs enjoy summer to graze and play.

But it's hard luck to be born male in the animal world. Many ewe lambs are kept for breeding but there's only one use for the wethers, castrated rams, which are aimed at the table. That is unless they have enough quality to be used at stud.

The lambs were responsible for a small incident of international understanding when two Japanese sisters studying in London booked a spring trip with their parents.

The couple, on their first visit to the UK, knew no English except thank you and good morning but in the Japanese way they bowed to us at every turn, deep bows from the waist and we found ourselves returning the compliment.

The concept of bed and breakfast seemed totally alien to them, apparently confused by it all. Early next morning I found the father seated alone in the rocking chair on the landing. At my appearance he rose and bowed deeply then followed me down to the kitchen.

There were three lambs to feed before tackling human breakfast and he watched in silence as I prepared the bottles of milk. When I fixed the large rubber teats to the bottles his face lit up in a wide smile. 'You know about this?' I asked, waving a bottle at him as he nodded agreement.

We went out to the pen where the little ones waited. Settled on a straw-bale he lifted one lamb to his lap and took a bottle from me, knowing exactly what to do. He was delighted as the greedy lamb drained its milk and we exchanged plenty of smiles as the job was done. He inspected the rest of the flock, nodding and still smiling at me and murmuring to the sheep in Japanese. I had no idea what he was saying but we had established communication and it was probably the highlight of his stay.

He and his wife enjoyed their English breakfast. His daughters explained that the family came from a country area in Japan and knew all about sheep. They left with even more smiling and bowing. They wrote a message in the guest book which was eventually translated by a London-based Japanese lady who came with her Scottish husband to stay several times in Red Kite, visiting local friends. She was much taken with the small herb garden by the terrace, particularly the lemon balm, telling me all kinds of esoteric things about its many uses, all new to me. She loved our home-made jams and on subsequent visits brought a bag of empty jars which were always welcome. One late September visit she went back to London with several bags of cooking apples, from the Bramley above the house and repaid us with a recipe for apple cake, simple and scrumptious, now often repeated.

The tree produces a huge crop and in September when they are ready and falling off the branches we ask guests to help themselves. Some have apple trees at home but many urban dwellers are thrilled to take some home, eager to make pies for the freezer.

They store well rolled up in paper and we turn some into a spicy Bombay chutney from a recipe given by one of our Gordon setter stalwarts who always made it to raise money for the rescue group. She kept it a secret for years until moving to a home with no apple trees.

The little Victoria plum tree gives a huge crop for its size. Planted in the early years it never grew very big, probably because of its dry and sloping position and the amount of rubble buried there. Its plump luscious pink fruit hangs in clusters, easy to reach and never so many that I don't know what to do with them. They appear in a bowl on the dining room dresser as an extra offering for breakfast, delicious when truly ripe, or maybe stewed and ideal to go with cereal or yogurt. We've always taken the breakfast part of b&b very seriously, feeling strongly that breakfast is the most important meal of the day for human health.

But pushing a hand up through the leaves to grasp a plum can be hazardous if the wasps are having a field day. Just as you are about to bite into a juicy fruit you notice there's a hole in it and the hole contains a wasp. I have a lot of respect for this maligned insect because they have a role to play like any creature in nature and if left alone they needn't be a problem. But the human reaction is often to start flapping hands and arms at the insects which naturally upsets them. If ignored they usually move off somewhere else.

Once, when my ideas were less tolerant I did a stupid thing after discovering a wasp's nest under the guttering. Climbing a ladder with a can of insect spray I attacked the nest. This provoked an immediate reaction as one made a determined wasp line for me and stung me just below the eye. No serious harm done except embarrassment and a sore swollen face for a week.

Such creatures are part of life here, mammals, insects or reptiles, they all have a place but not everyone appreciates them. However wasps seem to attract a special human hatred. One lot of Chaffinch guests left a dead wasp under a glass on the windowsill. A small act of cruelty which angered me, wondering if they watched it struggle before it died or just trapped it and left it there with no thought.

With a small flock there's more time to notice the characters of individual animals and some of them certainly were characters. There was Twidget — you really shouldn't name them but it happens sometimes —he was a twin but for some reason his mother wouldn't have him. She had plenty of milk but she just wouldn't feed him so he needed a bottle. He followed us around the yard, mixing with the dogs and if any were in the kennels he would stand outside waiting for them. He identified with dogs more than sheep.

We never had the heart to send him to the abattoir so he had a very long and happy life mooching about the fields, one of the Fat Eight, the remnants of the flock. When eventually he went off his legs and couldn't get up there was only one thing for it. When our farmer friend came with the humane killer it was almost a comedy. Fired close to his head the gun made no impact except a very puzzled expression on the old boy's face, looking up as if to say: 'What was that?' His ancient bone must have been exceptionally hard. The second shot was better placed and he died quickly and peacefully.

Years before, his twin had her own drama when still a lamb. With a ministry grant we had cut back the hawthorn hedges, planting new ones to replenish the line and fenced with a double row of posts to protect the young growth. A selected few trees remained to mitigate the impact but the whole project, which Beck did in his spare time in spite of his wonky shoulder, produced a huge pile of prickly thorn brash.

In a summer dry spell we set light to the pile which burned with a fury for more than a day and left a wide area of deep ash which retained its heat for nearly a week. A few days after the fire we were horrified to find Twidget's twin standing in the middle of it, ash nearly to her knees.

Her hooves were burning, literally red hot, but she seemed remarkably unconcerned. Cold water and various anti-burn salves saved her feet but it had affected the under tissue and although she lived to a good age and had several lambs of her own she was always tender on them. What induced her to try fire-walking was a puzzle, maybe she couldn't feel the heat through her hard little hooves.

Then there was Blackie, one of two Badger Faced ewes we took on from a friend. She was an escape artist and would disappear with her lambs in search of better pickings up and down the grass verges. In her fourteen years she produced a lot of lambs for a small black native sheep, mostly twins but also two sets of white triplets.

Twice she caused a stir when we were entertaining friends for summer supper. Someone looked out while the wine was flowing and did a double take to see this little black sheep strolling past with her three white lambs, waiting by the gate for one of us to leave the table and oblige her by opening it. The second time was hard to believe because it was classic deja vue.

We never discovered how she got out but she would take herself off to see what she could find and come back when it suited her. Triplets are hard on a ewe and usually one is taken away and fostered on a singleton mum but Blackie reared them on her own with the help of 'the long acre' as the gipsies' call it.

Supper parties were often interrupted by animals one way or another — there is a photo somewhere of a lamb at the dinner table — some crisis with a horse or dog or simply leaving the table before dessert to shut the hens in for the night, something which always annoyed Beck. A friend once said, 'You take good care of your livestock' and his wife retorted sharply: 'If she didn't they'd soon be dead stock'.

Before we got going with the accommodation Linnet spaniel made her mark at supper time. There were just five of us and the main event was a shoulder of venison keeping hot in the bottom oven with the door ajar, while we ate the starter. Beck went off to start carving the joint but was back immediately flourishing a 7-shaped bone with a few strands of meat clinging to it.

'Do you mean this?' he said with a grin to gasps from the guests and loud laughter from father.

Linnet had nudged open the door and scoffed the lot in short order, despite the meat being hot. The most annoying thing was that she suffered no ill effects from her gluttony. But what to do about supper? I told my laughing parent he could have an omelette which made him go very quiet. Fortunately on the day before I'd been to a press open day at the local abattoir and came away with several sirloin steaks which fitted the bill nicely.

But dealing with stock means facing hard issues of life and death which can be very distressing and for an animal lover there is a huge dichotomy in making these difficult decisions. At one period we were producing a good number of lambs which went to the abattoir in Craven Arms to be exported to the continent, mainly France. It was never an easy journey and heart-snatching to leave them there, waiting in pens for slaughter. But that is why they were bred and we were reasonably happy that their end was humane. It was better to send them on the hook rather than have them suffer a long journey by road and ferry.

Craven Arms was to us a slightly weird location. Billed as the gateway to the Marches it's a name remembered vividly from my Berkshire childhood. As a horse obsessed youngster I would pour over the equine magazines and one particular advert always intrigued me, the one headlined Craven Arms Horse Repository. This conjured images of horses, probably hunters, arriving by train in the old wooden livestock containers and presumably stabled at livery around the town.

When we first moved to Shropshire the town still had its wide area of stockyards, now vanished beneath ugly new developments which have changed the character of the place. The comment of a former colleague summed it up. Brendon Mulholland, was the once famous Daily Mail reporter who, with another, was sent to prison for refusing to reveal his sources back in the 1960's over the Vassall spy scandal. He came to live in Craven Arms and worked for a while doing subbing shifts on the Shropshire Star. Discussing the town one morning in a quiet moment he mused: 'I always expect to meet John Wayne walking down the street' — it had that kind of atmosphere. Sadly he died too young at only fifty-eight.

We kept a few lambs till the next year for ourselves and friends, preferring the older teg meat which is nearer mutton, a better flavour than young lamb. These were killed in the cold months on farm by a licensed butcher. This may sound horrible but these were the lucky ones. For the animal it was better to be brought a few yards in a place they know with no fear or unpleasant expectation and given a quick death. It wasn't easy to watch but as meat eaters the kindest end for animals was what mattered.

It's too easy to let the heart rule when dealing with animal problems and I learned this lesson the hard way. Our land was deficient in copper. The lack of this element causes problems in lambs, particularly swayback, a progressive hind limb weakness leading to paralysis due to damage in mid-pregnancy in copper deficient ewes.

This was solved by drenching the ewes with a copper supplement before tupping but one little fellow was born with wobbly back legs. He survived but could never walk too well and in that state I hadn't the heart to put the rubber bands on his testicles at a few days old. Inevitably he became a pet and we named him Wobbly. He managed very well and mooched about the place making friends with the dogs who weren't quite sure what to make of him.

But due to my misjudgment he came to a sad end when the ewes were ready for tupping. We found him dead in the field. He must have tried his luck on some of them and toppled off onto his back. Because of his weak legs he would have been unable to right himself.

The foot and mouth year was an appalling experience which immediately put a stop to any chance of guests. Just as we began to do it seriously the countryside was closed, the public banned from footpaths and bridleways in a bid to stop the disease spreading. We will probably never know the truth of what really happened that year but a lot of people got rich on it, while others had their lives destroyed. The slaughter was heart-breaking and the stench of burning carcases pervaded the air for months. Farmers lost stock lines and herds built up over many years, their life's work ruined in the ghastly campaign of slaughter and burn.

When we found lesions on the mouths of some lambs we had a decision to make. We knew from the early years that orf is endemic on the farm, a virus that affects sheep and particularly lambs. The pustules and lesions are unpleasant but it's treatable and usually passes leaving little ill effect. The virus, like ringworm, lives in woodwork and springs to life after being dormant for years.

We should have reported the lesions to the ministry and the flock would have been killed. But we were certain it was orf and not the dreaded foot and mouth. Financially we would have been better off with the compensation but every sheep in the area, all over the adjacent hillsides would have been added to the dreadful pyres which blighted the countryside.

It seemed so wrong. It's likely that many of the animals across Britain which were slaughtered probably only had orf because there were so few vets who had actually seen a case of foot and mouth. The last major outbreak had been back in 1967 and that started in Shropshire.

A group of lambs near Minsterley were penned in a lane overnight, against a holly hedge. In the morning their mouths were blistered and bloody, probably from nibbling the holly, but they were all destroyed. In autumn when all surviving sheep were blood tested, ours were clear.

My experience of orf was very personal. It's a zoonosis — people can catch it — and I did. My hands were always getting minor knocks and scratches which healed quickly. But a mark on the back of my hand, caught with a hammer, and a scratch on my forefinger both came up in big purple lesions. It seemed wise to visit the doctor, just in case, though I knew what it was.

A waste of time. He looked at my hand with a puzzled expression but agreed when I told him it was orf. Two of the bottle-fed lambs had mouth blisters which my hands had touched. I knew exactly what it was because I'd heard it on the Archers. There was no treatment, I just had to wait for it to disappear.

The blisters took a long time to subside. It also took a long time to forget because for several years I was reminded by the dark red marks which reappeared on my hand when too much alcohol had been taken.

Both working full time we struggled to fit in all we had to do. I changed to freelance shifts and later took the job as editor of the firm's monthly farming paper with a brief to manage it as I thought best. That meant some working from home, unusual then but helpful in coping with life at North Hill. But the whole set-up ended in crisis when the bed and breakfast got going and I muddled the dates.

The paper had a four week run-in with one easy week. Twice a year there was an extra week, a good time to take a holiday or generally relax. Business was now hectic and my mistake meant deadline week coincided with a busy week for breakfasts and ewes giving birth. It was chaos. Something had to give. With plans for a new room only in our heads it was a big decision to give up a salary to rely on accommodation income but we had faith that the upward trend would continue.

We soon had enough of the room switching routine and decided we must have another en suite room. The spider-infested outside toilet, used by the farmer when the house was a holiday let, was next to a small stone bothy, once a calf shed and another dumping ground for clutter. It offered possibilities. Its two battered oak doors were grey with age, badly fitting and awkward.

More of the stuff from Dad's home was dumped there, chairs, boxes still unopened from the move, two old paraffin heaters, demijohns for winemaking, a table and some chairs and other junk. Idly looking in there one morning I decided to be ruthless. Once everything was outside, destined for the dustmen or the tip, the empty space was larger than we realised and with the plumbing already in place the obvious thing was to knock through to make a new room — an answer to our problem.

Beck studied the little building from all angles and his imagination got to work. We agreed it was worth doing. 'We could make a feature of that corner,' he said. 'If we rounded the stonework it would add a lot of character and sort of lead people into the property. I can do some of it myself.'

We looked for a builder but though three came in turn to examine the project, not one of them grasped the concept of building the stonework in a curve. They seemed puzzled by the idea and in the end he said: 'It's ridiculous, anyone would think it was complicated, I'll build it myself.'

It was hard work, often at the end of a busy day. The solid concrete blocks for the partition wall were heavy and had to be lifted up about eight feet so it was no surprise when he began to complain of persistent aches in his arm muscles. Together we managed all the timber work, including wooden beams which were purely cosmetic but added ambience. We did the woodwork on the roof but found a tiler to complete the job.

The work was finished but aching arms still troubled him. The physio suggested it could be polymyalgia but blood tests were negative. He did so much physical work and that seemed to explain it, accepted as something he had to live with. A hot bath was the only thing which brought relief.

We were pleased with the final effect when Chaffinch was decorated and finished. We'd gone a bit overboard with the bathroom tiling, falling in love with some expensive porcelain tiles but it was worth it, an attractive cosy room ready to welcome its first guests in July.

The electrician was making final adjustments and he'd just fixed the TV in place on the wall. We switched on to test it and stared transfixed at the set, unable to take in what we were seeing, shocking pictures of dreadful carnage so unexpected in that casually normal moment. Sirens and screams and scenes of smoke and total confusion as the horror of the London bombings unfolded on screen. Perched on the bed I saw dreadful images of devastation on the underground and on the street around the wrecked bus.

Four legged guests

Dogs are an integral part of life here — the spaniels, English Springer variety, and Gordon setters, bred for the Scottish grouse moors. For better or worse, sometimes they bring embarrassment and occasionally complaints. They bark at people walking down the lane especially if they linger to take a look at us. The farm is on one of the printed walking routes around Church Stretton and at weekends and bank holidays walkers in groups, in ones or twos or sometimes a solitary figure tramp up and down. The dogs are doing their job, a good deterrent to unwanted visitors. As they say it's no good keeping a dog and barking yourself. They think they own the road and in a way they do since it's part of the property. Sometimes when they are lined up barking along the paddock fence I remember the line from Omar Khayyam: 'The dogs bark but the caravan moves on'.

Gordon Setters for me go way back but the spaniels were more unintended. Beck had a Springer called Flint before we met and we bought a bitch puppy for his daughter as a birthday present. That was Susie, a cross between show and working lines. When she had a litter we brought home a little bitch named Linnet — and the rest is history. We've been breeding them ever since in a continuous line for more years than can be told. Dogs are good for people, caring for them helps keep us healthy.

Once online with our own website we made it clear this is farmhouse bed and breakfast and as such, home to life of many kinds, the implied message being, 'don't bother coming if you don't like animals'. For many they are part of the attraction and often when guests call to rebook they say 'when we came before you had a litter of puppies in the kitchen'.

Puppies and paying guests have a somewhat symbiotic relationship in that people who buy a puppy sometimes decide they like the place and come back on holiday. So we get to keep in touch with our doggy family. On the other hand guests who come to stay often end up buying a puppy, such as the busy pair who run a nursery in Gloucestershire. They find it hard to get away in the summer because of watering all the plants. When they first discovered Red Kite Cottage they had a little West Highland White terrier bitch but fell in love with the spaniels. When Teasel had her first litter they bought a puppy and in due course, after the Westie had gone, they had a sister from the second litter. When they can manage two or three nights in the summer it's good to have the spaniels visiting.

Similarly the couple from Sussex who found us first as a stopover on their way to Scotland with their springer have become good friends and now have a black and white girl from Tawny, Teasel's daughter. It turned out that David was brought up in Shropshire and spent one night as a cadet marching on a route that took him through Cardington.

We tend to remember people by their dogs: Irish Water Spaniels from Northumberland and the same weekend four girls from Nottingham who came in the sunshine with a Portuguese Water Dog. Their stay was slightly hampered as the girl who booked the trip arrived on crutches with an Achilles tendon injury from playing football. Two Border collies came all the way from Denmark with their people, who loved Shropshire and came a second time to compete in sheepdog trials in North Wales.

As breeders of pedigree dogs it's interesting to meet different breeds instead of something with poodle in it. We attract dog lovers as one of the few places in the area that will accept canine guests. Among those we see regularly are a Dandie Dinmont and his little friend a Glen of Imaal terrier from Ireland. Both these breeds are rare and on the Vulnerable Native Breeds list, like our own Gordon Setters.

The Dandies were developed around the Scottish Borders but gained their name after the publication of Sir Walter Scott's novel Guy Mannering. In the novel Scott modelled the character Dandie Dinmont on a neighbouring farmer who owned terriers called Pepper and Mustard.

But not all guests appreciate having animals around. One disgruntled husband was very affronted to find a cat asleep on the stairs. The cat was unconcerned as they passed him. Black Sam, or Sambo as he'd been called before he came to us, was the most unusual cat we'd ever known. He had history, having started life with a sibling at the neighbour's house. Both cats disappeared and one was found dead at the roadside. The other turned up in the village and was adopted by the old colonel and his wife who called him Sambo. They were of a generation not bothered by political correctness and with family links to a grapefruit island in the West Indies they had no problem with that name because he was a black cat.

They had an elderly Labrador and the two were great friends so when infirmity forced them to leave their home he came to us. He was not in the least phased by the presence of several large dogs. In fact he appeared to think he was a dog and took to them very quickly. He stayed at first in what was then still the garage but soon took control of the kitchen, sharing a bed with whichever canine was the current incumbent and in later years tucked up cosily at night between Bryony the Gordon setter and spaniel Millie. He and Millie were especially close. When her first litter of puppies was due she was anxious and disturbed at the first signs of contractions during the evening but he cuddled close beside her until she began whelping.

Two ladies from Lancashire were expected in the days before Chaffinch and Kite were built. They were due on a Monday, always a busy day when Lyn comes to help with bed changing and cleaning. We were enjoying our mid morning coffee when a knock on the door announced the very early arrival of one of the guests, small, elderly and with a certain screwed up, grumpy expression.

The rooms were not ready and though we explained that guests were not expected till the afternoon, there was no apology. She made herself at home in the sitting room, making it plain she expected morning coffee and biscuits, not normally included in what we offer.

I didn't have the courage to tell her to go away and come back at the proper time. On the plus side Black Sam made himself happily at home on her lap which she didn't seem to mind.

This was the most inconvenient example but it has happened several times although the website and information issued to guests makes it clear that arrival is after 4pm unless by prior arrangement. About a week after they left a snotty letter arrived to tell us that while she had enjoyed her stay to some degree she didn't like the doggy smell. She got a polite reply to thank her for this information and assure her of improvements. Which we did.

Some years later more ladies came from Lancashire, they couldn't have been more different. One of them had old affiliations with Shropshire and knew the area well. Having found us, she returned with various friends. She became a friend and we would sit gossiping on the terrace in the summer evenings.

Certain dogs have also become friends but sometimes canine guests come alone when their people have gone away. Little Ross was one of these, a charming and well-behaved Border terrier. Both he and his owners Madeline and Peter are gone but he was a particular favourite and mixed well with our own dogs.

He was a real character but caused a few problems, particularly when the cattle were on the top fields around the reservoir. Cows and calves in this single suckler herd were used to seeing the setters and spaniels and took little notice of them but Ross came with us one day and they didn't like the look of him at all. His little tan coloured body caught their attention immediately as I was peering inside the reservoir to check the float switch. I looked up to find myself surrounded by most of the herd with the rest of them including the Hereford bull hastening across to see what was going on. Thinking to go the long way round just in case, I made for what is left of the hawthorn hedge about forty yards away. Ross followed me and the cattle followed him. Just in time I scrambled into the nearest tree as the whole herd thundered past on either side.

They galloped across to the far fence, calves kicking up their heels in delight and tail-swishing mothers bellowing in a mixture of anger and excitement, mainly excitement. But they headed back the way I wanted to go and hung around in a big group by the gate which meant a long detour to get home — and not a dog in sight.

Anxious for little Ross I needn't have worried as they were all waiting for me back in the yard. Cows anxious for their calves can be more dangerous than a bull who is usually content to carry on grazing and ignore human presence. The worst thing to do when chased by a cow or a bull is hang on to your dog. Let it go, it'll get away to safety.

Another time Ross disappeared overnight, or so we thought. A couple arrived with another Border terrier, a little bitch, which he greeted as if he knew they were the same breed. He usually slept in the kitchen with some of the others but had occasionally found his way upstairs through the wrought iron gate at the bottom.

In the morning he was missing and we were just starting to panic when the husband from Nuthatch came downstairs with his own little dog and Ross following happily. He explained that late in the evening as the couple were settling down for the night Ross had gone in through the half open door and made himself at home cuddling up with the little bitch in her cosy bed. They didn't mind and said he was good as gold all night.

An encouraging increase in bookings made us realise how much this comparatively unspoiled county generates a fierce loyalty in those who know it. Once visited it seems to draw them back. Shropshire people are generally friendly and welcoming, often sparing time for a chat.

Drivers speeding through between the hills on the A49 en route to somewhere else don't realise what they're missing. But those who stay a while are charmed by the elusive air of time warp. In literature Shropshire pops up in unexpected places, mentioned incidentally. Housman's Blue Remembered Hills and Mary Webb's evocative writing summon the essence of the wilder scenes.

In Precious Bane she introduces the concept of the sin-eater, a practice well known in Marches history, a burden taken on by her ill-fated character Gideon.

The last known holder of this dubious title lies buried in the small village of Ratlinghope. Both Webb and Malcolm Saville conjure the grandeur of the Long Mynd, the Stiperstones and the Devil's Chair in their work. And Winifred Holtby - writing about distant south Yorkshire - introduces Shropshire as somewhere desirable and far away.

Central on the UK map, families from different areas of the country and around the world find their way to us for reunions and parties, comrades who met at university come here to relive their student days and walk the hills. Travellers often book a night or two to break their journey up or down the country— it's a long way from Dorset or Devon to the Highlands of Scotland.

Not everyone comes back but this hillside spot has become a special place for many.

Early on two sisters came, from Norfolk and Bristol and their brother from across the Atlantic in New England. They became regulars, sometimes just the three of them or with children and extended families, turning up usually during the kinder months.

We got to know them and enjoy their company but one visit was less happy when the youngsters brought their Dalmatian which was very listless for a young dog. Off its food with no energy it was sick, which rang a warning bell. It was a lovely bitch, kind and obedient but obviously not right. The only possibility that made sense was poisoning from something picked up before they came. We urged a visit to the vet but they decided to wait until they were home. She had in fact picked up some form of poison and died from it. In rural Norfolk they lived near several large shoots and it seems likely the poor girl had found a rabbit or bird laced with poison to kill foxes or raptors. Strictly illegal but sadly something that still happens.

A keen biker with a big collection back home brother Daniel sometimes arrives alone at short notice on a powerful bike, a big bearded man in black leathers bearing a can of New England maple syrup. He made a delicious habit of the maple syrup and one gift arrived in the post. It was through him we discovered the more remote places on the west coast of Scotland and magical Applecross, reached by a high rugged pass over the mountain and known for delicious langoustines from the bay.

An unusual man he boasts three nationalities, British, American and Swiss due to an accident of birth, having a Swiss mother and grandmother. His family had strong connections with Craven Arms where his grandfather had moved from Norfolk to join a legal practice.

The family were great walkers, relishing the challenges of the Long Mynd and no visit to Shropshire is complete for Dan and his sisters without a pilgrimage to Ashes Hollow, rekindling childhood memories. One time he brought his whole family, including a toddler grand-daughter, who spent much of the time in the kitchen, sitting in the dog bed with Millie who loved the attention of children.

Memory tells me I was anxious about the hygiene aspect with the child wallowing among muddy paws and dog hairs though the parents were unconcerned. But then a bit of old fashioned mud, sand and earthworms are part of childhood. There's a strong case to be made that modern children don't get enough contact with such things and so never get the chance to build up immunity. Too much bleach splashed around. Similarly the obsession with washing everything. Nothing tastes better than fruit picked from the vine. Raspberries and strawberries especially lose much of their flavour in water and a touch of soil on a fresh pulled carrot shouldn't matter.

Some acquaintances turn up their nose if offered fresh picked vegetables and view wild mushrooms with horror. If it's not neatly packaged on a supermarket shelf they won't touch it.

Dan regaled other guests one morning with tales from America, including a trip into Canada when he was stopped on entry by border officials asking where he was going. The answer — Cambridge, Ontario — brought another question, where do you live? Cambridge, Massachusetts. Pressed further by the suspicious officers with the question, where were you born, his answer Cambridge, England caused them to detain him for further enquiries. They just didn't believe him.

He was keen to introduce his American son-in-law to the delights of English kippers. Daniel likes them in pairs and had demolished his while the younger man was still working out how to handle the fish, getting into a mess with the bones. There's a knack to it. He managed one but offered the other to Daniel who consumed it with relish. Kippers are a peculiarly British thing and hard to find across the pond.

Another American was not so amenable. Arriving with her English husband she made a big point of being vegan. Not a problem, although her husband, who had ordered a full breakfast, mentioned that at home they had two fridges because she couldn't bear the thought of having her food anywhere near his. That seemed a little extreme. But at breakfast next morning she watched aghast as the eggs, bacon and sausage arrived.

She sat a moment watching before pushing back her chair in a token of disgust to declare rudely: 'I can't stand this', flouncing from the room without even drinking her coffee.

What she did about breakfast we never knew but I saw a slight smile playing around her husband's lips as he ignored her antics and continued to enjoy his. There was no sign of her on the second morning and we wondered how that relationship endured.

Guests come because they were born in Shrewsbury or some small country village in the hills, drawn back from wherever life has led them to the place that will always be home. Some have family links from way back.

It's the hills that are such a fundamental attraction, the panorama of peaks and valleys is magical . Among the things that enchanted us when we first came south was the gathering of lapwings on the traffic island at Meole Brace. At certain times of year they were feeding on the grass, unbothered by passing vehicles.

But they have long departed in the wake of the town's development, part of the birds' dramatic decline both here and the rest of the. country. So many of their traditional breeding grounds in wet meadows and rushy pastures have disappeared.

The flat lands of eastern England send a steady flow of visitors drawn to the ridges and slopes of south Shropshire, walkers, would-be fell runners and cyclists, pitting themselves against the gradients in contrast to the level country around Cambridge and the Fens. It gives them a fitness edge for anything competitive, like horses which get fitter more quickly in hill country.

A family we called 'the tall cyclists' arrive regularly, father and sons all very tall and keen cyclists. One son would leave here on his impressive machine to cover up to twenty miles around the hills while his parents were walking.

In August they went blackberrying, picking on the sunny south facing slope towards Nant Valley. This unspoiled hidden area of our neighbour's land, a natural amphitheatre, overgrown with scrub and bracken is home for many small lives. In spring before the bracken reappears a soft blue haze drifts on the slopes as the wild native bluebells emerge, delicate and understated. The slopes are steep and hard for walking but one spring, venturing with the dogs as far as the tiny stream that winds its way downhill I found a flush of tight green foliage; wild strawberries, their tiny buds on the point of breaking into flower. These exquisite fruits can be found in hidden places among the less trodden paths in the hills.

This insignificant patch was the subject of a botanical investigation some years back which revealed a remarkable number of species including five species of fern, Wood Anemone and Wild Angelica, no less than eight types of sedge, golden-saxifrage, Crested Dog's-tail, honeysuckle and trefoils, the highly poisonous Dog's Mercury, red and white campions and Ragged-Robin, vetches and speedwells plus a range of trees such as the lovely whitebeam, aspen, rowan, maples, willows, elder and oak. From the hill above you can appreciate the thickly wooded nature of the valley bottom and more fields surrounded by trees.

On their excursion our guests returned with an impressive bucketful of shining blackberries. Grateful for this unexpected bounty I turned it into jam so they could take some home as a reward for their efforts. They seemed very pleased with the result — the flavour of fresh blackberry jam or jelly on hot buttered toast is another of life's small pleasures. August is the peak month for blackberries, though there are still plenty to find in September. Beyond that they go soggy; the old saying is that after the 30th the devil spits on them.

Jam making was something I'd never done, though I knew the rudiments through watching my mother. The vegetable garden has currants, both black and red, and raspberries and gooseberries among other things so it was a no brainer to turn the fruit into jams for the table.

The Aga makes the job so simple, simmering fruit efficiently and sterilising jars in the bottom oven. Unless they are confirmed marmalade fans who will have nothing else for breakfast, the sight of interesting ramekins of fruity jam is a winner with guests.

In my 'try it and see' style of cookery experiments don't always work. But the Gooseberry Gamble was a winner. The result of last year's dessert gooseberries still languishing in the freezer coincided with a good crop of raspberries and red currants. The guests loved it and much of the year's stock was sold to those eager to buy a pot.

Another success was also gooseberry-based. The label on the bush is long gone but its fruit, when it can evade the onslaught of the crows, ripens to a subtle red. We found a recipe which suggested trailing a few blooms of elderflower through the mixture during the boil to add a subtle flavour. But by the time the gooseberries were ripe the elder flowers had turned into green berries.

Then I thought of rosewater, used in the days of more adventurous supper party cooking. This 'rose hinted' gooseberry jam was another hit.

I learned to make even better use of the creamy clusters of the elder which decorates the hedgerows in early summer. They're best picked in the morning before insects harvest the flowers' pale yellow pollen and the delicate aroma begins to fade in the growing warmth. With only water, lemon juice and citric acid crystals the cordial is much nicer than anything you can buy and ideal with ice on a hot summer day.

The hills attract other visitors, helicopters and planes, mostly from the RAF station at Shawbury, north of Shrewsbury and we came to the conclusion long ago that North Hill is a marker for their training exercises, a precise spot on the hill in an expanse of open land. That's not official but it makes sense.

Helicopters are unsettling, the heavy grumble of their approach brings an almost atavistic sense of incipient panic, an urge not to be seen, to hide from the menace in the sky. This may be simply fear of attack from above but I imagine being a target chased by a chopper in some distant scene of war.

The loud yellow and black machines with winking tails often pass directly over the house, sometimes low enough to frighten the horses. They come regularly in ones and twos, often more, sometimes on nap-of-the-earth low-altitude flight training. As they fly up the valley towards Caradoc we look down on them before they are almost lost against the dark flank of the hill, rising at the last moment to clear the slope. In the early days huge Hercules transport planes would follow rumbling slower on the same path and vanish towards the Mynd. Higher up the sky shows white vapour trails of commercial aircraft.

From an equine point of view the hot air balloons which drift over mostly in the summer months are more worrying. These unpredictable craft, subject to the vagaries of the wind, sometimes drop very low and the loud whooshing sound of the burner blasting up to lift the balloon scares the animals.

But they also seem fascinated as they float by, rising like a mighty bubble from behind the hill. They stand watching, ears pricked till they decide they're frightened and gallop away to turn again for another look.

A ballooning colleague took us up once from the top field, rising gently to about two hundred feet. But with barely a whisper of wind we hung around over the valley for nearly an hour enjoying the view and speculating on what would happen next. Which was a sudden change as a brisk wind blew up from nowhere to send us moving fast eastwards down the valley.

I caught Liz's anxious expression before she said: 'We'd better get down or we shall be taken for miles in this.'

She was an experienced operator with her first balloon and we watched, exhilarated but slightly nervous, gripping the edge of the basket as she scanned the ground below for a suitable place to land. Wires are the big danger and farmers' fields are often criss-crossed with them, not easy to see from above.

As we lost height she spotted a welcoming pasture empty of animals just past Gretton and we began dropping nicely to a smooth landing. As the gondola was almost touching down a huge gust of wind took over and whisked us up again towards a big hawthorn hedge.

'Hang on tight!' Liz ordered as the basket was dragged through the top of the hedge into the next field, fortunately another pasture. We bumped along the ground for about fifty yards before the thing stopped, the envelope holding it upright.

As the adrenaline pumped we all grinned at each other, shaken but unhurt. Some time later she agreed to do a birthday treat for a local farmer who went up with his daughter. His wife and I were the pick-up team. Expecting from the last experience that the balloon would just hover about we stayed idly chatting for too long and then realised we'd lost it. Again the wind had taken control and the balloon was heading fast into the west. We scrambled to locate it, speeding down country lanes in generally the right direction just in time to see it coming down on the lower slope of Ragleth Hill. We got to them as Liz was hauling in the deflated envelope watched by her dazed passengers.

'Had to get down quick,' she said. 'We'd have been half way across Wales by now.'

Shell shock

In the cold months of January and February few people need a room, maybe for the odd funeral or a family party but not many travel in winter for the fun of it. The weather is so variable, sometimes these months bring mild, almost balmy days which fool you into thinking spring is almost here.

But one January in the new century was a real stinker, the temperature dropped to minus nine and the cold water taps in the kitchen and our bathroom were frozen and unusable for days. At the most exposed end of the house our room catches the full blast of the north winds. For nearly three weeks it was horrible, everything outside was solid, stable drinkers, water troughs and hose pipes.

We were boarding an extra horse for a friend and all water had to be hosed from the tap in the boiler room and the hose brought back indoors to stop it freezing along its length. We kept meaning to check on Chaffinch but somehow never got out there and we hadn't turned off the water. When the thaw finally began the water for Beck's hot bath was running very slow, so the pump was turned to constant. In the sunshine next day we checked the room to find it six inches deep in water, still cascading down the wall from a burst pipe in the roof.

The pump was still working merrily, sending the contents of the reservoir through the break in the pipe. The water drained away very slowly via the shower, a nightmare which took twenty-four hours to clear. Surveying the flood we found with relief that the electrics were safe but the carpet was sodden. It had to come out but moving it was a struggle, held in place by the bed. Beck had been feeling rough for a few days and unusually hadn't the strength to move it. Neighbour Phil helped drag the soaking carpet out to hang in the barn where it dried without shrinking. The original fitters came out and kindly refitted it at no charge.

A few days later Beck's debility was explained when he was doubled up with excruciating pain, landing him in intensive care for several days with sepsis caused by a blocked bile duct. At the time I had no idea how serious it was but the surgeon said afterwards it had been 'a close run thing'. He recovered well and we thought no more about it though he still mentioned the aching muscles. But the incident masked insidious unknown changes.

We often saw buzzards, kestrels and sparrowhawks but for years there was no sign of Red Kites. These spectacularly beautiful birds were something of an obsession with us. Newsworthy after the successful introduction of stock from Spain and Scandinavia they were still rare in Shropshire, with an occasional bird from Wales where what had been a very small number of breeding pairs close to extinction had increased to a healthy population. Gradually they appeared more often and now they breed successfully this side of the border, though their nesting sites are still kept secret as protection against inane humans ready to harm them or at best take the eggs.

They are around more often now and from the window three kites are visible sailing in a blue sky freed from the early fog. In some areas they can be a pest, like seagulls at the coast. They swarm over the Chilterns recalling black kites in Indian cities. Alfresco diners sometimes have their food snatched away by a swooping bird, a rush of mighty wings and huge outstretched talons at close quarters.

It would be sad if these stunning birds are endangered again through their own actions where they have become accustomed to easy pickings. At least here in Shropshire they are still shy of human presence. Their behaviour differs from buzzards which are usually seen higher in the sky, circling on the thermals as they watch for prey or sometimes on the ground pecking worms and insects from the soil. The kites fly low and more direct as they prospect for food, low enough to see the markings beneath their wings, the forked red tail and the beautiful grey head and yellow beak before they float into the distance.

When we decided to build a separate cottage this special bird was the obvious choice for a name. Since Red Kite Cottage was built the kites breed within three miles and are frequent visitors quartering the land.

The worst part of the farm was a decrepit concrete block 'garage' with a collapsed roof, full of the accumulated junk of years, an eyesore. The more memorable items included a pair of corsets, old spectacles, a chamber pot, items of kitchenware and a TV, along with barrels and boxes of old books and magazines. Presumably until the road was concreted rubbish had to be carted away to the tip because the bin lorry couldn't make it.

The redeeming feature was the black poplar tree whose branches partly hid this ugly building. For years Beck wanted to knock it down, 'tidy it up' but once gone we couldn't claim to be doing up an existing building. The idea came from an old stone farm we knew in Burgundy, b&b with a kitchen for guests' use. With so much great food available in Shropshire, real butchers and the famous Ludlow food festival, we figured guests might like to cook for themselves as a change from dining out.

The planners passed the design by the obliging nephew and work began one wet February day. His vision for a stone cottage and terrace turned out far better than expected. The eyesore and one section of the sheep house behind were demolished and the black poplar had to go, which was a pity but necessary. We were sorry to see it go, a living entity with a life of its own but it was just in the wrong place.

The decision to use stone probably helped with the planners. The soft chisel-kind sandstone of North Shropshire is now weathered into the landscape. We hadn't realised stone could vary so much in character and quality. Beck made several journeys towing a flatbed trailer, bringing tons of it in large chunks to be cut on site. It was hard to manoeuvre and unloading it by hand revealed an increasing weakness, where once it would have been nothing. One afternoon he made an uncharacteristic hash of reversing the trailer into position, drawing an unkind comment from the builder.

It was exciting seeing the foundations laid in the muddy ground and I was around to keep an eye on things — aggravation for the builders — but this time making my points before things went wrong. But kept well supplied with tea they were a good bunch whose skill with stonework was impressive. One of them was a man totally off the radar, with no car, bank account or national insurance number. Made homeless after a row with his woman he walked over the hill hoping we'd take him in — which we did for several weeks until we were busy again and he had to move on before becoming a permanent fixture.

Watching them work the raw stone, chiselling flat faces for the outside walls was fascinating. Once the foundations were ready the base arrived courtesy of several lorry-loads of wet concrete. Next morning a trail of dog footprints showed all across the surface, identified by size as one of the springers. But the building inspector triggered a bigger problem to delay the job, we needed a radon test. Parts of Shropshire have a high radon content, a gas that lurks in the rock and soil beneath us. This involved cutting out a rectangular lump of the fresh concrete to be left open for a few days to let out any possible emissions. This seemed absolutely crackers given the house had been there since the 1840s without any problems from this mystery gas.

By then we felt we belonged and watched with a small thrill of pleasure as the stone plaque carved with our initials and the date was mortared into the front wall facing the valley.

Other eyes were also waiting impatiently for the roof to go on. By the end of April it was ready for tiling and the swallows had arrived, prospecting for nest sites. Several pairs had renovated their usual spots in the stables and barn but others, perched on the power lines opposite, were eyeing up the possibilities of this new location. They chattered eagerly to each other watching the builders at work as if saying: 'Hurry up, we need to be in there.'

Even while the tiles were going on the birds began flying in and out of the window and door spaces, settled on the ceiling beams, deciding on suitable sites. They were very determined. The builders needed to fix the ceiling but the swallows didn't care. It was hard not to laugh as they moaned about the predicament and extra work. The woodwork wasn't ready so the only solution was to block all access with hardboard which had to be partially removed each day to get enough light to work. The little raiders were eventually deterred and found other nooks for their nests.

The new room was already on the website and we began taking bookings from July which put the builders under pressure. They worked hard to make it in time. With the carpet laid and the furniture finally in place the effect was pleasing. The final touch was the woollen rug we had bought in north east India, depicting the lotus flower in blue and gold. It was the year of 9/11 at a camp for Tibetan refugees in Assam where they earned a living making rugs. These were mostly garish depictions of tigers and lions, popular with tourists where they were destined to be sold. But we spotted something finer tucked away on a high shelf and asked: 'What about the one up there?'

'That's not for sale,' we were told, 'that's going to Dharamsala for the Dalai Llama.'

'Can we at least look at it?'

The rug was brought down and laid, not on the floor but on a table — it wasn't meant for a floor. The only thing in the place worth having, we really liked it but they insisted it was not for sale. I recall saying: 'Can't you make another one?'

The dealing took a while but in the end they agreed to let us have it. Back home we didn't know what to do with it. Its spiritual connections kept it rolled up in the corner of my office for nine years until the freshly painted long wall in the cottage just cried out for a hanging. So the lotus flowers found their home, intriguing those guests who notice and fitting well with the decor.

The first visitors to enjoy the new room were a large friendly couple with two very tiny Chihuahuas who helped by pointing out a few shortcomings.

They returned the next year. After them came an elderly couple, a retired army officer and his wife, who booked for a fortnight, wanting supper as well. My heart sank at the prospect because providing evening meals is a whole different ball game and it's difficult to charge enough to make it worthwhile. It takes a big chunk of time planning and executing a reasonable menu.

We succeeded in persuading them to try the local pub on some evenings but what they really wanted was the convenience of just popping across to the house. But they enjoyed their stay and seemed reluctant to leave. They left a peculiar mess in the fridge which turned out to be not nearly as bad as it looked. Several bottles of beer had exploded in the freezer compartment.

A steady stream of new visitors began, all pleased with the cottage and its situation, the views of Caradoc and the Lawley a big attraction. During the first few years it acquired a list of regulars which is the key to this type of business.

Among them in the first full year was a pair of unusual guests who arrived with two couples booked in Kite and Chaffinch. Zill and Gulliver are tortoises, both much older than their owners who visit several times a year. These loveable reptiles come during the warmer months to mooch about the terrace, a lovely sun trap for evening drinks, completed just in time for their arrival.

They are especially fond of dandelions and sow thistles, soft green plants also good in a salad. When they're due to visit we leave a patch of dandelions on the verge so there is a ready supply for such special guests. Very active when the sun is strong they cover a surprising distance in a very short time if not restrained, bringing back  childhood memories for me, hunting the garden for missing tortoises.

Nicky and Richard have tried every way to incubate the eggs Zill produces each year after Gulliver's travails but sadly they never hatch because the pair are slightly different species. They travel up and down the country remarkably unperturbed in the back of the car along with the family spaniels, one of them born here. Their intelligent, easy-going owners have become close friends and provided several ideas and suggestions.

The adventurous Zill caused a major panic one day. Left to browse on the cottage terrace she had barged her way through the temporary barrier and gone walkabout. In mid May the grass verge under the hedge was a riot of long grass, cow parsley, dying daffodil foliage and other rampant weeds waiting to be cut back. She could be anywhere. This small creature is more than a hundred years old and part of Nicky's life since childhood. She was frantic with anxiety and we all joined the hunt, slashing and poking among the greenery.

We widened the hunt to the field above the cottage. To everyone's relief the errant Zill was discovered in the short grass of the pasture heading with determination uphill. To get there she had crossed the road, crawled through mud and under the gate. We all tried not to think what might have happened had a vehicle come along and not noticed her in the road. Her mate had remained quietly at home.

That was also the year when we realised our buildings attracted migrant spotted flycatchers, nesting in the sheep house. One sat on the fence while excited guests were breakfasting on the terrace.

The cottage is available for bed and breakfast or self catering, the popular option for many, giving them the choice of chilling undisturbed. It hadn't been open long when a couple from a smallholding in Cumbria arrived. They were full-time foster parents who had been before with a variety of children and a black and white spaniel but listening to them was a terrible eye-opener into the darker side of family life. Booking their initial visit they asked if it would be okay to bring a young child, a little boy of about eighteen months who'd been neglected with no socialisation of any kind.

He hadn't suffered actual physical cruelty, just neglect, deprived of any form of stimulation, spending most of his time, day and night in a cot, fed and changed but nothing else. He had no idea about the world. Still in nappies he could hardly crawl, let alone walk and just beginning to react to speech.

It may seem odd to make an analogy with puppies but it is so important that they leave with an understanding and relationship with people, stimulated by play and cuddles, music and radio and all the things they will meet in their new homes. This child had been without any of this.

It was a busy weekend with six other guests at the breakfast table. From the highchair at the far end this delightful child watched wide-eyed to take in everything happening around him. He couldn't talk but when they talked to him his little face was wreathed in smiles as he basked in the attention of these unknown adults who addressed him like any other child. He blossomed before our eyes, his gaze alight with burgeoning understanding of what possibilities life had to offer. I have no idea what became of him but his time with this family and their dogs and ponies at least revealed to him the chance of a better future.

They came again bringing a young family of four and an extra spaniel which was one of ours. The two boys and two girls from early teens to a toddler were by four different fathers. They were great kids though very troubled. They loved the dogs but the older ones were in desperate fear they would be separated from their little siblings. They returned the next year, the foster parents by then very fond of the little family, hopeful they could be kept together.

Sadly the children were eventually split up and sent to different homes, a traumatic outcome for everyone and that may have been what decided the couple to give up fostering. There are only so many times you can have your emotions ripped apart.

Prospective visitors ask all kinds of questions trying to work out if the place will suit them. Among the most amusing came from a woman enquiring about a self-catering break in the cottage, emailing: 'Is there a toilet and shower in there?' Another enquirer was under the impression we had a fully furnished treehouse as an option.

The cottage has brought a whole new dimension to running the farm with frequent invitations from guests to join them for a drink and sometimes a meal. It's good to experience it as they do, either indoors or when the weather is kind, out on the terrace.

When friends stayed with their three Gordon setters, it was a busy weekend with people in Chaffinch and a couple upstairs in the twin room. After supper we sat chatting and enjoying a drink in our sitting room, not being especially riotous. At around nine forty-five, without a knock, the door slowly opened to reveal a frowning apparition from the twin room — a long haired woman clad in a thick sleeping garment the like of which I've never seen, complaining: 'Some people are trying to sleep.'

We stared at this spectacle mumbling apologies but pointed out that it wasn't yet ten o'clock and we were speaking quietly. But obviously too loud for that good lady. In the morning not a word was said by the couple and we thought it wiser not to raise the subject.

A young man who told us later that he had Asperger's Syndrome came several times after we built Kite. He came first with a girlfriend, staying in Chaffinch. We were embarrassed that they were still around during the day when the tanker arrived to empty the septic tank, a procedure which is best done without guests present. However Richard was totally fascinated with the operation and watched avidly as the tanker sucked out the waste through the fat snaking pipe. When he came again his companion was canine.

Several guests in Kite have reported other visitors, a family of weasels. While enjoying supper in the evening sunshine they've been joined for an instant by weasels popping out from the holes in the stone retaining wall. These holes are drainage pipes built in to release water which could build up behind the wall and possibly bring it down. It's topped by flagstones and a small garden border but the loose rubble filling is another world, an ideal home for the little mustelids and I imagine them inside their one up, one down house. They run from the moss covered front door along the paving and into the other hole, firing my imagination to picture their life style. There are certainly plenty of rabbits about to keep them going.

Other non-human guests include the occasional cat and sometimes horses, their riders drawn to the hills and especially the Long Mynd. We advertise dogs and horses welcome but it takes a lot of effort to organise travelling with a horse.

We were very dubious about a booking for several people with four ponies and a trap. Ordinary guests for bed and breakfast are out most of the time but those here with horses can be much more intrusive. But this party took care not to impinge and take the place for granted and were good company to be with. The majority of guests with horses tend to be female. Possibly men can't face the hassle or they go for more strenuous forms of horsemanship.

Some riders come to explore the local rides but others come for just one night following the long distance bridleway the Jack Mytton Way, which takes about a week to ride.

Two women came with their beautiful palominos on this trek, their arrangements and requirements laid out in a precise schedule which included the transfer of luggage to the next stop. The day they arrived we were staggered by the quantity of luggage delivered in a very large taxi. They seem to have brought everything but the kitchen sink, including a bag full of Prosecco — obviously trying to cover every contingency.

The well-kept mare and gelding, golden coated with white manes and tails, made a brilliant picture out in the paddock, with the chestnut tree in the full flush of its pink blossom and the glossy dark leaves of the copper beech shining in the sun.

They were booked for a night each way. When they returned for the second night their stuff had to be moved to the next stop the other side of the Stiperstones. On a glorious June morning I took the scenic route across the Mynd, down into the vale past Ratlinghope and up over the Stiperstones. I had forgotten the beauty of that valley between the two ranges of hill, the vista of rocky outcrops against the soft green of pasture; dotted with hawthorn still in full bloom after a late spring, the whole scene was bathed in sunlight shimmering on the blossom. I had to stand for several minutes just breathing in the scented air and the grandeur of it.

Another horsey group turned up unexpectedly following an early morning phone call looking for somewhere to stay when one of the ponies had gone lame. This was a woman riding from John O'Groats to the south coast for charity, basically alone but joined for stages along the route by various companions.

The small tough ponies looked pretty much exhausted, spending most of the afternoon lying down in the sun. They stayed two nights, deciding the lame pony couldn't carry on and another must be fetched from the Scottish border to replace it. This required a very complicated set of journeys when one friend went by train to somewhere near Uttoxeter where they had left the horsebox to then go north to collect the fresh pony.

Horses and riders of all shapes and sizes have turned up, varying greatly in standards of care. Most are very particular about attending to the needs of their animals but not all. Two nice but scruffy and very sweaty cobs arrived one evening for a two night stay. Their riders dumped all the tack on the concrete and were about to turn them straight out into the paddock as they were. Both ponies had dirty sweat stains around their ears and between the hind legs with the shape of the saddle outlined in dark sticky hair on their backs.

Hastily grabbing a sponge and a bucket of water I thrust the sponge at one of the girls saying: 'Maybe you should wash them off first, get rid of the saddle marks.' In the morning they saddled up without any attempt at grooming — presumably they hadn't been through the stringent test of Pony Club training.

Two kittens stayed in Kite with people from Kent who were regulars for a couple of years and a bedridden lady from London who came several times with her husband and carer, brought her special pet, a lovely Persian cat who made herself very comfortable in the cottage.

Tracks and trails

Walking the hill is a distinctly sensual pleasure. In late winter the moss filled turf creates a plush carpet, easing down beneath the pressure of a boot. Sphagnum moss, which mixes so readily with the grass, is common on this upland, efficiently absorbing carbon from the atmosphere. Mosses generally are under-rated plants, so beneficial ecologically, conserving water and aiding pollution control. The farm has more than its share and before we realised its benefits made efforts to reduce it. But now it thrives untouched among the grass both in the field and on the lawn, loose strands tumbled by the wind where the birds have pulled it free for nesting. The strong beaks and claws of the jackdaws have done much of it though the long-tailed tits and many other species make good use of this soft and malleable material. Rabbits too and badgers scratch it up to carry away to line burrows and setts.

Ancient hedge lines are marked with twisted hawthorns, warped into eerie shapes by the wind of years, probably planted back in the nineteenth century or even before when the land was first put under cultivation. Time has formed a natural bank along these trees and their thick roots delving into dry sandy soil are tunnelled by the rabbits into an extended warren. Rusted pig wire lies in several places embedded in the earth, half a fence left here and there, relics of a time when the hill was divided into separate fields where now it is an open sheep or cattle run.

These dry hillsides are well drained with rock so near the surface it shows through as outcrops, ideal for the wild ones to make warm, dry homes. The grass is marked by tracks of sheep and other creatures. The badgers' regular route is a wide path from the pasture down onto the gorse covered bank and a narrower trail shows where rabbits pass conveniently beneath a water trough.

Badger numbers have increased and they can be a nuisance, their powerful shovel-like front paws dig holes in the fields and gardens and sometimes vandalise newly dug graves of dogs or cats. Guests are keen to see them in the flesh and a walk with a torch across the top land in the dark is usually rewarded by the sight of a badger caught in the beam, hurrying away from intruders. They are protected and it's an offence to interfere with a sett but at one point we had no choice as they took over a rabbit burrow beside the road. It was soon in danger of collapse as they continued to undermine it with their excavations. They were deterred by the smell of diesel.

The steep slope of Cardington Hill is vibrant with the full yellow bloom of gorse — but then it usually is. Back in the day neighbour George laughed at my ignorance as I told him the gorse was flowering along the track to Middle Hill. 'It's always is,' he said.

It clads the hillside where previous owners have done battle to clear huge stretches which once cloaked the land, its roots now rest in bare ground where rabbits have cleared anything green. A strange plant, it's lovely in some ways but its thorny leaves are wicked at close contact. In flower for much of the year it provides shelter and food for many insects and birds, including stonechats and yellowhammers and a vital source of nectar for invertebrates which depend on it when nothing  else is in flower. Its unappealing appearance belies the fact that it's actually edible, part of the pea family. The flowers can be eaten in salads and make an unusual tea and its pickled buds can be used like capers, maybe in a fish pie. But too much can be toxic and the seeds should never be eaten.

We see brown hares more often now, staying silent in their form, hidden behind a tussock of grass, relying on camouflage and speed until disturbed by the dogs, who, if they spot one, set off in pursuit in a hopeless chase. They have no chance at all of matching the speed and agility of my favourite wild creature. There is something very special about hares, almost mystical. With their long ears and powerful hind legs they're evocative of all that's best in the natural world. At least on these sheep grazed uplands they're safe from the perils of valley fields where leverets can fall victim to the vicious blades of mowing machines and harvesters. The instinct to crouch and hide means they often leave it too late to benefit from their speed.

Under snow cover the landscape is transformed, green to the east, white to the west, the top of Caradoc glistening, its summit nestled in cloud and for once no wind to blight the scene. From up here the pond at Field House gleams with ice and the cold air echoes with the cries of wild geese. At the edge of the field the ash tree's bare branches are stark against the first real cold.

The winter world of unblemished snow reveals a fascinating picture of the hidden life about us here, tracks of small animals criss crossing on their mainly nocturnal business away from human attention.

Marking the trails before they're obliterated by dog paws, a multitude of rabbits and the larger prints of hares show up with other more interesting marks left by stoats, weasels and more often now the distinctive five toed print of a polecat. We discovered these are present after the poodle down the hill caught more than one and the awful morning when the hens and guinea fowl fell victim to these vicious killers.

One strange double track looked as if something had been dragged by a very narrow creature with no footmarks beside it, a continuous trail only about a quarter of an inch wide. It seemed odd and we puzzled over what might have made it, possibly some kind of insect. Sometimes the slots of deer cross the ground. There are many more than are ever seen, feeding in the steep slopes of woodland, especially on Wenlock Edge.

Sometimes they leap into the road unexpectedly in the path of unwary drivers and may have caused more than one fatal accident which have never been explained. In my office car early one summer morning Beck watched a lorry hit a roe deer which jumped out of the woods. The lorry carried on but the deer lay dead in the road. Unwilling to waste this bounty he popped it in the boot and carried on. By the end of a warmish day the body in the boot was starting to smell but we hung it and it was duly butchered and stored in the freezer.

Unfortunately the incident left a lingering odour which would not disperse and got worse with time. The car was due for replacement and when it went into the works garage the foreman said: 'What on earth have you had in here?'

'Don't ask!' was the only possible answer.

Footprints in the snow were what made me begin to realise that all was not well with Beck, that feeling when something seems not quite right, an uneasiness at the back of the mind, a nagging you can't quite put your finger on.

Gradually it became obvious that something was happening, a fundamental physical change; among other things he was losing his balance and having problems with his right foot, which was stiff and unresponsive.

It's a human trait to see what you want to see and close your eyes against unpleasant realities. The fact was that my strong and athletic partner was never quite the same after the gall bladder operation put him in intensive care.

He took up horses late, in his thirties, but became a confident jockey happy to tackle anything. He joined our local hunt in Yorkshire, the Rockwood Harriers, whose country in the southern Pennines had a mixture of moorland and pasture, stone wall country which meant a lot of 'leaping'. On his ex-racehorse Pythagoras he was like a duck to water. He loved it. Out with the Grove and Rufford over in Nottinghamshire, hedge and rail country, he took his Cleveland Bay cross Thoroughbred gelding over enormous hedges with ditches. When he discovered team chasing he was an eager competitor both in Yorkshire and here in Shropshire.

He wrecked a shoulder early on at the farm, bucked off onto concrete by a sad little dun horse who'd been difficult to break in and would leap or buck horribly. Roland had a bad history and buying him was a mistake but he was such a sweet natured animal to handle in every way except when you were on his back. We thought he would come round but the cause of his behaviour was pain. The bastard who bred him had left him unhandled until a two year old and we learned later had beaten him when naturally he proved difficult. It's likely that this cruel treatment had injured the horse's spine and sadly we never got to the bottom of it.

In another incident the feisty chestnut mare Vale slipped on a wet rock on Hoar Edge and she and Beck came down together. The sound of galloping hooves approaching sent me rushing to the gate as the mare arrived home, hot and anxious, without him. That caused more damage to the bad shoulder which meant he couldn't raise this arm above his head. But he still enjoyed it, including two trips to Exmoor with Sonny and each of the mares. It became a worry when he rode out alone as he seemed less secure in the saddle.

For those who don't know, balance is very important for a rider. I began to discourage such excursions and came the December day when we were hacking along the top road to Wilstone during the annual village fell race. One of the white-clad runners was moving quickly up the field track towards the road and the bay mare Opal was startled and shied away. Beck came straight out the front door as we call it, falling off over her shoulder to hit the deck.

He wasn't hurt but that was a turning point because such a small incident would never normally have brought him down.

His hip was also causing pain and that seemed an explanation. This was supported in mid winter as we trudged through deep snow with the dogs. On the way back we crossed some strange tracks, human footprints with one foot at right angles to the other. 'That's queer,' he said. 'Who's made those?'

Realising they were his I said: 'I'm afraid it's you.' We decided it was time to seek advice.

By now plenty of guests were finding their way up the hill and on at home days he helped with breakfast, preparing it himself if someone asked for his special way with smoked salmon and scrambled eggs. Beck's Special on the menu is a popular option, often chosen when guests see others presented with it. 'Ooh, that looks good. Can I have that tomorrow?' is a frequent request.

He enjoyed chatting with new people but you can do too much talking with the visitors as we discovered on more than one occasion. Deep in conversation about all kinds of things, politics or history or the birds — then returning to the kitchen to find sausages are overdone or the bacon is too crisp. The one thing you can't leave unwatched is scrambled egg which will quickly lose its succulent fluffy quality if neglected. The chat could be about mushrooms or porridge, both mentioned in web reviews, gratifying words about the porridge which we make in the Scottish way. The way my father made it, almost every morning of his life — you could say his signature dish.

Breakfast might bring laughter or problems, you could never be sure. People vary so much in their requirements, some will drain a pint jug of milk, others use hardly any, orange juice on cereals is also surprisingly popular and we had to learn about flat eggs.

An American woman first requested a flat egg. I must've looked confused and she probably thought I was stupid. But when I admitted my ignorance she explained what she wanted. Very simple really, all it needed was the egg mixed together before it hit the pan — in effect a mini omelette.

Then there was the girl who asked for her toast to be well done. I let one batch go too far, talking again, burnt in fact. About to bin it, with a sudden thought I asked Beck to take it through and ask if it was too far gone.

'You can't give her that!' he said but took it in and came back stunned. She was delighted, saying: 'That's just how I like it.' It's a bit like that with bacon, the majority definitely prefer it well done. We serve smoked bacon which has more flavour and only twice have we had complaints, most guests saying 'great bacon'. But one lady from Yorkshire didn't approve at all, complaining because it was smoked. As they were booked in for four nights we assured her she would only be offered green bacon next day. We promised the dogs a treat but the offending rashers didn't come back to the kitchen. Her husband apparently had no qualms and was happy to eat hers as well as his own.

We soon realised one of the problems in this business is that people sometimes don't understand the difference between bed and breakfast and a hotel, assuming they are run in the same way, expecting hotel facilities at b&b prices. But the old image of the boarding house is long gone, the days when the seaside landlady would strictly enforce her rules on when guests were expected to be out of the house. You couldn't get away with that approach now, although a surprising number of visitors still ask if it's okay for them to return during the day. We encourage them to make themselves at home and use the garden, the summer house and the terrace.

More and more people have allergy issues, usually either gluten or lactose averse, mostly genuine but sometimes you wonder if it's just a passing fad. It's puzzling when someone requests almond milk while taking semi-skimmed dairy in their tea.

We have always served breakfast in the traditional style with full cutlery and linen napkins which guests appreciate. Many comment on the crockery which we found originally at a vineyard on Box Hill. Its attractive green and cream grape design looks good on the oak table. It's been long discontinued by the makers but we have plenty, found and collected from a variety of sources.

Breakfast reveals an enormous contrast in manners, especially some Americans who leave knives and forks scattered on the plate so you can't tell if they've finished or not. Placing the cutlery together on the plate isn't an outdated fad, it tells the person serving that they've finished.

Another early lesson concerned alcohol. Cooking a full English breakfast with a hangover is not funny. But however much you feel like death warmed up you have to contrive a brave face and a cheery smile from somewhere. That's what the guests expect.

From the kitchen you listen for the buzz of chatter, frequently rising to a crescendo of voices and often laughter which means the guests are enjoying themselves and each other's company. The downside is if they linger a long time at the table chatting when you want to clear it all away but a good crack at breakfast is a bonus that brings them back again. You also soon learn never to leave the dining room empty-handed, some finished-with item is one less thing to clear away. Similarly things that need to go upstairs are left on a step ready to be carried up. The only problem can be helpful guests who, seeing something on the stairs, bring it back

But a stoney silence at breakfast is bad news, like the uncomfortable pall of quiet broken only by the slight clatter of crockery we endured from a couple of singers. They had come with an augmented choir to sing in the village church but ate breakfast totally ignoring the other people at the table. We tried some light hearted comments but they were disinclined to make conversation, obviously not happy sharing. These occasions are awkward for us as hosts. Coming as they were to sing in church we presumed they were Christian but their behaviour was not my idea of how believers should behave.

North Hill seems to attract people of faith, of one kind or another. Maybe there is some subliminal message in our website, though the only overt indication of church affiliations is the unobtrusive little palm cross which has perched for many years above the fireplace in the sitting room, tucked into a tiny plaster Tudor rose from Ironbridge.

Two committed Christians from Surrey are always welcome, originally just Chris, who came first with a young German friend to visit an elderly acquaintance in Church Stretton, sharing the twin room with two collies. With husband Keith she has stayed in every room on the place and they arrive every year or so now enjoying the extra space in Kite but these days with only one lovely collie. Religion is never mentioned among visitors but a bible on the bedside table and other reading matter in the rooms tells its own tale and sometimes a certain quiet attitude makes me cautious in the language I use around them, not wanting to offend with my sometimes colourful expletives.

It's very disconcerting when you're serving breakfast and spot something unwanted on the window sill. Do you carry on regardless and hope the guests haven't noticed or do you make a joke of it and hope they think it's all part of the rural charm? Definitely unwanted – mouse droppings in the dining room are not what your average punter expects from AA four star. Later you find evidence elsewhere, on bookcases and the carpet.

It's a puzzle until Black Sam gives me the nod with his head on one side listening by the fireguard. There's a rustling noise from beneath the pile of dry logs awaiting the next time the day is miserable enough for a fire . Moving one log at a time reveals a comfy nest of paper and the pert round ears and large shining eyes of a field mouse glaring defiantly at the intrusion.

We tend to chuck waste paper into the empty fireplace – fine in winter when the fire is lit most nights but it accumulates in summer. With the cats shut in the kitchen we set out to catch it, or get it to depart via the terrace door.

The little creature has done no harm – or nothing the vac can't cope with. So we begin a game of hide and seek. Back and forth behind the grate, it considers running up the chimney but decides against and we think it's cornered till it makes a neat side move and hops over the brass fender and legs it across the carpet. Then it's a torch job, lying flat to peer under furniture. Until you spend a wet Tuesday mouse hunting you don't realise how inconvenient furniture can be. A low fronted Jacobean dresser, the three piece suite and the sofa in the dining room – all an inch or so from the floor — and carpet-hugging curtains make ideal cover for a tiny fugitive.

The double doors are open and we move a curtain behind the sofa to find it looking up from the top of a case of wine. But it shows no inclination to use the open door and heads off in the other direction, back under the dresser.

We nudge it out with a cane, almost catch it in a jam jar – it goes in twice then whips out sideways – then it's back in the sitting room. Searching all round again and then you wonder – we're funny about TVs so ours sits inside an antique radiogram. But it's got no back. Our little friend is right at the front watching us. It lingers awhile then scuttles past the TV and dives behind, leaving its tail in view. We manage to grab the tail and are pulling it back in triumph wondering if it will whip round and nip. But it's not held tight enough and gets away.

It's a good thing there are no guests about. I've seen screaming women literally standing on chairs because there's a mouse in the room. We give up the chase and set the humane trap with a course of muesli and peanuts, leaving the door open. The trap remains untouched so the quarry has had enough and departed. Meanwhile the two cats are happily asleep in the kitchen.

Another downside of paying guests is the laundry work, especially if you hate ironing. The problem came to a head one October half term when we seemed to have an endless number of changes and my sister, here on holiday, found herself on ironing duty. This was no good and we either had to find somewhere to send it out or get a means of doing it at home. We decided on a press which turned out to be the second best thing ever bought. Careful folding is the key and you can get a lot done in ten minutes. As Margaret Thatcher said: 'Never underestimate what can be achieved in ten minutes.'

Many city people these days don't keep a car, relying on public transport where it's regular and reliable. Most hire a car when visiting places like Shropshire where the buses are few and far between. Occasionally guests come by train and we arrange a taxi or meet them at the station. They don't understand that taxis here don't hang around hoping for business, it doesn't work like that. Some are brave enough to walk it —a brilliant trek over the top from Church Stretton, via Wilstone but tough going with a pack of luggage on your back, especially in bad weather.

A GP who arrived this way on a second visit earned my lasting gratitude. Her husband makes harpsichords and they keep bees on the roof garden of their London home, explaining when we expressed surprise, that the bees find a wonderful choice of nectar from the window boxes and small gardens in the city. They promised to send a sample. As they stood at the front door saying goodbye, she asked if the small lump near my eye had been checked. This was something I'd mentioned to my own doctor who'd dismissed it as nothing to worry about.

'You must get it checked,' she said. 'It looks pearly, I think it's a BCC'.

Confessing my ignorance she explained it was probably a basal cell carcinoma, or rodent ulcer, by any name a common form of cancer. She was right and it was successfully removed but if she hadn't spoken I would have carried on in ignorance until it became more obvious.

In the autumn a small parcel arrived, a pot of aromatic London honey — a generous present since it had been a very bad summer for the bees and a poor harvest. The maker of beautiful instruments said just keeping them going was an achievement, so it was more than kind to spare some for us.

It was our habit for several years to leave the kitchen window open in the summer months; with a dog in the kitchen we felt fairly secure and it was handy for Black Sam. Coming down one morning I noticed that the radio on the windowsill was slightly displaced, which had us wondering. The puzzle was solved when the guest in Wagtail came down for breakfast. He was one of a trio, his friends staying out in Chaffinch. Coming back towards midnight he was relieved to find the open window. 'Hope you don't mind,' he said 'but I had to climb in the window last night, forgot to take my key.'

Another hardy visitor was a teacher from Bonn who came for two nights in May spending time as part of her sabbatical year, tramping the countryside with her belongings on her back. She also arrived by train and was proposing to walk it but agreed when I offered to fetch her. Good decision. It had poured with rain all day and when she eventually arrived in Church Stretton, by bus because the line south of Shrewsbury was closed, the rain was torrential and the walk over the hill in that would have been unpleasant if nothing worse.

One part of her trip was the coastal path north of Berwick on Tweed towards Dunbar. On a stretch with no bed and breakfasts around, she found herself at Fast Castle on its remote headland above the crashing sea beyond St Abbs. Having gone far enough that evening she crawled into her sleeping bag and spent the night among the ruins of the medieval castle. That took a lot of courage and something I doubt I would've done.

One couple and their teenage son found enough to occupy and please them for a whole week here without a car. The train brought them from Kent, probably with several changes, and though we offered to give them lifts to anywhere they wanted to visit the only trip they needed was back to the station. They brought enough supplies of food and drink and everything they needed in their luggage. The boy especially seemed to appreciate the landscape, the wildlife and all the walking — just doing their own thing, chilling for the week.

Adam's ale

The most important item to sustain life is water, yet mostly it's taken for granted. Taps are turned on without a thought, often running away to waste. Our supply deserves a mention for its many issues and the hours lost dealing with it, especially in the early days. It is delicious, running underground through the limestone from Wenlock Edge to the aquifer in the valley below, where our borehole taps into it. Then it's pumped six hundred feet up the hill to a reservoir at the highest point on Cardington Hill.

Despite the hassle-filled we wouldn't change it for the mains at any price. This fundamental liquid varies enormously in flavour and ours is pure with a sharp edge to it, just right for whisky. As good as anything you buy in a bottle and better than many but for years we wondered why we bought a place with such a liability. Believe me, you don't take it for granted when you're the one tackling the problems.

Dealing with the reservoir is tedious and we've cursed it many times but the view from there is magnificent with an almost three hundred and sixty degree panorama taking in the Clee Hills, the length of Wenlock Edge and our own nearer hills. It's a wonderful place to take the dogs when the sheep are absent.

Up there on the shortest day the sky is a deep cobalt blue, the only marks faint remnants of vapour trails while a skein of calling geese cuts across the valley. The scene shows a landscape changed, the valley drowned in thick fog. The Wrekin's summit stands clear above mist as smooth as water, like a volcanic island in an inland sea. To the east beyond the trees towards Stone Acton another strange inversion creates a mirage to transform the view. For a while the veil is lifted, the church tower appears, among fields and hedges dusted with ice, wisps floating slowly away driven by the growing warmth of the winter sun.

The passing of the shortest day has meaning in rural life, as it had for ancient people yearning for longer days to return. Imagine the cold and darkness in a village hut and the need for a celebration to bring hope of brighter days. The December sun feels warm but the temperature drops by mid afternoon as it sinks towards the solstice and on the tops the mist is rolling back to reclaim the land.

Originally the farm was supplied by an old brick well across the fields on the edge of the hill, gravity fed from one of many springs. Still used by sheep and cattle it's become home to common newts. The 'new' system was put in during the 1970s by a former owner who claimed he dug the trench all the way up the steep hillside by hand to bury the pipe and its armoured electric cable.

Unfortunately, probably for convenience and speed, they didn't bother about stop taps, let alone a map of the system. The important junction where the line to the house joined the main supply wasn't even marked, nor any layout of where the pipes ran. We had to dig a hole and hope.

It's laughable when you consider the modern requirements for selling a property. The pipes cover a wide area and supply our neighbours below, plus field tanks on the surrounding land. The power control box is on the other house because the two properties had been owned by relatives in the same family and it seemed easier to do that — never mind future inconvenience.

Those many metres were the old black pipe, thousands of miles of it laid all over the country, with a tendency with age to split lengthways along the join and leak. But leaks only show as a wet patch in the ground or if the electricity bill suddenly shoots up. Tracing them is a nightmare and the only way to handle it is digging to insert a fresh section with the appropriate fittings. Simple. You'd think so but what in theory seemed straight forward never worked out like that.

Beck spent a Christmas morning in a muddy hole down in the valley repairing the main supply pipe. Another time, when at least it was summer, he was paddling in mud in the same field with the power off to stop the pump, the reservoir already emptied.

Our neighbour then was an awkward little man who disliked paying for water. He had the idea it was freely available in the earth — which it is —but he seemed unable to grasp the concept that the tricky and costly bit is delivering it out of the ground to his taps. He came home and turned on the power, creating an uncontrollable fountain of muddy water under full pressure which drenched Beck in the trench.

The air was blue when I accosted the culprit, before donning a swimsuit to climb into the fast-filling reservoir to turn off the tap at the bottom while it was still shallow enough to get in without drowning. Not a happy day.

A moorland fire on the hill produced another hefty bill when for nearly a week several fire engines trundled by all day, filling up from a main in the village to run long hoses over the heather to fight the fire. The weight of all this on the concrete road caused another leak in the pipe beneath.

Many of the water problems originated at the other house and when it was on the market the driveway and surrounds were dug up for weeks while they struggled in vain to find the leak. We never found that pipe let alone the problem and meanwhile water was running away down the hill wasted and costing cash with every litre as the pump kept working to fill the reservoir.

The original owner's business was groundwork and he had spent hours on his JCB creating a level area on what was very steep land. In doing so he buried the pipe far underground. The solution was to replace the line completely with new blue pipe from the house to the junction with the main supply. At that point we insisted on fitting a stop tap; a simple task you might think but in order to fit it we had to uncover a long enough stretch of the pipe.

There is an art to using a mechanical digger, some operators are brilliant, working the ground with a delicate touch, scraping the soil almost tenderly, others simply attack it. Enter an attacker with a JCB, biting into the gravel just outside the neighbour's gate with a bucket too big for the job. Having watched the pipe put in I knew it wasn't far down at that point before it went under the road and away up the hill.

'Go carefully,' I said, 'it's not very deep here.'

The bucket went down again for another deep bite instead of gently scraping the soil aside. I was half way through saying: 'Do be careful, or you'll split it' when a fountain of water shot into the air between us. One of the bucket's teeth had struck the pipe. We'd found it. Much argument and swearing and rushing about to find the right fitting to repair it. Needless to say we didn't have the right one which meant a drive to the building supplies depot. Meanwhile the water flowed away.

While Hillside was still seeking a new owner it was Christmas again and we were without water — again. So that was Christmas Day spent with sympathetic friends. This time it was purely electrical, a broken cable from the supply pole had cut off the power but because the house was empty there was no one to report the problem.

Then there was a vandal attack when someone thought it clever to wreck the float switch in the reservoir, the vital component which triggers the pump and again the water was off. The trouble is that until the tap runs dry you don't know there's a problem, that's when you start to ponder what it might be this time. We had a near miss when BT planted a new pole next to the road right on the line of supply. They hadn't bothered telling us what they were doing and missed the power cable by a fraction.

Gradually the black pipe was replaced with modern blue and it was startling to examine old sections carrying a thick layer of sediment which reduced the space for water to pass through.

The water is tested each year, very important with the responsibility of guests but most of the issues were before we started doing b&b seriously. As a rural county Shropshire has many farms and homes with a private water supply, either boreholes or springs, because the cost of getting mains water to some of the more remote places is prohibitive. Facts we discovered when forced to fight off a scheme to bottle water at a nearby farm. This was in the period when the Ministry of Agriculture was urging farmers to diversify, with a special pamphlet telling them how to go about it. One of the first instructions urged farmers to consult their neighbours about any proposal in case it affected them. Unfortunately the group behind the idea, dreamed up in the pub, took the approach that it had nothing to do with anybody else.

Because the new borehole was on the same aquifer as ours and others, had the scheme gone ahead it would probably have left us all without water and forced to go on the mains supply. In all fourteen families in the area were on private supplies. The whole thing and the attitude of 'let them go on the mains' created plenty of bad feeling in the village at the time. What names we were called in private are most likely not printable but a couple of comments got back including 'that rabble in the village' and 'the witch on the hill.' That was me. While there was no actual planning reason to turn down the project we made the point very strongly to the councillors that they had a moral obligation to ensure these families were not deprived of their water supply. Our vigorous campaign in the press and via the council succeeded in preventing the scheme.

Now when we are all so aware of the implications of global warming and we begin to see the real effects of climate change the issue of water becomes ever more prominent. It is the most important thing in our lives, without it we die. In the future wars may be fought not over oil but to get control of water. We need to value it, conserve it and use much less of it.

We have several water butts and a large bath by the stables for rain water. It's much easier to dunk a bucket to water plants than mess about with a hosepipe. The down side of these is the unfortunate habit of many insects to fall or climb in, often little black beetles and sometimes the increasingly scarce stag beetle. It's worth checking in the mornings hopefully in time to fish them out. Baby birds, especially the blue tits which nest in the roof above the bath have drowned and we've also found tiny pipistrelle bats.

The water passes its annual safety test but sometimes it comes out brown if the reservoir is low or there's been disturbance in the system. It's only sand drawn up by the pump from the surrounding ground but it can be unsettling; like the lovely hotel in Cumbria with signs in all rooms warning that the water is brown because it flows through peat. One year it failed its test because the old tank was crumbling inside, the internal render flaking off and tainting the water. The massive boulder which came out of the hole for the replacement now sits by the rockery at Red Kite Cottage.

The water system cost us both one of our nine lives and could very easily have ended badly in a messy heap. Needing to check the reservoir on a late winter Sunday morning we decided to go up in the Discovery rather than walk. It was snowing, a very wet snow, cold and miserable and the thought of walking was not appealing. He drove in low box down the rough track at the back overlooking Nant Valley and across the breast of the slope through only a few inches of snow. Approaching the crest of the hill the vehicle began to slide away downhill to the right, wheels slipping, unable to grip on the slushy service. As we headed straight ahead on the steepening slope I said pointlessly: 'Turn the wheel!'

'I am turning the fucking wheel!' he shouted.

The speed increased as, totally out of control, we were carried towards a broken fence, probably the most frightening experience of my life to date with the prospect of careering on down the next steeper section to crash in the tangled woodland at the bottom. Flashing through my mind came the grim thought that it could be days before anyone found us and neither of us had brought a phone, that and the image of Amber, the Gordon puppy, waiting in her crate in the kitchen. Unfastening my seat belt I got ready to jump — hopefully a safer option, urging him to do the same. As we approached the fence and braced for impact I saw the top strand of barbed wire was set very high. That saved us. As we hit the wire it caught the top of the windscreen and slewed us to the left, down into a hollow lined with a few small scrubby hawthorns which brought us to a shuddering halt.

With legs like jelly we scrambled out, gasping deep breaths, then laughter took over. My husband glared in puzzled anger till he too began to grin, sheer hysteria from shock. The snow had stopped and the sun shone with sudden warmth us as we trudged back up the hill and completed the task we set out to do.

Back in the kitchen we knocked back whisky and hot water and thought about it. Later there was an embarrassing telephone conversation with our neighbours, the landowners, asking them to haul out the vehicle with a tractor. By the time the brothers arrived the snow was gone and it was hard to believe what had happened.

They were shocked by where they found the Disco, saying unnecessarily: 'You were bloody lucky!'

They told us that long in the past a shepherd's hut had stood on that spot, dug well into the hillside for protection against the wind. The shallow remains of its foundations certainly protected us.

Once settled we realised what a special village we'd chosen, big on flowers and big too on community spirit, people working together with dedicated enthusiasm to celebrate every jubilee and national anniversary.

The village gardens open in summer in aid of historic churches, including St James'. Weeks of hard work and loving care produce an amazing variety of styles, some very formal and others with a wild unsculpted beauty. The event covers a wide area and it needs fitness and determination to visit them all. Like the fete the afternoon draws visitors from all over the county and beyond, many for the delicious cakes and sandwiches provided in the village hall by Cardington's brilliant bakers with a big reputation to maintain.

A couple came from Dublin especially to see the gardens. With their little dog they had stayed in Kite for Easter, very taken with Shropshire and the village. They were able to see an extra garden which wasn't officially open because of the owner's advanced age. It displayed several unusual plants and a gorgeous blend of colour in the borders. A highlight of their trip was the rose in the hedge opposite the cottage.

Called Kiftsgate we'd planted it several years before to fill a gap. The Irish lady had spotted it at Easter and was determined to come back to see it in bloom.

Its vigorous spreading growth yields masses of clustered small, white flowers each facing outwards, exposing pretty yellow stamens. The musky fragrance scents the evening air. That year it was particularly lovely, a mass of flowers covering the hedge They were also intrigued by the flourishing gooseberry bushes in the hedge. Unable to answer their query I could only surmise that past occupants had made the most of their surroundings — or a blackbird had dropped a fruit to germinate there.

A decade after we arrived the village set out its stall in earnest to mark the 50th anniversary of VE day with a special tea and an exhibition of wartime memorabilia. It was an amazing display, helmets and uniforms, posters, flags, even weapons, with the tea ladies in character, their heads scarf-wrapped in the mode of the forties.

In the evening we climbed Caer Caradoc to watch the beacon fire. The farmers worked for days ferrying loads up the slope to build a huge pile of wooden pallets and the scouts finished the job on the day. From the valley the outline of the hill changed with what looked like a newly-erupted rock formation. Before they lit the beacon the noise subsided for a short but moving memorial service. The drinking began on the hill and continued in a long and boisterous night at the pub, packed by the biggest crowd for years.

With the new century came a fresh idea in the village, an annual pantomime. The first one was an amazing success and it developed over the years, offering a brand of mad comedy as actors make fools of themselves to the delight of others.

Late one afternoon in high summer a glance through the front window spots an unexpected car outside. Almost all our bookings are pre-booked so a strange car at this time of day is unusual. From behind the vehicle a blond teenager emerged, looking hesitantly at the house but seeming reluctant to come further, so I went out to him. Despite the sign on the wall proclaiming us as a bed and breakfast he replied to my query: 'Can I help you?' with 'Is this the bed and breakfast?' frowning with an expression of deep anxiety.

'Yes, that's what we do," I smiled at him 'Are you looking for a room?'

'Would that be possible?'

Chaffinch happened to be empty and I indicated the door close to where he stood.

'You can have this room if you wish. Please go in.'

The boy went into raptures as he looked around, seeming particularly thrilled about the bathroom. The tiling in here is attractive but his eyes lighted on the toiletries, body wash, shampoo, body lotion and of course a bar of soap. 'Can I use those?'

Laughing I said: 'Of course, that's what they're there for.'

'Thank you, I will love to stay — I will pay you now.' Told the price he handed over the requisite number of pristine sterling notes, straight from a bureau de change.

'How far must I go to get breakfast in the morning,' was the next question.

He gasped when told the price included a full breakfast, explaining he was on his way from Switzerland to meet his parents in Ireland. They had flown over but he wanted to make the journey by land and ferry. In the morning he revealed he'd only just passed his driving test and this was something he'd planned for a long time. Although we asked how he had found us we never did know what had brought him to this remote dot on the map.

By the way he was eyeing the shower I realised he was itching to clean up and discovered why next day when he related his journey to the other guests. He'd been travelling for three days and so far had spent his nights in the car, cramped and feeling grubby. After a shower he was outside staring at the view and particularly at the crags on Wilstone Hill. 'Is it possible to walk up there?'

'It's an easy walk, especially for a young man like you, just go through that gate and follow the path.' He asked what time the sun would rise, — in late June around 4am. After again raving about the toiletries he asked directions to the pub and set off to walk.

In the morning I saw him return around seven, assuming he had been for a stroll but when I brought his breakfast the other guests were listening to him enthralled. He described in terms of wonder the crimson streams across the sky from the rising sun, illuminating every edge and filigree of the clouds in glory while the golden orb was concealed below the horizon. He told them the moon was still just above the hill defying the sun, pale against an azure sky.

He'd made coffee in the flask from his drinks tray and walked up the hill in the dark to be by the crag in time to watch the sun appear behind Wenlock

Edge. He seemed overwhelmed by the experience, extolling the beauty of what he'd seen between mouthfuls of bacon and eggs. He was also fascinated by the swallows perched chattering on the wires above the lane.

It seemed strange to be so moved, coming from a country of magnificent landscape. But listening to the boy the comments of another Swiss family came to mind on the subject of hill country. Yes, the Alps have a majestic, perhaps frightening splendour but their size makes them not easily accessible unless you're a mountaineer. The hills of Shropshire, like those in the Dales or the Lake District mountains are pleasurably attainable offering an intimacy between the human foot and the land beneath, drawing them into the heart of the place. We hear this same appreciation of the English landscape from other guests who live with high mountains.

Another Swiss family were forced to cut short their first visit when their son, a little older than the sunrise boy, had to rush back to Switzerland, called up for his country's national service. He had to go home first to collect his rifle. In Switzerland all healthy men must do military service, recruits generally do eighteen weeks of boot camp, sometimes longer. They are then required to spend several weeks in the army every year until they have completed a minimum 245 days of service. They have assault rifles or pistols, kept at home, ready for action.

Way of the wild

The move to Shropshire introduced Beck to shooting with a small but efficiently run group whose members observed the niceties of dress and manners, proper breeches and flashy garters on the woollen socks — he favoured olive green with red tassels. The lunches were the main attraction, always joined by the WAGS, with an interesting bunch of men including a surgeon and a Czech freedom fighter who was officially dead. It produced some good crack along with the port and whisky as much as the shooting itself, though eventually we got tired of eating pheasant. We began skinning rather than plucking the bird or just taking off the breasts.

It's good meat, with a tendency to be dry if roasted but delicious casseroled in wine, especially finished with a cream sauce. When dad was still with us one of his favourite meals was when we cooked a brace of birds one day and next day's treat from the pressure cooker was pheasant casserole with dumplings. Real peasant food but brilliant on a cold day.

Boxing day lunch at the shoot was always special, extended and good fun but I didn't make it the second year, stopped by a crisis which nearly ended in tragedy. By this time Cloud was old and ailing and his son Cloudborne, known as Sonny was five and at stud. The weather was bitterly cold, wide stretches of ice in the paddock, mud frozen in deep ruts. For exercise Cloud was loose in the barn and Sonny in the paddock while I mucked out.

Hindsight is wonderful. I should have stopped it immediately as father and son were playing over the metal door, nebbing at each other like foals. Suddenly it became more aggressive, the gentle biting turned to riving, mainly from the young horse, both of them crashing violently against the gate. As I tried to grab Cloud's head collar to drag him away, cautious of being crushed, the door burst open to let him loose in the paddock.

Any aspect of play was gone, the roles were clear. Cloud was fleeing the young pretender who had murder in his brain. You could almost smell the testosterone. Watching them charge back and forth across the rock hard paddock was horrible, both screaming, into the barn and out again, hooves slipping on the ice, the younger horse tearing at his sire's rump. My sister, here for Christmas, rushed out to see what was going on and I yelled at her to keep well clear.

It was as if the childhood book, Thunderhead, had come to vicious life before me, the young stallion driving off the old Albino. It's the way of the wild, happens all the time but to see it in domestic horses is appalling and it would end in disaster if I couldn't stop it. To get in their way would have been suicidal. Both were drenched in sweat but Cloud's breathing was laboured and he looked near collapse. Standing near his pen as they rushed back into the barn towards me I threw open the door and bawled at him: 'Cloud!' He heard me, saw the opening and shot in. Before Sonny could follow I slammed it shut. The poor old boy stood trembling, shivering in the corner while his son seemed to come to his senses and stood still, staring from wide eyes. He allowed me to catch him and shut him safely away.

It was hard to access Cloud's injuries — not a mark on Sonny — and with no question of joining the lunch party I called the vet. There was no severe damage but the old horse had lumps of skin torn from his hind quarters and a bad case of shock. He was shaking with stress and cold. The vet administered several injections, including a sedative and instructions to keep him warm.

The guy who ran the shoot was particular about not wasting the birds, insisting each gun must take his share. Pheasant shooting is a major part of the rural economy but many of the big shoots attract urban people who come just for the sport. They have no interest in the life or habitat of the quarry and no inclination to take home even one brace. Thousands of pheasants are still buried each season on large estates and it's unusual now to see birds hanging outside a butcher's shop. It's wicked to see tasty healthy meat going to waste.

Beck was a competent shot and enjoyed those long cold days in the woods and fields. But the nature of the shoot itself began to change, internal politics brought friction, some of the more interesting guns were gone and the ambience was lost. All things pass and he began to find his hip hurting when trudging across wet fields and through deep plough. But more than this he worried about being a danger to others if he was unstable while trying to fire. At the end of the next season he reluctantly called it a day.

The Boxing Day battle was the beginning of the end for my much-loved old horse, we noticed increasing symptoms of weakness and he was losing condition. He went to a friend's farm for better grass but nothing improved and the new vets decided he had some form of cancer — wonderful Roger had himself succumbed by then to the Big C. In late spring we brought Cloud home. The trailer tyre went flat on the bottom road and he had to walk up the hill beside me, head down, a shadow of what he had been. As we passed the red candle blossoms on the lane-side chestnut trees, he suddenly realised where he was, his head came up and he began calling, neighing continually, drawing a response from above. He was coming home.

The vet comes next day and I lead him up the field wearing his special head collar with CLOUD NINE on its brass plate. The young horses in the next field, his offspring, flock to the hedge to see him and he tries to pull towards them, so occupied he doesn't notice when the vet takes the rope from my hand and puts the gun to his head. Death is instant, barely a muscle spasm or a protesting kick as he goes down. My face screws up with gritted teeth but I can't hold back the tears. Beck's away from home, somewhere up the Irrawaddy on one of his explorations.

As I wait, looking beyond the body, the clouds seem not to move, hanging over the Wrekin, tinged with grey and white. The low drone of the forage harvester sounds from the valley where four men are making silage, rising to a harsher squeal on the turns. Two tractors work side by side, one pulls the harvester, gobbling dried grass with its spout above the big green trailer alongside, like the mouth of a rearing dragon disgorging its prey onto the growing pile.

The trailer fills up quickly clearing the field in a matter of minutes. One unit is away at the farm unloading while another tractor takes its place so the greedy machine is never idle. Meanwhile the fourth man rows up the cut grass in the next field like giant corduroy, dark green on the now yellow land. Hopefully there were no rabbits or nesting curlews among the standing grass. Its's a vicious business, done so fast it leaves little time for the wild things to get away. Modern equipment played a big role in the demise of the corncrake, too slow to escape the scything blades cutting grass or corn. No birds are following now, they had their feast at cutting time, crows, buzzards, seagulls sometimes if the weather is bad at the coast. All find good pickings among the victims, sliced and laid out by the fast moving machinery. Then the noise of another engine tells us Vince is climbing the hill on his JCB.

The vet moves to take off the leather head collar but I shake my head. It's supposed to be acceptable to bury even a human on your own land as long as it's not near a water course. Legal or not we were going to bury this horse at his home. It needs a big hole to do that and the required depth is fifteen feet but on this hilltop the rock is near the surface. At twelve feet the bucket hits solid rock. 'If you want to go deeper I'll have to get a different bucket,' says Vince. 'But I reckon that's deep enough.'

Peering into the chasm it looked a long way down. 'That'll do.'

Like the vet, Vince starts to unbuckle the head collar but again I stop him.

'Leave it. If in the future someone digs down to see what's here they'll know who he is.'

The powerful machine is incredibly gentle as it nudges Cloud's body to the edge and down into the pit. He falls neatly into place at the bottom of his grave, limbs and head laid out as if he were sleeping. Staring at him for the last time a rapid stream of memories flashes through my head before nodding at Vince to fill it in. As the sandy earth and rocks rain down I wait until he's covered and can no longer see the shape of him.

After the busy year building Kite we were determined to get some time away. As the business grew it became more difficult to escape from North Hill and essential to have a house sitter to cope with animals and sometimes guests. It's not easy to find someone to leave in your home and feel you can rely on to handle a crisis. They are like gold, incredibly valuable for peace of mind. We needed to plan well ahead in order not to take bookings when we would be away. Many b&b owners tend to go away in the quiet months after Christmas but that restricts your own enjoyment and we were determined that the accommodation should not rule our lives. By then Beck was spending time at different hospital appointments relevant to the hip but a date was fixed for an operation in late spring.

We were shocked to be told the op was off because the blood test showed he was profoundly anaemic. He needed a blood transfusion which sounded ominous. A succession of tests never revealed a cause for the anaemia but the hip operation was rescheduled for October.

In a June heat wave we left for a few days to explore Suffolk from a fascinating old Tudor house which had recently begun taking guests. We had a glorified summerhouse in the garden surrounded by fields, home to gorgeous thoroughbred mares and foals, a common but lovely sight in that swathe of the country around Newmarket.

In mid October we headed for Croatia and that lovely coastline which was so popular with Brits when it was cheap and cheerful Yugoslavia. He had images of youngsters diving off quaysides into clear blue water where fish and crabs were easy to see. We wandered through the intriguing interior of Diocletian's palace at Split for a dose of culture. Then lunch at a small cafe with beautifully tiled marble floors and a marble bar. We ate outside enjoying the sun and before we moved on Beck went inside to the gents.

It was a while before I began to think he'd been a long time and was getting. concerned when a worried waiter appeared to call me inside. 'Your husband has had an accident, nothing serious.'

Seated on a bar stool he was holding his forehead with a lump of gauze, a small anxious crowd gathered around. 'Don't make a fuss!' He said immediately. 'It's nothing.'

'What happened?'

'Not sure. I just fell, must've tripped. Caught my head on the edge of the bar.'

The young waiter who had fetched me said in a quiet voice: 'He seemed to lose his balance for a moment.'

Just a small cut running up into the hairline it produced plenty of blood around his face and in his hair. They were all very concerned, probably partly self interest in not wanting any repercussions to affect their trade. He was cleaned up before we went on our way, shaken by the incident, though of course he wouldn't admit it. Afterwards we told people how he split his head in Split.

The trip so far had given us no chance to swim. We missed out on some of the lovely sandy beaches this coast can offer but moving down to Dubrovnik the hotel had beach access down a long series of steps. It wasn't sand but an expanse of big round pebbles. He watched dubiously as I negotiated the approach and plunged into the deliciously balmy water. It was late afternoon with sun shining on the sea and very little wave movement.

As I swam back towards him he was trying to cross the rocks, hanging on to a low stone wall at one side. His uncharacteristic caution surprised me, he was struggling for balance, afraid of falling before the water could cushion him.

Eventually he got in and swam around for a while, enjoying it but certainly this wasn't the same man who dived into the Nile. I went in again next day but he sat on the wall to watch, his confidence shaken.

As we drove home from Manchester Airport a couple of days later the news was just flashing that Muammar Gaddafi was dead, found hiding in a drain.

The operation when it finally happened was straight forward and Beck recovered well, slightly lame but getting around with ease on crutches, help which again masked the reality of the problem. He was soon walking around the farm and beyond, though he took a stick when out with the dogs or on longer walks.

With the new hip he took to more walking in the winter, trudging through the January snow. Intensely cold at the month end, six below zero and deep snow and by the following week a layer of ice covering everything. Behind him in the snow the footprints were unchanged since the operation, still the strange angled impressions.

It was naive to think the new hip would somehow be a magic trick to solve his health problems. It certainly hadn't resolved the foot problem which he now called a drop foot.

He showed little concern about his condition though what he really felt we'll never know, carrying on regardless throughout the busy spring and summer. Still doing several days a week at different pharmacies interspersed with hospital visits — to the hip surgeon and various other medics, along with tests, trying to work out what was wrong with the foot.

Bookings for the next year were particularly good though the early Easter was blank, right at the start of April. Just as well because it brought a heavy fall of snow blocking the road for two days. The previous week we'd stayed at a farm deep in a Derbyshire valley where it snowed all night and in the morning the power went off just as we were finishing breakfast. The steep roads were bad but we set off in the car to visit the places on our agenda only to find it was impossible to leave the village. Every road was blocked by drifts. With no power the room was cold and the only option was to retreat to bed for an enforced rest. Our host came round in late afternoon with tots of whisky. Fortunately the power was back by early evening in time for the pub to produce hot food.

But the snow brought a bonus next morning. The Peak District landscape seen glistening under a blanket of white was magnificent and returning over the moors we watched a Short Eared owl hunting among the heather close to the road. He continued questing low over the ground, oblivious of our presence.

Back home we had guests booked for a wedding party which meant eight for breakfast. There was near panic when we realised all the Aga switches were off and it was going cold, both oven and hot plates too cool to cook sausages or bacon, let alone fry an egg. The small portable cooker was dragged out. It does the job and at least the party all wanted full English so there was only one set of ingredients to cook, and the ovens were still warm enough to heat the plates.

The Aga's rare breakdowns always seem to coincide with busy times or bank holidays. This time it was entirely my own fault, I hadn't told my friend Nettie who had kindly stepped in to house sit that the switches are never turned off.

Autumn brings longer nights and dark skies and with it the stargazers. Though not as perfect for astronomy as the wide open spaces further north the hills here are free of light pollution and very dark on nights without a moon.

Orion appears in the southern sky, Mars is bright in winter and in spring Venus beams at us in the early evening. Darkness does alarm people. We mention it in our blurb and guests visiting the village pub for supper sometimes moan about the darkness and lack of street lights. They seem surprised there is no artificial illumination in our conservation village and more so to hear that nobody wants such intrusion. For visitors from towns and suburbia — probably the bulk of our customers — this blackness is unnatural. Indeed it sometimes causes friction in the village with newcomers who find the darkness difficult. But they buy a torch and get used to it.

We were disturbed late one chilly evening by the couple in Nuthatch, the double room in the main house, when we heard them go downstairs at bedtime, returning very soon after. Later they were off again and outside in the darkness for a good hour. Puzzled, we should have realised they were out in the lane and up on the grass with heads craned back to look at the stars.

They were full of it at breakfast. Wrapped up well they stayed out in the still, chilly night for longer than we realised, entranced by the brightness of the constellations and lucky to spot the space station on its orbit. They hadn't mentioned their interest in astronomy when booking but we were glad our stretch of the firmament had fulfilled their expectations. People sometimes arrive with expensive telescopes but the weather doesn't always cooperate.

The stars bring back memories of childhood out in the garden with my father on dark winter evenings as he pointed out the figures in the sky. No street lighting in rural Berkshire then, the sky was dark and free from orange light. Before the fields were swallowed by development, the stars were seen in brilliant clarity and their patterns were like friends.

The Chaffinch room with its wide window gives those who are interested a sometimes close-up view of wildlife, especially the birds in the hedge across the lane. It's a very dense hedge, mostly hawthorn with some elder and ancient fruit bushes, ideal for nesting and fully utilised by these busy neighbours.

Most visitors love to watch them and hear their morning chorus but occasionally someone complains that the birds have disturbed their sleep. Rabbits often chase each other along the verge or sit chomping on the grass, unaware they're being watched but ready to dash into the hedge for cover at the first alarm..

It was guests in there who first alerted us to the presence of a little black cat and her two kittens who turned up during a July heatwave. Her arrival was very welcome as at the time we were without a cat and at the mercy of an increasing population

of mice. We don't mind a few about but they were showing increasing bravado. Until a few years ago there was always at least one cat here but when the last one died we decided not to have another in the house. The dogs had always grown up with and accepted them as part of the family but the younger dogs have never lived with cats and it's difficult to introduce them now.

These arrivals were very elusive but we often caught a glimpse of a black shape leaping into the hedge when a car approached. It was soon obvious that something was taking control of the mouse problem which over the last twelve months had got out of hand with both house and field mice rampaging through the buildings. They nibbled milk portions and orange juice, kept in the outhouse for cool convenience, chewed through a plastic lid to demolish the fat balls and worst of all they ate my apples. A particularly good crop of Cox's Orange Pippin had been carefully stored in plastic trays. Individually wrapped, they keep well into the new year. To me they are the best apple in the world for texture and flavour. The mice had a field day and consumed more than a third of the crop.

Hoping the cats would stick around I left food for them in the outhouse but feared the dogs' presence would scare them away. This was underlined when my attention was grabbed by a frenzy of barking in the barn and dogs frantically staring up at the roof. Well out of their reach on an iron beam were not three but four cats, glowering defiantly at the besieging canines, probably disturbed from a comfortable sleep in the hay.

The little mother must have been caught at a very tender age because she was hardly bigger than her babies, two black and a lovely grey tabby. Our neighbour had also seen them about and discovered they were camping in his lean-to garage with the Porsche.

If they were going to stick around four undoctored cats was not a good idea. Nick the neighbour got advice from the Cats Protection people who lent him a trap and one by one he managed to catch them and take them to be sorted by the vet. He kept two and the others were found a good home together.

They seem to regard North Hill as part of their territory and their efforts keep the tiny invaders under control. Rabbits which enjoy the young grass in Nick's mini orchard need to take care as these young cats are avid hunters. One year rabbits stole the purple sprouting. The late snow was marked with clear prints around the plants and when it melted only the stalks remained.

Feral cats tend to turn up here. One male who appeared looking for food had a badly infected leg, most likely injured in fighting. He was nervous but obviously needed help and allowed us to stroke him. We had a few young helpers then so with three of them hanging onto various limbs and head I managed to inject some antibiotics into his bottom. The infection eased and he stuck around being fed for quite a while until at last he decided to leave.

Months later we returned in the early hours from a trip to France and at about four in the morning the same cat was by the car, watching the house. We called to him but he vanished and we never saw him again. We don't know where they come from or where they go, always unable to settle; in the same way that some people prefer the open road.

Le Crunch

While the Olympics are on full throttle in London we're off to France, taking a spaniel puppy to friends on the Sussex coast en route. It proved to be a big mistake because we hadn't booked anything and finding places to stay on spec wasn't easy with most of the French population on holiday. But we found a bed each night, if not always exactly what we were seeking but more importantly, good places to eat.

At sunny midday rounding a bend in deepest Normandy we find a lake and sandy beach, with caravans and tents sheltered by pine trees. We've done it again, our knack of finding the way to a beach somewhere has triumphed as we find another gorgeous place to indulge our love of wild water.

'Wild swimming', so-called as if it's something new, is what people have always done, a lure so appealing against the claustrophobic atmosphere and cloying heat of modern pools. The frisson, near pain, of cold water brings goose bumps to the skin, then the soothing warmth of acclimatisation, followed by exhilaration.

Occasions like this have always been a joy, the chance to swim in warm lakes and rivers and of course the sea. We seem to have an instinct for finding a suitable stretch of water — a lane which led down to a tiny beach on the Boden See in Bavaria or a wide sandy stretch on an Italian island, the sand almost too hot to walk on with bare feet.

Or splashing around in warm deep pools beneath a waterfall in the Gorges d'Herique in southern France and the river at Roquevin where they were dredging as we swam.

And in the Nile near Aswan where Beck dived from the wrong side of the boat into deep and weedy water, seeming like for ever till he bobbed up grinning: 'Bit weedy down there.'

But we never found a way into Lake Trasimene — where Hannibal slaughtered the Romans. Its thickly reeded shores were probably a warning.

The Europeans turn water into fun places, creating beaches and safe spots to enjoy. Here in Britain we guard our reservoirs with fences and big signs shouting 'No Swimming' or 'Bathing Forbidden' or simply 'Keep Out'. But at least that's been given up at the old reservoir in Cardingmill Valley, whose shaded depths are a magnet for local swimmers.

With the hot August sun beating down from a sky as blue as a childhood dream, laughter rings out across the lake as little bodies romp in the warm summer water, splashing parents, siblings and friends. An arc of bobbing red buoys marks the safe area as we watch from golden sand under the trees and strip for action. To safeguard our gear we go in separately, me first, to join the laughing kids playing near the edge. The water is balmy but pleasantly cool further out where there is depth enough to swim. It's glorious. When I come out he's ready for a dip. He sits talking for a while, seeming reluctant to move but eventually I watch him cross the beach and walk into the lake.

Towel abandoned I stretch out as the sun begins to pink my pale English legs, missing what comes next. Lulled by the sleepy heat my eyes close for a moment to enjoy the sensual joy of skin exposed to reality.

I should have known something was badly wrong when I look again, expecting to see Beck swimming further out. The fact that an unknown man is helping my husband to his feet in shallow water rings a massive alarm bell. Even at that depth he's struggling to get a footing, the other man is lifting him, hands under his arms to haul him up.

He keeps a hold on his arm all the way to shore and even in such shallow water Beck is struggling for balance. The stranger smiles, saying: 'He's okay, he couldn't seem to get his feet'.

We thank him and Beck looks sheepish. 'It's all right, don't fuss.'

'I'm not fussing.'

Leaving him to recover and dry himself I return to the water knowing he won't be joining me, recalling all the times I had to ask him to wait or slow down as he strode ahead up some hillside in the north or on Exmoor, my unreconstructed knees making me hobble in his wake. The scene in the lake indicates some deeper issue, ten months after the hip job.

With hindsight the signs are clear, it all fits together, makes sense; but when you're living it the wood obscures the trees. Years of watching and helping as he built walls and steps and lifted huge beams into place made him seem indomitable despite the recent issue of aching muscles, first the arms, then his legs as well. But still I failed to register what the surgeon had said, that the hip was not that bad, meaning the problem was more than a worn out joint.

The hotel dining room menu has an ample input of apple derivatives, Normandy being the home of Calvados and full-bodied cider. For dessert they produced a wonderful sponge creation with a special ingredient Pommeau, a fortified apple wine. It gives the dish an exquisite flavour which I've never been able to reproduce despite taking a bottle home. As we sit enjoying this concoction he begins talking about the swimming incident.

'It was quite scary for a moment, I tried to swim but it was too shallow, then I just couldn't get my balance to stand up. It's this bloody foot.' He pauses for a few sips of white wine.

'If that chap hadn't helped me I suppose I would have crawled out. It was very humiliating.'

Not knowing what else to say I mutter: 'I should have been watching you.'

'Well you didn't expect that, did you?

'No.'

He finishes the dessert and pushes his plate aside, looking around the busy room, packed with the French enjoying life. He drinks more wine and says: 'Whatever's wrong with this leg it's getting worse. The operation made no difference.' He looks away from me and says quietly: 'I think it may be some form of degenerative condition.'

My response is a frown, not knowing how to reply. For the rest of that trip we keep to dry land and cut it short to spend a few days exploring Kent.

By now his foot is increasingly difficult to control, making him uncomfortable in bed and its appearance has changed, reddish and thick looking, almost alien at the end of his leg. I'd seen that look in the arm of a guest suffering from a form of ataxia. Walking is more difficult but he makes the concession of using a stick when following the perimeter of the fields with the dogs, now a daily ritual. The fact that it takes longer is a bonus for them as they run several times the distance he covers, bounding round him one minute then dashing off in another direction. But balance is definitely a problem.

Among friends having evening drinks he plunges headlong to the floor, with absolutely no warning, not even a stumble. Everyone is surprised, solicitous and embarrassed, him most of all but we laugh it off. He certainly isn't drunk, hadn't even finished his first gin. The crunching tinkle of breaking glass and the clear wetness of gin and tonic spreads on the hearth rug with fragments in the fireplace.

He carries on working, very good at it, popular with patients in the shops with a kind and helpful manner despite the fact that sometimes people come into the pharmacy with unnecessary time-consuming queries which common sense would answer. Such as a scratched finger when the only real response is 'go home and forget about it'. But of course that's not what you say.

Meeting a group of friends for a posh pub dinner we all sit waiting way past the booked time because he's driving back from Rhayader, in deepest Wales. When he eventually limps in they're surprised at the change in him and by his bad temper when we query the delay. He needn't have gone, having accepted the booking after the meal was arranged. Soon after this he announces he's decided to retire at new year. That's good news and long overdue and after all the years of him being miles away most of the time I envisage the chance of more time together and doing the things we never got round to.

Having made this decision he seems happier in himself and looking forward to less stress. He suggests we have a party at Christmas, not just one but two, one for our village friends and another the day before New Year for staff at the shops where he spent most time. It's down to me to organise it but that's the way it is and both events go well.

A lot of his time in the new year is taken up by an increasing number of trips to hospitals and clinics, investigating his anaemia, always testing different bits of him for different reasons. Scans and scopes and clever little cameras down his gut transmitting findings to a screen, which tells us very little.

Every day incidents underline the changes, an insidious weakness in his muscles which means he can no longer tackle tasks requiring a man's strength. Between us we manage to fit a new fridge freezer and everything starts to add up.

The muscles that had lifted a huge stone lintel into place at our Yorkshire cottage had lost most of their power. He becomes gradually weaker and when fitting new units in the boiler room he can't help the plumber carry the worktop. It's down to me and it's heavy.

The spring is harsh, an onslaught of heavy snow late in March leaves frozen drifts lying against hedges on the hills for nearly three weeks, though the water butts thaw sooner. The early Easter passes without guests which is a blessing. The fields have never looked so tired and the daffodils, usually wilted by now, are still only in bud. It's as if the land is holding its breath, desperate for a touch of warmth in the soil to launch the green flush of new growth.

So different from how the month began, arriving like a lamb, with us down on Exmoor, staying in the cottage at Withypool. On an incredibly warm sunny day we're outside eating lunch at the Hunters Inn in the Heddon Valley after walking to Heddon's Mouth. This gap between towering cliffs that are some of the highest in England is where the river flows out over a pebbly beach into the sea.

The Devonian sandstone is around 400 million years old. We sit in the sun and talk about the weather, wondering if later on we'll pay for this unseasonal warmth. Sure enough, we did, when bitter March departed like an angry lion.

The walk is my idea, a little over two miles, and he's eager to do it. But it's hard going for him on the undulating stoney path above the river. He's a long way back and again I recall the times I had to yell at him to hang on because I couldn't keep up.

He makes it as far as the sea but struggles coming back and I leave him to come at his own pace, hurrying ahead to fetch the car to save him the last mile on the road. By the time we reach the pub he's had enough but pleased he made the effort, though a far cry from the days of the Three Peaks and the Lyke Wake walk over the north Yorkshire moors.

April brings a breath of warmer weather and a green shadow begins to colour the fields, deepening day by day. Soon the tractors are moving up and down with rollers and harrows, priming the growing grass ready to cut. The fields are left in broad stripes as perfect as the smartest lawn.

Tilly spaniel, or Water Lily to use her posh name, has five puppies and by the time they are ready to go outside into the stable for more room the swallows have hatched their first brood. They arrived mid month, prospecting past nests and quickly begin renovating some while another pair starts building from scratch. Constantly on the move they speed in flashing arcs across the paddock where patches of drying mud left from the snow give them plenty of materials to build with.

Now in a constant feeding routine they dash through the stable roof space to fill the gaping yellow beaks visible at the rim of the nests, indifferent to the noisy young dogs playing beneath them.

Before the puppies are ready to leave for their new homes the swallows have fledged, testing their wings up near the roof, lining up on the beam at evening.

Eventually the orthopaedic people say they can't find anything physically wrong with his hip and leg but I don't realise the implications of the next move, to see a neurologist — and Beck says nothing to enlighten me. Most terms concerning human health have passed me by, never one to dredge the internet for gloom and doom unless for something specific.

So while the late May sunshine is blazing outside I sit at the back of a consulting room watching my husband, naked to the waist on a chair, as the neurologist stands behind him eyeing his muscles and flesh, prodding here and there, asking desultory questions. He's a tall lean ex-army doctor, not given to small talk, brusque and businesslike. Not a man to waste words on pointless sympathy.

Sitting there like a victim Beck is somehow diminished, the back no longer well muscled, the shoulders less broad. My anxious mind flits away to a beach scene with that torso above tight swimming briefs and strong legs picking a way gingerly down the steep shingle bank towards the waves in Dorset, the picture framed by the majestic arch of Durdle Door.

A man towards middle age but muscular and smooth skinned, the back tapering to a trim waist above firm, slender thighs. The friend sitting next to me in the sunshine follows him with her eyes to the water's edge where he hesitates before wading in to make a shallow dive into the sea.

'Beck has a lovely figure,' she says.

'Yes,' I smile.

Back in the present as he puts on his shirt and the sports jacket, smart as always, the neurologist sits at his desk and faces him a moment in silence before saying in a deadpan voice: 'I'm sorry to tell you that you have Motor Neurone Disease.'

Beck, sounding unsurprised and apparently unfazed, says simply: 'I thought it might be that.' But for me there is cold shock as the implication sinks in. Like a fool I ask: 'What are motor neurones?'

The look of scorn on the consultant's face reveals utter   for my ignorance. His condescension is cutting: 'They are what makes the muscles work'.

That simple. Like a jigsaw, all the pieces fall into place and we see the pattern of this creeping killer, hidden all along, making sense of the incremental events of the past few years.

His role in pharmacy must have brought him into contact with such things across the years but he had never mentioned those particular words to me and the diagnosis comes as an appalling blow. Diagnosis is incredibly difficult and it seemed to me then and now that when everything else is eliminated MND is what you've got. I quote: 'a progressive neurodegenerative disease that erodes motor neurones — those little 'imp-like' neurones that act as spark plugs for the muscles to make it all happen —until it becomes difficult or impossible for a person to walk, talk, speak, swallow and breathe'. Or live.

There are many theories about the causes of MND but basically we still don't really know what triggers this horrible condition. But nothing will alter its course.

As our GP said most family doctors will probably only ever see one or two cases in a career and diagnosis within the confines of a standard consultation is extremely difficult.

The neurologist prescribes Riluzole, the only medication available, which has shown a survival benefit for MND patients, thought to slow down the progressive damage to the motor neurone cells by reducing their sensitivity to the nerve transmitter glutamate. But at best it only extends life by a few months and the side effects are unpleasant.

Many people experience symptoms for months or even years before finally getting a diagnosis, very much the case for Beck. We both find it frustrating that the doctors ignore what we say about his early symptoms, as if it has just popped up out of the blue.

In fact it was there for years, stone by stone as he worked on Chaffinch, unknown, untracked; a silent relentless death approaching. In retrospect it's impossible to say when it started. Insidious casual happenings seeming at the time inconsequential but adding up to a grim reality.

Only later did the sequence of small or greater incidents begin to fit into place, until the day the truth is there. A horrible reality to be faced and dealt with. We all know we must die but it's hard to know it will be soon.

We don't talk about it much, there really is nothing to say but I can only imagine what he's feeling, much like the dreadful emptiness of depression overwhelming me when it takes nothing to turn a good day into dark despair. But we're busy with bookings which is a blessing since we must keep up appearances with people coming and going. The cheerful front, the brave face are essential but that's not how it feels, trying to stay calm while throwing myself into a frenzy of activity, anything to shut out the facts.

When we talk he sometimes comes out with strange notions, such as a dream from way back which he remembers as a premonition, about a house behind a parapet, a place something like this, motioning with his hand where we sit on the terrace while his eyes are on the distant crag. He looks so well, tanned and deceptively healthy but physically weak, unsteady on his feet, liable to fall, even on level ground. He begins collecting glasses from the table and next thing he's down, tripped on the concrete.

All this while the place is alive with activity from the creatures who share it with us. The wood pigeon siblings, bustling around with their mother, are unconcerned by us and only take flight if we get too near. A distraction for Beck who watches their interaction, one minute close together pecking at the same object, then a sudden quarrel and a mock fight with frantic fluttering of wings. These will be the youngsters I saw being fed last week, probably born in the holly trees or maybe the nest I look into from my office window. It's amazing how they survive given the shambolic nests they build. One of the pair is often eyeing me from the Chaffinch roof with a flimsy piece of dried grass or twig in its beak.

In contrast to the sunny days when we can enjoy being outdoors, we light a fire to brighten a cold wet windy June weekend. Comfortable warmth but always we come back to the same gloomy topic, the future — or lack of it.

Periodically we have guests who come to stay to learn how to make boxes, beautiful boxes, intricate and delicate on courses with Andrew Crawford at his workshop on the Acton Scott estate. Andrew is internationally renowned as a craftsman and teacher and the author of three books on box making. Beck is fascinated by the end result, not totally finished but destined to be a gift, a jewel box for a lucky wife. He spends a long time chatting with one man, here for several days learning the diverse skills required, asking all kinds of questions. It's always men who come for the courses.

And it was Beck who was there to reassure a desperately embarrassed father at breakfast after spending the night cleaning up and washing sheets in the bath after his young son had wet the bed. A charming blond boy he was

118

obviously at a tricky age. This kind of thing is a rare event and easily put right in the washer.

Across the hill at the far side of our land the underlying rock, never far from the surface up here, breaks through the thin soil in a small knoll. The grass is sparse and it's where we leave the chain harrows to lie so they don't get bound into the turf by more vigorous grass. The bank falls away steeply onto our neighbour's land and down into Nant Valley.

From this point the view due south looks over Wenlock Edge and Apedale — the valley of the bees — towards Ludlow and to the west the dim outline of the Welsh hills in the distance. Beyond the Edge the long wavering outline of the Clee Hills is a dark shadow against the sky except on very clear days when you can make out the tops of the Brown and Titterstone Clee hills. Clee Hill is the only named hill in England on the Mappa Mundi, the medieval map lodged at Hereford Cathedral.

Beck likes to be here — to simply contemplate and absorb the beauty of the valley landscape. With the aid of two sticks he can walk that far but needs a rest before coming back. From Yorkshire we brought with us the heavy cast iron Victorian garden seat which he had found somewhere on his travels. On a day of damping rain with a grey view down to Ludlow we heave it into the back of the truck and he drives it up there. It drops out onto the rocky lump and by now the rain is lashing us and it's too cold to linger. Next day I return with the dogs to manoeuvre it into place. It's not easy to set it safely with no danger of rocking or tipping backwards.

If the weather is fit he goes up every day, to sit and stare, until he's ready and strong enough to come back. The downhill trip is easier. One July day he returns smiling, to report four red kites prospecting the valley. After waiting so long in the hope they might nest here this small excitement means a lot to us.

Patience

My notes refer to this period as 'learning patience' — in capitals — and I still need to learn it. The ragwort is in bloom, its yellow flowers mocking us among the grass and I waste time pulling it out, a task both strenuous and frustrating but an excuse to escape from the house. There was no ragwort on the land when we came but years without sheep next door have let the dreaded yellow weed take hold and now it crops up everywhere.

This daisy-like flower is pretty to those who don't understand but when cut and dried by mistake in hay grass it becomes very poisonous, a danger to livestock, especially horses and cattle. Sheep will eat it at the rosette stage when it's hardly noticeable. It's an important host for the cinnabar moth whose caterpillars feed on it. But the plant is common along roadsides and neglected fields so I feel the moth has plenty of places to pursue its lifestyle without troubling my conscience.

Yanking ragwort from the ground, planting runner beans and fixing nets on the fruit to deter the birds, is all stuff that could be left but is part of the effort to maintain normality. It sounds selfish, the need to get away into fresh air for some time alone to reboot the ability to cope.

Once we have told the people who matter it feels easier, everyone saying how brave Beck is. He does show a very brave face, laughing off his increasing debility. He spends as much time as possible outside and has decided to plant a wildflower bank, purple poppies and wild flower seeds, plenty of them— but it's hard. His increasing weakness makes it difficult to bend down and he struggles with the watering can. And always the implied but unspoken thought between us, will he be here next summer to see it grow. He orders plants for the borders, penstemons and calendulas and different coloured foxgloves plus the forget-me-nots and aquilegia which come up each year uninvited.

It's difficult to relax when he's outside because he's so unsteady, easily knocked off balance. Walking is slow, one step at a time and each step on uneven ground could trip him. He falls on the grass slope by the gate trying to start the mower for me. That's a job I've never done and the smaller mower is light and efficient but the pull cord is hard. None of this stops him taking the dogs into the fields, one morning tramping in his slippers through the hay grass thick with buttercups. Teasel dives into the water trough for a dip and they all return stained yellow from the pollen, slippers, trouser legs and dogs.

The diagnosis prompts a frenetic summer trying to do things we always meant to do, like a particular garden in Herefordshire, lovely in early summer with hidden corners and sudden vistas. But the intrusion of hospital visits and tests impinges on the pleasures we find, along with the arrival of officialdom in the shape of the motor neurone disease coordinator for Shropshire. A young woman just doing her job but a shock emphasising the harsh reality of the situation. In the coming months she appears at intervals, checking his progress but there is nothing she can do except reassure us about future help. Numerous persons come with advice, nurses, an occupational therapist, and the coordinator again, all well-meaning but basically unable to help at that point. We have begun a journey which only leads downhill.

While I'm filling in the form for attendance allowance he's in the barn chopping logs, or trying to, every lift of the axe a hard breath and a rest needed in between. Tommy the farrier comes to remove Sonny's shoes, because I won't have the time or the motivation to ride as this moves on. He is kind and concerned and I wonder if I shall ever ride my lovely old horse again.

Our GP writes expressing his sorrow at the diagnosis, laying out details of special nurses and other services who will help. The intention is kind but the impact is horribly depressing though Beck is philosophical, unlike me. At the surgery around this time I ask the question: 'What's the form when someone dies?'

'We're a long way off that,' says the doctor.

'Maybe, but I need to know.'

The visit to Wolverhampton hospital is a bad day, more nerve tests. The point of this exercise is never made clear but it seems to me an unnecessary cruelty which does nothing to help. It's horrible watching him stoically endure needles stuck into various bits of him and electric shocks on chest and limbs testing nerve responses. We can only hope his pain in some way assists with research.

He admits later that the electric shocks really hurt but next day reports feeling a bit better, joking that the shocks have done him good.

The first visit to the University Hospital at Stoke was a lesson. The deterioration is incremental, though as yet we don't fully appreciate the extent of decline. I don't think to grab a wheelchair and he tramps valiantly down an enormously long corridor, exhausted by the time we get to the relevant clinic. He is happy for me to wheel him back, a taste of things to come.

Appointments with the neurologist are troubling, the hassle of simply getting there seems a pointless exercise as the consultant is presumably only assessing the decline.

We watch a gardening programme one evening but Alan Titchmarsh is creating a garden for an MND sufferer, a guy helpless in a wheelchair. Beck shakes his head and switches off — a bit too close to home. Especially as he is ready for a bath, which is rapidly becoming a fresh issue, a struggle to get in and out, though we manage to make it light-hearted.

July kicks off with ten very hot days and buzzards drifting on the thermals. We count eight of them spiralling upwards into the blue while at roof height two kites come drifting by, prospecting in a wide circle around the farm. We see more of them now with several pairs nesting in the county, some as close as Hope Bowdler Hill. He watches them intently, as if to retain the image, until they float away.

We don't talk about it much, there really is nothing to say but I can only imagine what he's feeling, much like the dreadful emptiness of depression overwhelming me; when it takes nothing to turn a good day into dark despair. But we're busy with bookings which is a blessing since we must keep up appearances with people coming and going. The cheerful front, the brave face are essential but that's not how it feels, trying to stay calm while throwing myself into a frenzy of activity, anything to shut out the facts.

After the rain-sodden hours of spring the land is alive with the scent of fresh cut grass . The front field produces enough sweet hay for the horses and sheep, a mix of grass and herbs with lots of clover and plantain since it was reseeded in the early years. The weather is ideal and neighbours have rallied round to cut and turn it. The long grass is down, lying in leafy swathes already drying in the heat. The evocative fragrance of grass wilting in the sun is intoxicating, the very essence of summer and with the luscious draught of honeysuckle and dog roses in the lane, it scents the evening air.

Beck has gone off to Lincolnshire with his brother to a Lancaster bomber gathering, a mutual obsession with them since we found the grave of his cousin's father in Holland, killed when the plane was shot down. Beck loves the heat but I worry that the event might be too much for him. He wanted the sun and now it's come with a vengeance.

So I am relaxing here alone, a big round moon glowing above the fence, rising a little before eleven in the windy dusk. The face is so clear, like glistening eyes gazing down from the wild sky. I'm out late waiting for it and watch a flock of maybe forty starlings dive bomb in one great swirl into the hawthorn tree. Their raucous chatter is soon stilled as they settle to roost. Satisfaction that the grass is cut and the weather set fair. In this heat on the slope it will dry quickly and probably bale in just three days.

The couple staying in Chaffinch are on a freebie, they won it as a prize we offered at a country fair. At breakfast they're full of the kites they've seen on the hill, the birds flying alongside them, revealing their colour in close-up. In the vegetable garden the crows have eaten all the gooseberries so no Gooseberry Gamble this year.

The evening light on the hills is especially glorious as we drive over the Long Mynd with the Stiperstones and Welsh ridges in our sight. On down the winding road to Bridges to meet friends for supper, waiting for us, drinking outside in the sun. It's many years since we've been there, recalling Cloud in the river but somewhere Beck particularly wants to revisit. Or wandering through the halls at Compton Verney, to see the Van Dyck exhibition where he's told off by an officious steward because the stag horn thumb stick he's using is missing a ferrule. Its soft wood end isn't marking the floor but the man appears to have no sympathy with someone struggling to walk. He manages the long trek from the car park but when we've seen all we want he's happy to return in the courtesy car.

We're doing again the things we like best, knowing it may be the last time. Cartmel races — always fun, especially the year I jumped the stream that runs the length of the members paddock. It seemed a good idea after several glasses, white wine with lunch and fizz to follow, but maybe my judgement was impaired. They all watched as I took a run at it, landed badly on the far side and fell backwards into the water. How they laughed. Roy dined out several times on the tale though he always forgot to mention that I went back and did it three times successfully. But that would've spoiled the story.

It's a busy year for guests, more bookings as we become better known and plenty of them returning, a good sign that we're doing something right. Despite his condition Beck is helping, laughing off his increasing debility and on the Sunday when we're off to Cartmel he cooks the breakfast for five while I'm the waitress. Stopping for lunch as he struggles out of the car the seat is covered in wisps of hay and stuff and it's all over his trousers. He puts on that sheepish look and tells me he fell on the concrete getting in the car while I was locking up. There's a bruise on his bare arm, coming out dark near the elbow.

'How did you do that?' I ask.

'I just tripped', he says. 'My foot got in the way.'

When I ask why he didn't wait for me he just shrugs. 'I can still manage on my own, I want to manage. I didn't want to tell you'.

When we land at the Drunken Duck to join our friends they're out at the front, having tea. They comment how well he looks, brown and happy too, gazing across the valley with the mountains behind. We have fresh strawberries from the garden for the racecourse picnic next day, with fresh salmon and salad in a cold box. But the hot afternoon at the races seems to make him weaker and he can only sit in the canvas chair and watch.

We move on to Settle where we stayed before, to go down Gaping Gill, the immense cavern under Ingleborough Hill. They lower you by winch three hundred feet through limestone, soaked by water from the diverted Fell Beck which normally pours over a lip of rock. In the moss and greenery around the pothole entrance a yellow wagtail had a nest, busily ignoring the unusual human activity. The long walk up from Clapham to this hole in the side of the hill had been nothing to him then.

We had often talked of taking the train from Settle to Carlisle over the viaduct at Ribblehead to see a different perspective on the Dales scenery. A taxi takes us across the city to the castle and he reckons he can walk to visit the cathedral on the way back to the station. Big mistake. He's very anxious, worrying we'll miss the train and moving very slowly with his stick.

Beck goes on ahead while I dart into the cathedral for a hasty look around the red stone interior, no time even for a prayer. A woman approaches trying to show me things of interest. She means well but takes up the little time I have, anxious to be left alone for a moment's peace. Then I'm running through the crowds, almost panicking because he's much further ahead than expected. We catch the train but his sigh of relief as he sinks into the seat reveals the massive effort it's been. Too much.

Next stop Wensleydale, a hotel down the valley from Middleham and the castle where Richard III grew up; horrified when shown our room, a little converted bothy up a flight of narrow and steep stone steps. He grimaces, then smiles and follows the boy, climbing carefully with one hand on the flimsy iron handrail. We hadn't mentioned disablement when booking and the room is charming so we decide to make the best of it for the two nights and minimise his use of the steps.

We tour old haunts in the upper dales, Dentdale and beyond, hot and lovely in high summer, winding lanes between dry stone walls, wild flowers along the roadside, pale blue foxgloves on the limestone and everywhere a gorgeous blue geranium. We pick flower heads for seeds, knowing they're unlikely to retain the colour in our soil. On the road from Hawes to Ingleton a sudden spatter of rain creates a rainbow ahead, a complete arc across the sky. He says you have to make a wish when you can see both ends. So I wish that he won't suffer too long and for inspiration which I'm always seeking. He doesn't say if he's made a wish and we don't ask each other.

Up through Swaledale and on towards the Durham border to get lunch at the Tan Hill pub. The highest in Britain and even in summer a sharp wind blows across the wide bleak moors. It hit the news again when Storm Arwen brought nine foot snow drifts, stranding guests for three days of quizzes, board games and karaoke.

But we feel trapped in the car, frustrated, aching to be out in the land, not just looking on with longing. Each of the Three Peaks in view at some point only emphasises the contrast between past and present.

Lighter moments en route to Norfolk to see his cousins, zipping round the extensive grounds of Anglesey Abbey on a buggy, fun even at five mph max and eating ice cream in the rain. Touring the coast in search of crab sandwiches and swimming at Wells in the deep channel when the tide is out while he watches from the beach. We leave strange tracks in the sand and a trail where the stick has passed.

Back home a wheelchair has arrived, just the simple sort you push. 'I don't need that yet,' says Beck and pushes it out to loiter in a loose box. He doesn't like taking the drug which has weird side effects, especially affecting his sense of taste. Always greedy for chocolate suddenly he doesn't like it any more and the same with whisky. He thinks it makes him very tired and decides to stop taking it and see how it goes. Sometimes I find myself peering into his face when he's not aware, looking for signs of change. The tablets are designed to extend life for at least a few months but we don't know what that means. Presumably it depends when you start them but the condition doesn't begin with the diagnosis. All along I've been angry because the doctors ignore anything we say about the gradual changes over the last decade. There is a lot of anger.

Next morning there's a bat clinging to the wall above our bedroom door, probably flown in through the open window after an insect, caught away from its roost at dawn. A little brown long-eared bat, it stays put all day, trapped by the daylight and as the light fades it begins to rouse and move its ears. My hand covers it gently and I feel it tremble on its short journey to the open window. Free to go, it shakes itself casually before taking flight into the deepening dusk.

We're home to several species of bats, though it's impossible to identify  them as they skim above us in the half-light and sadly we only see them at close quarters when they're in trouble, drowning in water butts or caught up in some way. Not long ago a dead bat lying close to the house on a wet morning was puzzling. We're used to birds flying into windows or walls, often with fatal consequences. But it seemed strange that a bat would be killed in this way, given the power of their inbuilt sonar system. Was it possible it had been attacked in flight by an owl? Unlikely, given their speed and surely the bird would have swooped to collect its prey. I studied the fascinating little body, with its dominant ears and long, undamaged wings, reluctant to dispose of it.

Totally harmless, it's hard to understand the often manic fear they induce in some humans. As with the dislike of toads, frogs and snakes; it's as if they have no right to exist and interfere with human activity. An elderly friend told us once she'd found a slowworm in the garden and described with some pride how she killed it.

Appalled, we asked: 'Why did you kill it? Were you frightened?'

'No, but they're poisonous. I didn't want it in my garden and I don't like snakes.'

For one thing it's not a snake and it's not poisonous, we explained. They are protected by law and in the garden it's helping to get rid of a lot of what she would call pests. She was of a generation with little compassion for other creatures

Out in the paddock grass, a puffball has grown in our absence, nearly football size but not yet turned to spores. A couple who've been before are here and they enjoy wild fungi with breakfast. The puffball's creamy white interior has a delicate but distinctive mushroom flavour, sliced into strips or chunks and fried in butter it goes well with a full English or in a velvety omelette.

Wild mushrooms are one of the delights of the farm and its surrounds. Until we came here we had neither the time nor the inclination to pick and eat them. As a pharmacist Beck would in some countries be expected to have the expertise to advise his customers on what they collected. But we soon learned to find and enjoy the local bounty. When the b and b really took off we liked to offer them in season to appreciative guests.

A striking semicircle of fungi comes up some years in the far field where rabbits once started a burrow. They have a look of St George's mushroom which is one of the very few that appear in April, in time for St George's Day. I've only seen them before on our neighbour's land where parasol and horse mushrooms come in late summer. But they haven't surfaced in recent years. Excellent eating but I have doubts about these new arrivals, dubious colour, slightly more tinged with beige.

One season we fed the guests on home picked mushrooms from mid July through to the end of October plus gifts for friends and neighbours.

Parasol and shaggy parasol mushrooms arrive as little bulbous brown heads, eaten only when they are small, neat and juicy. Once they've grown into huge umbrellas, hence the name, they become tough, still edible but not good. The true parasols are less common but delicious.

The large and luscious horse mushrooms are my favourite, their white heads and pink gills occur in a certain spot on the hill. Sadly the chanterelle isn't found much here, being more at home among conifers. But on a wild wet walk in Scotland we found them growing in profusion, enough to fill the hood of Beck's raincoat.

Our friend watched in horror saying: 'Why are you picking them, I wouldn't eat them if you paid me.' But he did. Back at the hotel our hostess sautéed them in butter with a sauce, producing a tasty side dish enjoyed by everyone.

The morning walk with the dogs has added interest when the first field mushrooms appear. After hot weather with the grass turning brown a good soaking stimulates the mycelium to make small white buttons push up through the soil from one day to the next and if left they will soon be two or three inches across.

Ours are mostly from the agaric family, agaricus campestris, the field mushroom, but there are many other edible species. They can be mistaken for the deadly Destroying Angel which is sometimes picked as a field mushroom and the most common cause of death for the unwary. Its shiny white appearance should be a warning, both gills and cap are very white, unlike the pink or brown gills of the field mushroom. The spotted red one of fairy stories, the Fly Agaric, is said to be what Elizabeth Woodville gave Edward IV as a love potion.

The thing about wild fungi is you need to be one hundred per cent certain that what you pick is safe. Ninety-nine per cent isn't good enough — that one per cent will kill you.

Recent research shows there is much more to fungi than meets the eye, an extraordinary hidden world beneath our feet. They belong to a kingdom of their own, not plants at all, their DNA is much more akin to ours and the rest of the animal domain, going way back in time to our evolution from ancient microbes. The hidden mycelium, the greater part of any fungus, has an intimate symbiotic relationship with trees which use this amazing network to communicate with each other.

The mycorrhizal threads pierce the tree roots which helps the uptake of nutrients from the soil and in return the fungi get the glucose sugars they need which the trees produce through photosynthesis.

Through this network trees can send food to each other as well as warning messages via chemical signals released from the roots. They can also attack rivals by spreading toxins through the woodland web. Many gardeners have discovered this new ally and mycorrhizal plant foods speed up the establishment of roses and other plants.

It's wonderful to find and pick wild food, one of the mysteries from the earth; the force that brings a pale flush of green from dull brown furrows, followed by exuberant young emerald corn and finally in high summer the golden glory of harvest.

In September we head for Pembrokeshire for another break, whatever the weather, at my nephew's cabin in Manorbier. But that turns out not such a good idea because the quirky place has issues for someone whose legs are packing up. The entrance steps are sawn lengths of tree trunk, very dodgy for him and he can't risk the deep step down into the kitchen. We return to find most of the swallows have gone, disappointingly early with only the late brood remaining. Maybe they know something we don't, having fed well this year and feeling strong enough to leave because the weather is already chilly.

It's cold for mid September and we light the first fire and drink champagne with sea trout and salad to celebrate farewell to the mortgage. Beck has been very rocky without the drug and decides to take it again.

The whirl of doing things goes on but he's less keen and it's obvious he's scared of not coping. At Boscobel House and the church at Tong, another site we always meant to visit, he can't manage two steps up from the ground floor because there's no handrail. 'I'm best off at home,' he says, 'where everything is what I know and I can get around easily holding onto things.'

On a lovely sunny day he stays in bed till ten and is still tired and rocky when he does get up. This is the day we write to the DVLA for the form to give up his driving licence; a bitter blow because he's been telling himself he's okay to drive but now knows he shouldn't because of weak legs.

October finds us back in Yorkshire, at the community owned pub we found in Coverdale in the summer — Coverdale, home of a delicious cheese, smoother and more creamy than Wensleydale. Again the stairs are steep but manageable but it's the trip to Whitby which finally brings home to me the speed of decline. Beck wants fish and chips at the Magpie Cafe, said to be the best in the country. The town is packed with people drawn by the autumn sunshine and I leave him to wait on the quayside while I park on a disabled space, first time using the Blue Badge. I find him cowering against a wall with his sticks, looking really scared, something I've never seen before. His relief when he sees me is palpable, he was afraid of being knocked over by the heedless crowds. I watch them stream by, laughing and chatting, often pushing their way through. It's a lesson for me, realising for the first time how disabled people are so disregarded.

The cafe is busy and he struggles to reach the upper floor but the fish lives up to its reputation so he reckons it was worth it. The staff are very kind and send us down in the service lift. He manages to walk to the car but the day is spoiled by the sight of a parking ticket fluttering under the windscreen wiper. Pissed off with myself for not having taken sufficient notice how the badge system works I realise I hadn't set the clock thing and been booked for that.

Luckily for us someone at Scarborough Council had a heart and my letter of explanation got us off the fine with a warning not to do it again.

Help from above?

The wheelchair still waits unused in the stable with Beck reluctant to admit he needs it but in Swansea at the Mumbles restaurant we watch a woman wheeling her husband to a table. We arrive by taxi after at last making the journey we've so often talked about on the Heart of Wales train from Church Stretton to Swansea through all the small remote stations in the mid-Wales countryside. She sees us looking and smiles. We return her smile but our eyes meet as we turn away and he says: 'It won't be long.'

Back home the wind has whipped more dried holly leaves from the base of the big hedge, wicked and sharp to unwary feet. The holly is a good wind-break for the house but its dead leaves are a year-round chore. They flock like frightened hens at the front door and around Chaffinch, drifting thickly in autumn when joined by the rest from the sycamore and apple trees, leaves huddling into heaps ready for collection.

Remembrance Day is sunny and everyone is kind and pleased to see him but he doesn't read out the names of the fallen this time, afraid he might fall and make a fool of himself. Sir John Taverner on the radio talks about his old presbyterian pastor who said: 'Life is a slow creeping tragedy so you have to keep cheerful'. How true that is. Steadily his weight is dropping. I spent years trying to stop him taking sugar now I'm piling it in to keep up the calories.

An Australian couple are booked in Chaffinch for two days and they stay chatting to him for a while after breakfast, talking of the places they plan to visit while they're over here, including York Minster. For years he's wanted to go back there for the Christmas carol service but in our busy life it's never fitted in. He loves organ music and the glorious tones sounding through that beautiful building are very special. This conversation renews his longing and knowing it's now or never I say nothing but decide to organise for him go with his brother. Tickets are still available with the bonus that places at the front are reserved for wheelchair users while the pusher, as I call it, goes free. He doesn't like resorting to the wheelchair but accepts that he'll struggle with the cathedral aisle on his own two feet, so that clinches it and I order tickets and arrange a room for them for two nights — all settled.

He tries out the wheelchair in the kitchen, we both do, brief moments of fun which help the coping. You need to seek the lighter side and forget the encroaching disablement. The chair is hard work on the concrete but we manage — later they will send one that's powered. We improvise a ramp to get in and out of the house. Fortunately the ground floor is all one level and the back door is the easiest exit with a low threshold. The farm being what it is, there are odd bits of timber about, of different size and thickness, and these work well to make a convenient slope.

Come the day, brother David is here and desolation dawns, it should've been me going with him. 'I wish I was coming,' I say.

'Well come, I'd rather it was you, just tell him'. But that's not possible, we have guests who need breakfast and it's too late to make arrangements for a house sitter. Above all it would be both unfair and unkind to disappoint his brother.

They're almost ready to go and I'm doing the fireplace when a crashing sound brings me rushing to the kitchen. Beck is on his back surrounded by broken crockery and glass, fallen against the worktop and then to the floor. Naturally he says he's fine but he's cracked a rib, a pain he doesn't mention till they're home again.

Outside the wind has risen into a howling gale, remnant leaves whirling around the car but the wheelchair is stowed and he is safely in the passenger seat. I watch it all, conscious of an overwhelming sadness, just managing to hold back tears as I kiss him and wish them a good trip. As the car disappears down the hill a deep breath releases the tears and the remains of the day are an intense lonely misery. Through the long months of deterioration not going with him to York is what I most regret.

The poor dogs wonder what's going on, their dinner is frequently late, because there's so much to do. The dogs are good for us both, a lot of work, but they keep me sane and get me away from the house because I can't bear watching him all the time. Friends invite us for supper but we can't wait to get away, at least I can't, but I know he feels the same. They mean well but I just can't relate to them any more. We still argue, small disagreements when I try so hard not to get cross and irritable but it's difficult. One time I say: 'You being ill doesn't make me a saint!'

They want him back at Stoke hospital, this time for several days, to learn how to use the ventilator. He doesn't need it yet but they tell us it's a matter of time before the condition starts to affect his breathing. They have given us two machines, which indicates the looming importance of the things and lots of paraphernalia to go with them. There's a choice of masks to fit his face — and of course instructions for me, as carer.

In the ward next to him is a young Indian constantly attended by his mother who stays in the hospital. He can move only his face and hands but talks very brightly though struck down by muscular dystrophy. He's very clever, still doing the accounts for his family's business and they are all around his bed much of the time.

Only one visit from me: he keeps saying it's a long way to come, don't bother. After five days he can come home. On a dark cold December evening we can't face the M6. This proves to be a good decision because the clutch goes as we come round the last roundabout above the hill on the Ironbridge bypass, meaning we can freewheel down into the lay-by to summon help. Breaking down on the motorway would've been a nightmare. It's fortunate he's home as it snows heavily on the Friday before Christmas and the road is bad for a day or two.

Three days before Christmas we're in Little Stretton for drinks which he enjoys with old friends. Our host's grandson is there with his girlfriend and as we chat about family it turns out her mother had bought Hoppy, the lovely grey horse who was Cloudborne's son — we called him Cloudhopper. How small the world is, unexpected links crop up all the time and it cheered the day to know the horse is still well and being ridden by a youngster in the pony club.

Everything now comes down to a succession of visits, specialists, doctors, physios, nurses, dieticians and our lovely lady vicar whose calls he finds a comfort. She has a little travelling kit of silver artefacts for communion and on the first occasion I join them and take the sacrament but after that I shy away, feeling strangely uncomfortable. Stupid things, silly things that don't matter, wind me up. I can't let it become a problem, can't do with anything happening to me.

He needs crutches now to get around outside and they send a zimmer frame which he needs but hates using. One day I think he's not so bad, then he seems much worse. His voice is changing, quite different in tone and much weaker, a voice no longer his own. And day by day if he attempts to write, the script becomes more random and will soon be as bad as mine.

I dress the chimney breast with greenery and lights because family are expected some time over the holiday. It's very effective and worth the effort and he's very taken with it. But tears are never far away and through wet eyes the white fairy lights on the tree create long twinkling rays like entrancing images from childhood.

On the big day we do the posh scrambled eggs with champagne bit in the morning but it's a strain. He enjoys the goose later but he's distressed and in tears some of the time, saying he isn't afraid to die but doesn't want to leave me. By the evening tiredness makes him repeat that several times.

New Year is better, though we ignore what it might bring but it's a good evening spent with friends from way back and he's more relaxed. The night is wet and very windy but midnight sees me up the lane shouting into the dark as a four day panic sets in. Bryony, the oldest Gordon has gone missing. She went out for a pee mid evening and didn't come back. In the night I go down three times to open the front door, hoping to find her waiting on the mat, then lie awake listening to the howling weather, thinking of her out there, dead or trapped and dying of hypothermia.

The only thing worse than looking everywhere for a missing dog would be hunting a lost child, that dreadful feeling, knowing it's pointless but being unable to stop at home and wait. Calls to everyone we can think of, including the dog warden, brings no word. The expanse of countryside around us, much of it rough and hilly, covered with bracken, gorse and other vegetation gives endless cover and searching is hopeless.

During the next three days in almost constant rain and wind I trudge high and low, exhausting myself while he sits at home and worries. We both go out in the Land Rover on some of the further tracks, driving round the lanes in case she's been hit, wondering if someone has picked her up.

But there's no trace. She's old and full of cancer and we fear the worst out so long in the elements. The gate into the field opposite is open and she may have gone that way. We're convinced she's dead and contact the hunt to look out for a body.

The stress has a real physical impact, fatigue and loss of appetite and it would be better to know she is dead than just not know. Beck keeps saying: 'I just want her to be here to give her a cuddle.'

On the fourth day a guest who lost his glasses on a previous visit calls to ask if he can come and search again. David had taken a wrong path on the slope below the farm and dropped his specs somewhere among the bracken. We think he doesn't have much chance of finding them but he's welcome to come. We provide him with a bill hook to help with the undergrowth and tell him about Bryony.

When the vicar arrives we tell her the sad story. She commiserates and begins her prayers, including a special prayer that God will help us to find Bryony. As she prepares the communion there's a loud knock on the door. It's our guest back from his search, saying eagerly: 'I can see a dog down there, on the path right at the bottom'.

With a rush of hope we both ask: 'What colour?'

'I haven't been right down but it looks black.'

That's it. Boots and mack dragged on, slipping and stumbling down the muddy field, knowing from a distance by the shape that it's her. She is ecstatic to see me but can't walk, her body thick with mud, obscuring the tan markings. It looks as if she's been dragging herself along and I fear she has a broken leg or dislocated joint. What to do? David is keen to help but there's no way we can carry her up that hill.

'Will you stay with her?'

He nods. 'What can we do?'

The field below is muddy and running with water after all the rain, slightly downhill to the rough track at the bottom. 'We'll have to drag her across. I'll get something, be as quick as I can.'

By now the short January afternoon is closing in, it will soon be dark and the rain is heavier. Struggling back up the hill, horribly out of breath but just concentrating on getting her home and thinking what we've got that will do the job.

Beck and the vicar are waiting anxiously, both delighted it's her and of course she gives the credit to the Almighty. Perhaps she's right. Thrusting the car keys into Beck's hand and helping him into the vehicle I tell him: 'Take it down to the lane end and wait. Don't try to get out, just wait for us.'

With a big plastic ballast sack from the barn I head back down the hill in the now torrential rain, slipping twice on the muddy grass. Our gallant guest is waiting patiently with the poor old dog lying beside him on the path. We manhandle her onto the sack and start to drag it between us across the field. It's hard going, even on the slope, easier where there's more water lying but she weighs more than normal being so plastered in wet mud.

The worst bit is getting her along the deeply rutted lane but we manage it and heave her into the back of the car. Beck drives us carefully up the hill, he's very fond of Bryony and desperately pleased to be useful. This is the last time he drives before his licence is surrendered.

The exhausted animal is hosed down to clear the mud and lies, wrapped in blankets, by the Aga. She takes a small feed with some analgesic and is left to recover before we examine her properly. The kind helper is splattered with mud but feels better after a shower and a bite to eat. He never found his specs but has been back several times and reminded me not long ago that we gave him a free night's stay as a thank you for his help.

Bryony sleeps soundly for a few hours while we worry how badly injured she might be. Eventually she stirs, wags her tail and tries to stand. With help she gets on her feet and walks to the water bowl. The hind legs seem to be uninjured and we decide the apparent paralysis was just pain in the hip joints from cold and fatigue. For the next few days she hardly leaves her bed. Where she'd been those four days we'll never know but she'd made her way back that far. Fired by her determination she might eventually have crawled home but we can only conjecture what sparked her disappearance. There were deer slots in the mud by the open gateway and perhaps she picked up the scent and followed.

Friday's joy evaporates on the Sunday when Kitty and the youngest bitch Amber also disappear, vanishing within minutes of going out into the yard. It's hard to believe it could happen again but it adds to the theory that deer were leaving strong scents to attract them. Kitty has always been prone to wandering, led astray at an early age by mother Bryony but it's devastating that they've both gone. They're not back by evening and I mix a gin and tonic for consolation. But some inner voice warns me 'don't have a drink', some superstitious thought that it might help. Within half an hour the phone rings, our neighbour saying they had seen on Facebook that someone had found what sounded like our dogs. The guy — who runs a taxi service — is suspicious and careful, asking what breed of dogs we have. I explain that we live just over the hill from him, though nearly four miles by the road.

His daughter had found two dogs coming along the road in front of their house. They had come to her happily and were put in the barn with some food. It seems they were heading in the right direction for home. As soon as I'm out of the car and speak there's a loud wailing from the barn which I know at once is Amber who does a wow-wowing kind of talk, not a bark. She goes berserk as I enter the building and he grins at me: 'There's not much doubt about that.'

They're thrilled to be home, making a mega fuss of Beck. Outside with them all in the dry clear night the flash of intuition about the gin seems weird. Staring up at the bright pattern of stars a rush of relief and momentary happiness washes over me, my deep breaths expelled in rising puffs of warm air condensing in the cold.

In the long boring January evenings I'm busy repressing everything and the horrid weather keeps Beck indoors. He feels the cold, though it's not that bad. During a brief spell of sunshine he's watching from the window a flock of starlings on the holly trees opposite, where the berries have all gone, stripped by the redwings and fieldfares. He refuses the offer to go outside in the wheelchair; on a morning like this the fresh air would be good for him. It feels as if life is suspended, on hold. I long to spend more time outside with the dogs and animals, relishing mundane tasks like raking up dead leaves to leave the soil free for the snowdrops to emerge, pure and lovely in the harsh winter.

The MND expert from the hospice visits and tells him he must use the ventilator more often, especially at night. Maybe he will take notice of her. She says it will increase life expectancy though the prognosis is dubious.

He wants to revisit Tenbury Wells, the little time-lock town where he's worked so often. We go for lunch and drive back over Clee Hill through deepest south Shropshire on a mild sunny afternoon. We come across a long ford near Clee St Margaret and I get out to check the depth, walking along the footbridge. It's hard to judge but two tractors come splashing through and it's not that deep, so we get through safely.

It reminds us of getting stuck in deep water at Tarr Steps on Exmoor and the large clump of soot which was sent sailing off down the Barle when the engine spluttered back into life. We felt guilty about polluting the river.

My youngest nephew comes to visit with his wife and small son who is disconcerted and hesitant around the invalid. The boy doesn't remember Beck as he was, whispering to his dad: 'Has he always been like this?'

It's been snowing and they find a distraction outside with the sledge that's been so long unused. The wind has whipped the fine snow, running it down the car windscreens into tight scrolls at the base of the glass. When the snow stops we watch the mist drift in fine skeins across the face of Wilstone Hill, moving closer until it almost obscures the oak tree in the hedge.

When the beasts from the east arrive, and we've known plenty, the bitter winds from Russia and Scandinavia give a whole new meaning to cold. The wind chill factor is vicious, freezing the land hard like iron and the water really does resemble stone as the temperature drops low enough in a truly bleak mid winter. The harsh cold scorches the skin like a burn and snatches the breath from your throat. When at last the wind direction changes, a slow thaw begins but all the bucket shaped lumps of ice lying in the yard take days to melt away.

With stock to feed lugging water is a misery. But there's compensation in small pleasures, such as watching thirsty hens rush to taste a bucket of warm water in the barn. They come with flapping wings, half flying, to gather round like children at a party, bending to dip their beaks, then with heads thrown back and eyes closed they savour the water trickling down their throats in obvious enjoyment, shaking themselves in satisfaction.

.

The murky days of winter make everything outdoors clammy with damp and the dogs seem constantly muddied. When depression sits like a weight on your shoulder even a glimpse of the sun brings a lift. You find energy to go outdoors and tackle some small garden job and the views and more frequent visits from the kites make it all seem more manageable — life may have some prospect of hope.

A brighter February day on the cusp of spring and the air feels almost warm but from the upstairs window the village is white with frost though the fields here and on the surrounding hills are green in the rising sun. Trudging uphill through sparkling dew to retrieve the old ewes trespassing on the wrong land the sun in my eyes is blinding. Coming down it casts a long, thin shadow ahead of me.

Beck can still get around the house with a stick and the worktop and other bits to hang onto. But when the weather improves comes a glorious day of blue skies when he sets off with crutches to go up the field to his seat with its misty view of hills and the blossoming valley. He is back within ten minutes, having gone as far as the gate by the sheep house but unable to manage the incline. So after that I drive him up in the Discovery, easier to get into than the car.

Returning one afternoon after rain the Disco starts to slide on a muddy patch and with a sharp sense of deja vu we're slithering out of control towards the bottom fence.

No real danger this time as I turn the wheel and we're moving parallel to the fence but the heavy vehicle continues to slide and ends up tight against it. There's no way he can get out the passenger side but with great determination he contrives to move across into the other seat and out. The effort exhausts him and he leans on the bonnet, trembling.

'My legs just don't want to work,' he says.

After a rest he summons all his strength and makes it as far as the sheep house but the slope is too much. 'I don't think I can do it,' he says.

'What about sliding down,' I suggest, thinking of Bryony.

'Suppose we could try.'

Back with a plastic sack I find him clinging to the gatepost but he sits on the sack and I start to push him like a child on a sledge. The grass is wet and muddy which helps the undignified progress towards the concrete. Uncertain how I'll get him back indoors, at that very moment one of the nurses appears on an unscheduled call and she stays with him while I fetch the wheelchair. Between us we get him safely back to the kitchen.

The wheelchair is becoming more necessary. A van arrives with another chair, a complicated electric affair which needs a short seminar on how it works. I tell the man we don't need it yet, to which he nods and smiles: 'Well it's here now, ready for when you do.'

In the past, as if he had a premonition about it all, he's joked several times about Beachy Head and wheeling himself over the cliff if he was ever in a wheelchair. There's no answer to that. I would only say: 'You'd have to get there first.' He's also mentioned pillows but I could never do that — or could I, if he begged me?

Water everywhere

Late winter is plagued by long days of storms and heavy rain with serious flooding around the country but we decide on a trip south for his birthday. We'd often talked of visiting Selbourne, nestling under the Sussex beech hangers where Gilbert White spent his life studying the natural history of his locality, the first ecologist. We arrive eventually after several diversions to avoid flooded roads and he can access the museum in the chair through the heavy rain. He can't make it to the upstairs rooms which commemorate the life and heroic death of Captain Lawrence Oates on Scott's ill-fated South Pole expedition of 1912 — the man who said: 'I am just going outside and may be some time'.

White's house has a beautiful garden, part of an extensive estate and I leave him a moment to go outside and assess possibilities but it's raining more heavily and the grass is sodden. No way can I push him around on that. On the return trip to Devizes there's an hour delay at the top of a steep hill on Salisbury Plain where the road at the bottom is flooded, only passable one car at a time.

I snatch three nights away on Exmoor, putting aside the feelings of guilt, for two days riding on a part of the moor I don't know, interesting but not the same as riding Sonny. Skylarks rising in song and a white-bibbed dipper as we ford the river. David is in charge and I return to find he's left the barn gate open and the poultry have stripped all the lettuce and tomato plants. Beck seems worn out and aggravated, not least by being served mushy peas with the wonderful pizza from the deli.

His brother manages to get him out into the sunshine for a few hours with Black Sam on his lap, watching the swallows dashing in and out of the stables and swooping to gather more mud from behind the barn. And he saw a kite which made his day.

David shoots the white cockerel, which seems harsh but necessary He attacks the others and flies at people, flashing beak and spurs — nasty, especially if children are around. Without him the other three settle together with the old rooster still in charge.

The trees this spring are especially lovely, the hawthorn and the whitebeam, bearing pale silvery leaves and sprays of tiny sweet smelling flowers which attract an array of insects during their brief appearance. Before long the cascade of honeysuckle which clings to it will be decked with yellow blooms and on the red chestnut tree the blossom display is the best it's ever been.

In late spring it's Galloway, a small hotel in Portpatrick with good views of the harbour and the sea. From that coast on the Mull of Galloway you can see both the Isle of Man to the south and across to Northern Ireland. With three steps up to the door and a handrail he can just manage to get in if I park by the steps. Our room is on the ground floor and he can walk across to the dining room for breakfast and supper.

The talk inevitably turns to the referendum coming up in the autumn, the big decision on Scottish independence. Our hosts are vehemently against it, telling us that most people in the hospitality trade think it would be a disaster. With Scottish blood on his mother's side and affiliations in the borders from his father's connection with the wool trade, Beck is passionately against the idea. 'I hope I'm still here to know the result,' he tells them, a sentiment he repeats several times in the coming months.

Most of our stay is spent driving around and the weather isn't kind with yet more rain. An abundance of wild garlic amongst a sea of grass create a landscape incredibly green and strangely alien though bluebells are still about in the woods and Ailsa Craig is a dark peak against the grey of the sea and sky. Cattle are everywhere, pensive contemplative beasts hock deep in the grass, lush grass, untroubled by weeds, no dandelions showing bright golden heads to break the monotony. It's man-made grass but on the rocky outcrops there is gorse and yellow flowers, maybe buttercups. The stones cleared to create this green desert are piled at the edges. In one place a digger has gouged out cliffs in the black peat.

We're both disappointed not to see many Galloway cattle, dun, black or belted which we expected to find in their native territory, only large herds of dairy cows. The area has some lovely gardens and we attempt a visit but once away from the main track most of the paths are grass, wet and very soft after all the rain. We manage one short circuit but it's impossible to carry on, to push the wheelchair on boggy turf is beyond my physical capacity.

Down in Portpatrick we book supper at a recommended fish restaurant. The car park is some distance so we use the wheelchair, causing a small commotion when we arrive. I had mentioned the chair but they're unprepared and it requires some rearrangement of the tables to get us settled. Again we learn how the interests of the disabled are never a priority. It's good food but he opts for the chowder which turns out to include whole mussels and other shellfish as nature made them, not an ideal choice for someone whose hands have lost most of their dexterity. But with patience he gets through it and enjoys the dish.

Best part of the trip is the journey up the coast towards Ayr and the Burns country with the rocky lump of Ailsa Craig always in view. Then turning south on the mountain roads over the top of Galloway Forest Park. This is more Beck's style and brings back good memories of challenging treks in various Land Rovers, vehicles he is ridiculously fond of. The car wasn't meant for such rough tracks, mostly unsurfaced and in some places I fear we might get stuck but once we're over the top and heading downhill it's easier going, back to civilisation at Newton Stewart.

Now he can no longer tackle the fields on foot the idea of a mobility vehicle arises, an all terrain machine to tackle the slopes and the grass. If I mention it he immediately says it's a waste of money: 'I won't be using it for long.' We had the same argument about buying a riser recliner chair, 'waste of money.'

In Shrewsbury on some errand we pass a mobility equipment store. 'I'm going in to have a look,' I say, 'let's just find out what's involved.'

The salesman is there in an instant as I'm looking around and in the middle of the floor is a large vehicle which looks robust enough to tackle our land. 'That looks the sort of thing we need but I guess it's a lot of money.'

With a smile he says: 'Altogether, including its rain cover, they work out at a bit over £6,000,' he pauses, 'but this is secondhand.'

'How much?'

'£2,500.' For once fate is on our side. 'Can you take it outside to the car, it's not easy for my husband to get in here.'

'No problem.' He opens the big door and drives the vehicle out so Beck can see it. He says grumpily:'I can't see the point.'

Ignoring his objections I follow the salesman back inside and agree the sale. 'Even if you only use it for a few weeks over the summer it'll give you some independence to get around the farm.'

The machine is called a Breeze, which seems appropriate for where it's going to be used. Pretty much like new it has very few miles on its clock, and is a real bargain.

A few days later it arrives in bright sunshine. He can climb into it from the wheelchair and test drives it round the paddock with a smile on his face which is good to see. He christens it Dolly. It's a great piece of kit and easily tackles the steep slope up past the sheep house into the field or the other way up the lane and in through the top gate. We start a regime with me seeing him off and closing the gate and when he's coming down he summons me by phone, driving the Breeze right up to the front door to climb back onto the wheelchair. In the warm summer days it can only do him good to be out in the fresh air for as long as he feels like it.

The horses are alarmed at first when he tries to get close enough to offer them an apple or a carrot but they quickly get used to it, reassured once they realise it's him

But indoors things move on. Until now he can still get upstairs to bed, though every day it becomes more precarious and it's only a matter of time before he can't make it. A hospital bed is already ordered to go in the small sitting room which will be easier for him as he gets worse. Each day makes me more anxious as he climbs the stairs, carefully step-by-step hanging on to the handrails at both sides and often staggering at the top to make the turn onto the landing.

Sharp intakes of breath from me but it's impossible to help, certainly not going behind to support him in any way because if he fell backwards it would be a disaster for both. It's weird to recall him fixing a new rail some years back to make it safer for disabled guests. Ironic that now they are vital for him.

It gets worse each night, especially if it's late and he's tired and comes the night when he's swaying so much at the top I fear he'll fall back. Without comment I watch but later in bed he turns to me and says: 'I can't do that any more, you'll have to sleep alone from now on.'

'We'll move into Chaffinch tomorrow, we'll be cosy in there'. But I know it can't be for long because it's booked the following weekend. And it's not ideal, although the bathroom and shower are set up with handles for semi-ambulant guests, simply getting him from the room back to the house and vice versa is difficult. The wheelchair barely fits through the door and he struggles now to walk the few yards back to the kitchen.

Frantic calls to the hospital about the bed reassure us but with only one night left when Chaffinch is available we're increasingly anxious, thinking about a mattress on the floor as a stop gap. But our wonderful health service doesn't let us down and early on Friday afternoon they arrive with the bed, with all kinds of clever bits to alter things like height and angle designed for his comfort.

It's all set up by early evening with the ventilator at one side which he can reach easily, now increasingly necessary for breathing. Black Sam quickly decides it's a good place to sleep. A few days later a man arrives with a big case to set up a buzzer system so Beck can contact me instantly when I'm upstairs. It sits on the heavy oak shelf in our bedroom and makes a horrid noise vibrating on the wood, like a frog in pain.

There is an incremental reduction in what he can do. No more washing up, the fingers are clumsier and less able to manipulate. The dogs are upset by noises from the new bedroom next door. They can't understand what's going on and it takes a whole new length of time to get everything done. I can't get to bed till he's settled but it must be hell for him to be so bored and feel so useless. It's an awful thing to have total control over another human being and alone in bed I need the Moroccan blanket to replace his warm body.

When the sun shines he's keener to be out and is finally persuaded into shorts instead of thick trousers. But the summer subsides into a succession of medical happenings, trips back to the hospital at Stoke for 'assessment', visits from doctors and nurses, physiotherapists and dieticians at home and at the hospital. The orthotic department provides made to measure supports for his legs to aid stability — but they make no difference. Then there are occasional appointments with the neurologist which become more and more trying as getting him in and out of the car and into the wheelchair is an increasing challenge.

These dates in particular begin to make me angry and we agree to defer them, with various excuses as the dates approach. He doesn't want to go and I can do without the struggle. These uncomfortable visits do nothing to help him and the cursory interviews cannot add much to the total knowledge about this awful condition.

Friends offer use of their swimming pool thinking it might help. But it just exhausts him and getting his damp body back into clothes is awful, just to get the shirt over his head is a problem. So we don't repeat the exercise.

Guests are still arriving, both bed and breakfast and increasingly for self catering in the cottage. People ask how I cope with doing that and looking after Beck but having people around is helpful, the normality of it is oddly reassuring and the income is handy. Meeting new people and talking with them is a tonic for both of us and takes us beyond the ever-tightening bubble engulfing us.

A recurring theme is the number of people who visit Shropshire seeking a new home, often staying several times in the process. One guest who became a friend was an endoscopy nurse from the south coast who had discovered the joys of the county and planned to move here and work at one of the hospitals. Suzanne was well up the NHS nursing ladder but looking to downgrade for a less stressful life. A cat lover with four cats to consider it was important to find the right property. With her impeccable English I couldn't quite place her origin and thought she might be South African but eventually she spoke about her German background so that solved my puzzle.

She has lived here and worked in our health service for thirty years or more but when Brexit came along she was required to jump through several hoops to stay.

She enjoys her visits and the atmosphere with our dogs and cats, Black Sam especially. But this intelligent cat is ageing fast and increasingly plagued by epilepsy, which at his age the vets say is untreatable.

Poor old Bryony shows more signs of pain and is diagnosed with kidney cancer, embarking on a regime of painkillers. There is nothing else to be done because we would never put a dog through the kind of treatment given to humans. They can't understand what's being done to them or the horrid side effects and it seems kinder to simply make them free of pain.

A couple arrive from Edinburgh on a tandem and Beck gets into a long conversation with them about the referendum. They seem unsure which way to vote but he impresses them with how much he cares; maybe it will make a difference.

A bumper crop of strawberries is ripening fast in the veg garden, giving thoughts of strawberry jam. Double cream waiting in the fridge, I go bowl in hand to pick some but none are ripe enough. Those which were turning the previous day have vanished. But there would be some tomorrow – or so I thought.

Puzzled and frustrated I try again next day and discover a large hole in the netting. Surely the crows can't break the netting like that. But the thief has four legs.

Next day I notice a squirrel squatting on the slope behind the car looking woozy. It's drunk on my strawberries. Millie spots it and gives chase but it flees into the crabapple tree. She sits beneath as it stays there for several hours while I fume at the lack of an airgun.

Instead I set the cage trap which only creates a Sunday morning horror. The noise of a commotion, the racket of angry crows, sends me rushing out --

burning the bacon with guests at the table — to find the remains of a female blackbird, just a leg and a fragment of wing.

The poor bird had gone in after the strawberry bait only to become the victim of a gang of crows whose long vicious beaks had reached in from all sides to rip her to pieces. An unpleasant start to the day and not one I wished to relate to guests.

In July its Norfolk, planned for May but the spring floods had wreaked terrible damage on the north Norfolk coast and the ground floor flat we had booked needed total refitting. Things had changed radically for us since the original booking. His breathing is becoming so bad we wonder if we should go. We chose it because it's right next door to the crab man's cafe, so we could spoil ourselves on his fresh seafood. But the way we remembered the place didn't take account of the current situation. My courage nearly fails pushing him from the car over rough ground and manoeuvring the wheelchair through a really awkward turn to get in. Inside there is an even bigger issue, the bathroom has been raised about a foot above the rest of the flat, so there's no way he can use the facilities. At that point we wonder if we should just go home. But it's only three days and we'd arranged to entertain his cousin for lunch. We've brought a mobile commode and outside there's a skip full of furniture items and waste decorating stuff so we improvise — where there's a will.

It isn't the happiest holiday, the struggle to get in and out and his growing despondency make it hard going. But at least we're in the same bed again for a few days. The crab salad lunch goes off well and I leave them for a while, hoping to get a swim. But the nearest beach has a steep bank of pebbles down to the sea and the crashing waves are not inviting. The angry sea deepens my rising sense of desolation and I drive around, reluctant to return. He looks cross and after the guests have left he demands to know where I've been. Who knows what he was imagining? Next day we have another row about it, sitting in the car watching the boats at Morston Quay. The situation made more sad as it brings back good memories of leaving from here to visit the seals at Blakeney Point.

The evening before we go home we book supper at the pub, almost next door but approached up sloping gravel. Again I underestimate the difficulty and really struggle to push him uphill. I almost give up at halfway, thinking we can't make it.

My frustration is compounded by a guy sitting at an outside table with his family watching my efforts in obvious amusement. I'm on the point of saying something abusive when a young man appears and takes over the chair to push Beck right to the pub door. The other individual gets my most scornful scowl as I pass. Returning to that pub more recently I noted ruefully the new tarmac path up from the car park.

Back in Shropshire an adapter gadget arrives from the NHS which plugs into the car and means we can use the ventilator away from home. He spent a lot of time doing locums at Rhayader, in the land of lakes and reservoirs and it was the journey he always enjoyed, eager to go back. We take a longer route so we're not covering the same ground but after an hour he's become very uncomfortable, struggling for breath.

In a lay-by beneath a tall cliff it takes me several minutes to set up the equipment with the ventilator behind him on the back seat. He's impatient and almost gasping before we get the mask in place. By the time we get to Rhayader he's feeling better and we park by the river but when I get the wheelchair ready and bring it to the door he looks at me with an apology. He can't summon the energy to make the effort. He stays in the car while I go in search of fish and chips.

After we've eaten I follow the path for some way along the nascent Wye through the trees beside the fast flowing river, hoping to glimpse the blue flash of a kingfisher or spot a dipper fishing from a rock. It would be good to get to the waterfall but I can't leave him that long.

'What would you like to do now?' But he just shakes his head at the question.

'What about visiting the kite place?' A farm not far from the town attracts a host of red kites for a daily feeding ritual. 'If you like.'

There is half an hour to wait before the appointed time but a few birds are already overhead circling the site. He tries to watch them but he can't lift the binoculars to his eyes any more. It's obvious he's not comfortable being there.

'Let's just go home,' he says. He hardly speaks, sleeping for a while and immensely relieved to be home. This is the last time he goes anywhere in the car.

After supper once Beck is settled watching TV I slip away with the dogs. The last rays of the sun behind Caradoc gild a mackerel sky into crimson bands while a full golden moon is already rising above the line of Wenlock Edge. The lie of the land makes the bright face in the sky seem very close. Before we came here I never noticed the moon as a presence — took it for granted, it was just the moon — never considering its vital impact on tides, weather and the hours in our day. Now it's a constant fascination.

With little light pollution its commanding presence dominates the sky and on clear nights demands attention, effacing the stars, or perhaps half hidden as it sails among fleeting storm clouds, often softly muted behind a veil of cirrus. The ancient face still watches, observing our futile machinations and probably will still be shining in vain on the wreckage when we've destroyed its planet.

It's in such moments that we're most alive and connected to the real world of nature. Moments that soothe, a reminder that life goes on, in an ancient world beyond what we've done to it. The still air is filled with the sounds of evening, sheep bleat for their lambs, flocks of black birds fly overhead, crows, jackdaws and rooks clamouring before they settle to roost. A cock pheasant crows and the hoot of a tawny owl close by in the lane is answered at once from across the valley. We linger, the dogs and me, in the deepening dusk and the bats are suddenly around us, flitting overhead so fast they are just a blink and gone.

An August evening brings an amazing red sky, grey clouds etched with deep crimson, waiting for the back end of a hurricane called Bertha to land from America. But Beck is not interested, only the swallows attract him. At bed time he's miserable, saying he wishes he might not wake up. This is the first time he's said that. And I have this sort of suspended disbelief, that it's not actually happening — as if I've been waiting all my life for this grim tragedy. He has no energy, saying he only gets a third of each breath, so needs the ventilator more and more. And he's always cold, sitting by the Aga wearing fleece gloves even in a heatwave.

The weather is unkind, not fit for him to get out on the Breeze and each time it's more difficult to move from the wheelchair. He's finding it harder and harder to make his legs work, will power isn't enough, they no longer respond to instructions from his brain. The neurones have been got at by whatever chemical reaction it is that causes this invidious invasion of his body.

He decides to start using the electric wheelchair and we fetch it indoors from its hiding place in the stable. Getting used to working the powered chair is entertaining for both of us and in reverse it sets up a loud bleeping. It means he can get around the house under his own steam and outside, if I hold the doors open. It's better in many ways and he can move around the yard and into the lane at will. The dogs are confused by all these changes, they can't understand what's happened to him. Poor Bryony, spending her last summer between sun and shade, keeps approaching him to commiserate and Millie simply looks sad.

This means redundancy for Dolly, as he's now too weak to manoeuvre himself from the chair, so she's banished to the stable. Sensible consultants advise patients with any form of degenerative condition that there's no point spending a lot of money on a brand-new vehicle. Better to look around, as there are many bargains to be had. The sad fact is that few of these vehicles put many miles on the clock with just one owner.

The hand of authority

Various medics keep arriving to make further assessments and they tell us he needs a hoist. When it arrives we watch with distaste and alarm and our GP happens to be here. I must be looking a bit tired because he starts talking about respite care and the possibility of Beck going into the hospice for a short break. He doesn't seem to mind the idea but we don't expect anything to happen in a hurry.

But early on Monday morning there's a phone call to say there's a bed available in the Severn Hospice if he'd like to take it up. That puts us on the spot and he looks reluctant and asks what I think but it has to be his decision. After some thought he says it's probably a good idea so I call back and they confirm that an ambulance will collect him in the afternoon.

By the time they come he's worked himself into an unpleasant mood. He wheels himself out to where the ambulance is waiting with its ramp ready for him to ride up. His dislike is obvious — can't blame him — but then he steers the chair onto the grass, by mistake or deliberate, who knows. Soft after rain one wheel sinks in and it takes several minutes to free it before finally he's safe in the ambulance. I'm to follow on.

When I arrive he's already in a pleasant room fussed over by two nurses and our vicar, who was due to visit that afternoon. I had redirected her to the hospice and she made an effort to be there when he arrived. Then more staff appear. There's a problem, something to do with the hoist, the room is too small and they decide to move him.

Led by a nurse he sets off along the corridor with a trail of people behind and me. The nurse opens some double doors and we enter a large room with wide glass doors opening onto the garden. It's obviously a room meant for more than one patient but they've decided that with the wheelchair and the hoist they need more space. He looks bemused and tired but surrounded by women he produces some of his old charm.

They ask how we've been managing with the hoist at home and he says we haven't used it yet. They seem aghast but in fact we've coped with all the issues of getting in and out of bed and to the bathroom and all the basics that involves. He's done it with his upper body strength and mine and we just got on with it.

But the hand of authority changes everything and two people are required to hoist him. He hates it, the indignity and the feeling of utter helplessness which so far we've avoided.

The few days respite turn into a month because now we are constrained by the system and we no longer make the decisions. He wants to come home but now they say he needs full care at home, two carers four times a day but this requires funding. I am assured we are eligible for full support under the NHS continuing healthcare system. This is a relief and good news but of course the bureaucracy involved takes time with many forms to fill in and decisions made elsewhere. The hospice staff are incredibly kind and helpful but they won't let him come home until the package is approved and ready to roll. Being there moves the situation up a gear — or in reality, down.

So through the lovely days of September he's there in a sunny room — and there are certainly many worse places to be ill. Once secured in his wheelchair in the mornings he is free to go outside as much as he likes and can wheel himself out into the fresh air to sit in the sun or move along the paved areas and sometimes further around the extensive lawns. A succession of visitors pops in to see him along with the usual coterie of medics. He has another date with the neurologist but we cancel that as unnecessary hassle. For me it's a trip every other day which takes quite a chunk of available time and we are still busy at home with visitors. The facts of his condition are not something discussed with guests unless they know him from previous stays. It would only make them uncomfortable, embarrassed, unsure what to say and after all they are here to enjoy themselves. So it's all about putting on a brave face.

The Shropshire hospice is a wonderful place. Apart from our own experience we've known several people who've gone there to end their lives in peace and comfort and its staff and facilities are always gently reassuring. But Beck's condition is not something they're equipped to deal with in the long term as he doesn't require palliative care as such. In any case he doesn't want to stay there, he wants to die at home. But being there accelerates the loss of power in his limbs. When he went in he could still stand and move from bed to chair but since they hoist him all the time, his muscles are now useless and all his independence has gone.

Back home the glorious late September sun lures me outside with a drink, sitting with only my friend the Wrekin for company. I try not to think of him alone in that bed under the mask that gives him breath and holds the slender diminishing thread of his life. But being out there prompts an idea that will cheer him for a little time.

Medics and others now realise the beneficial effects of animals on people, reduction in stress and the simple pleasure of having them around to touch and stroke. The hospice is brilliant over this, allowing dogs and other pets as visitors. Beck is very anxious to see the dogs and I decide to take Bryony. She trots happily along the corridor on a lead and at the door I let her off, assuming he is alone. Opening one of the double doors I let her pop through and bound into the room only to be greeted by hysterical screams.

One of the nurses is cowering behind the bed as the old dog is ecstatically greeting her dad. Mortified I hasten to reassure the poor girl who it transpires is terrified of dogs. Thoughtless of me and big apologies but I do get her to make friends with Bryony before she disappears. At least it's entertaining for the patient but Bryony is ill at ease, it seems to increase her anxieties so I don't take her again.

Millie comes next time. She's been pining for him, being a real daddy's girl who used to spend hours cuddled close to him on the sofa. She's been puzzled and bereft since he vanished. Her delight at seeing him is over-whelming and he is equally thrilled. Soon she's up on the bed, snuggled close to him, a terrific boost to his spirits. Another time I take Amber who manages to disappear up a corridor but is soon found in another room.

It's decision day in the Scottish referendum, something he really cares about and very interested in the outcome. But he's not well, restless and very uncomfortable in the wheelchair. The nurses hoist him back into bed as he seems to have reached some sort of crisis. Really worried I go home to deal with animals and guests and come back later in the evening to find they have fitted a catheter; more indignity and less control, one more downward step. They say they can fix me a bed so I can stay but it's impossible to leave everything at home unattended.

The outcome of the Scottish vote is what we both hoped and I arrive late morning bearing a half bottle of champagne with some special cheese he likes to celebrate but his heart isn't in it. He takes a glass of champagne but his mind has drifted away from the Scots' decision.

Once I've read through all the forms and signed everything, the Clinical Commissioning Group confirms they will pay so we think great, we can get him home. But there's a fresh problem, finding a care company to do the job. The first one approached turns out to be too expensive, or so they tell me, and the other, which is actually more local to us, has no staff available until the end of the month. So he must remain in the hospice until October is knocking at the door, somehow shrinking down into his chair, very poorly, increasingly reminiscent of Stephen Hawking. The catheter is affecting him badly, it needs frequent changing and the pain is wearing him out. The nurses are bemused when I mention that yoghurt pots will be very useful for emptying. The carers too, until they see the little buckets complete with handle which are just the right size to fit under the tap on his leg, having contained a kilogram of Greek yoghurt from a certain supermarket.

The homecoming is chaotic, bad communication causes a muddle and the carers we expected to be there to get him settled don't turn up. His favourite nurse has come back with him and between us we manage to move him from the wheelchair into the bed. The first two of his carer team arrive an hour later.

From then on it becomes a tedious routine with carers arriving first thing after his breakfast, to get him up and deal with all the personal necessities. During the day he's in the chair. They come again at lunchtime for a repeat performance and again at teatime and yet again to get him back into bed for the night. This visit is a major issue because they come so early and he's angry about being in bed sometimes as early as seven o'clock. We set up a TV at the end of the bed and he has his DVD player and radio but it's the lack of freedom and choice that bugs him.

His life now is confined to bed and wheelchair as the new month brings deteriorating weather and October turns unseasonably cold. In the morning the rising sun glints on the silver landscape of a really sharp frost. A family of ravens are floating on the air currents, enjoying the sun, calling as they roll and tumble together.

But it turns mild again and the grass keeps growing and needs a cut at the end of the month. A bonus in the situation is that one of the young carers is also trained as a hairdresser which solves the hair cutting issue. He can't stay long outside, soon feeling cold but small things please him, like the sparrows having a splashing party in the birdbath and when I show him two eggs that the spaniel sisters Tilly and Teasel found in the hay and brought to me.

The sheep have gnawed the bark on his red chestnut tree, the one he planted early on and so beautiful when in bloom. Better that he doesn't know because it will only make him angry. Nor do I tell him I've taken his walking boots to the dog shop. Expensive leather boots, hardly worn, replacements for the ones stolen with all the other gear along with the Land Rover when he was doing a locum in the Black Country.

Then it's wild and windy, very wild, the back end of another hurricane lashing across the Atlantic from Bermuda. The wind excites me. I like to hear it bang and crash at night; the open window and the billowing curtains are disturbing but oddly comforting -- like an old friend waiting to come in. It's still blowing in the early morning with the shadow of the house outlined on the field as a flock of pigeons fly fast uphill, colours bright in the burgeoning sunlight.

Around noon I realise Sam is missing and immediately think he's gone off to die, something cats do, creeping away to be alone. We both get upset, thinking the worst, then at teatime I find him in the washing basket, asleep on the clean laundry. He's been there all day. Poor cat is sick most days now and I should do something about it but he's such a character, so genuinely loving to people and dogs, unlike most cats who are innately selfish.

Three whole days of rain and gales depress us even more and the catheter keeps blocking which needs the nurses to fix. By mid morning the sun is out and it's warm. The catheter is blocked again so he goes out in the wheelchair to bump up and down the road. The rough concrete frees the blockage, a good idea but it must've hurt. He tells me he saw the raven family, rolling in the sunshine, calling to each other. The next night there is so much blood in the catheter I call out Shropdoc to fit a new one. Unlike the nurses the doctor shows me how to do the needle and flush it.

Brother David is here more often, sometimes staying for several days which is mostly a blessing because he entertains the patient, leaving me free to do all the other stuff. He's a lovely man but quirky, one trait being he never sees what needs doing. On dustbin or recycling days he'll walk past the bins all day and never think to bring them in unless it's mentioned. But he's kind and helpful, devastated by his brother's condition and worried for me. We ask him to join us for Christmas.

It's late in the year for guests but a man from Suffolk calls wanting a couple of nights and proceeds to tell me all his wife's requirements. Something in my gut tells me let this one go but I ignore the feeling and book them in

Chaffinch because she supposedly can't manage steps. The morning before they are due the wife calls to say she needs to sleep on the floor — something not mentioned by her better half. Explaining Chaffinch is not a huge room but she could sleep on whatever she brings at the bottom of the bed her reply is indignant.

'I'm not sleeping at the bottom of his bed!' she says in an unpleasant tone, then proceeds to tell me that her gluten-free toast must be made separately to avoid contamination from ordinary bread. I should know better and tell her our facilities are unsuitable and book elsewhere. But I don't and change the booking into Kite, explaining that its steps are negligible.

Beck can't be left alone for long and gets worried even if I'm just doing something outside. I've arranged to buy a new car and collecting it is another issue. But kind friends from the village offer to sit with him while I'm gone. I plan to be back before four o'clock when the guests are expected but they arrive before the prescribed time and have already made several complaints. The husband, who acts as errand boy, appears in the kitchen to say she cannot use the shower or the bath in Kite. Instead of telling them to leave I say she can use the bathroom in Chaffinch.

They arrive for breakfast with her special cushion which she leaves in the dining room both mornings so the poor chap has to scurry across to collect it. But the meal goes reasonably well though she moans about the lack of choice in gluten free cereals. Her husband has booked the smoked salmon special which he enjoys. I particularly make the point that they should let me know in the evening if they want anything other than the full English next day.

Unsurprisingly in the morning she wants the smoked salmon which her husband is having again. Apologising I tell her there's not enough available because she hadn't booked it. After a lot of huffing and puffing she opts for full English minus the sausage.

Her gluten-free toast is on a plate well away from her husband's when I make the mistake of asking them if they would like some more. He asks for more butter and I take away the little dish to refill it. He calls to me: 'You must use a clean dish, it will be contaminated.'

My patience is running out fast and I retort heatedly: 'It wouldn't be if you hadn't stuck your dirty knife in it.' The only occasion when I have been less than polite to a guest. This supposedly disabled woman appears perfectly agile during her stay which leads me to think her one of those people who enjoy ill health and wallow in the attention of others. This is another husband who earns our sympathy.

Thank God they are leaving and away in good time. The poor husband comes across to say goodbye and actually thanks me saying 'we may see you again'. I refrain from articulating what's in my mind: 'I don't think so'.

Some while later an email arrives from TripAdvisor: 'North Hill Farm needs attention on TripAdvisor.' What she has posted is upsetting, a very nasty review of her stay; not only critical of us but also of the local pub which is reached by a couple of very shallow steps. The comments are totally unjustified. It's a nasty blow, coming at a time when we are at such a low ebb with Beck's condition moving towards an end. And a shock because I hadn't been paying much attention to what's on there.

But fortunately it caused great amusement for other guests with sufficient understanding to realise this was a woman who likes to write bad reviews. One small consolation is that on checking her profile we find she is in the habit of leaving unpleasant reports and is very hard to please.

A natural reaction in this situation is to hit back hard but with advice from friends we refrain, merely saying we were obviously not the right place for these people but in their two night stay they managed to use all the towels and toiletries in two bathrooms.

The cold, wet mornings in early December are dispiriting but despite his condition there are other things to care for and the horses need hay and hard feed. Heavy rain deters me and I wait, hoping the weather will improve but instead it gets worse. After a wild night blowing entirely from the west, there's water in the summer house and the front of the barn is sloppy with mud but nothing like was bad as they've had in Scotland. They call it a weather bomb.

I set off on the quad bike with an empty chaff sack over my thighs because I can't find the waterproof trousers. The rain eases as I get off to open the gate and a change in the sky makes me look up to see the sun struggling behind clouds and small patches of blue appearing.

The warmth of the unleashed sun is startling and its brilliance catches raindrops clinging to the hawthorns, so they glitter like diamonds. Down in Apedale the remnants of mist drift upwards, drying to nothing in the sun. Away to the north from total gloom the clouds roll away and the church and the caravans across the valley are revealed.

In the distance the top of the Wrekin is unveiled, then the rest of its grey cloak is banished and the hill is seen complete.

Such magical moments keep me sane and outdoors is a lure to freedom. Indoors the whole thing clamps us down with all the daily issues to contend with. Now it's all about coping and the lid has been well and truly lifted on the underworld of illness and disablement — the world of knowing death when most are oblivious to those worse off in life. The shell I've built around me helps but the situation brings foolish moments such as getting a loaf out of the freezer and leaving it on top. It's forgotten till the morning when I find the package on the floor, just three slices left and all nibbled. Possibly a rat, or even jackdaws but in the feed room something's in the bird seed bag. A flash of brown up and over the wall is a young rat.

As the year drags itself towards Christmas Beck is increasingly crippled and almost totally reliant on the ventilator, usually under the mask for eight or nine hours overnight and much of the day. Sometimes it gives an unpleasant whistling noise and makes his face sore. We settle into the daily pattern of carers and medics coming and going. Now it's easier for him to drink through a straw, it's hard to bring a cup or glass to his lips. The straw seems to have a life of its own, wriggling around in his mouth, hard to control. My back and feet ache with standing by the wheelchair. He's muddled about the time the girls are due, asking where the hell they are and demanding to know where I've been.

Gradually his world reduces, shutting him in -- kitchen, sitting room and bedroom, 'shades of the prison house'. Coming downstairs each morning is a dread, wondering what I'll find.

Several times they come from Stoke to 'assess' him and as he finds it more difficult to move in bed they provide a new piece of kit which moves him automatically; it seems to help.

All this unwanted association with illness reminds me of a guy who stayed in the early years. He came down to breakfast in his dressing gown and I told him we would prefer him not to do that.

Later I regretted the admonition and when he came again he had lost a significant amount of weight and was obviously ill. He probably had cancer and after his second visit we never saw him again. Tolerance is a hard won virtue but life and age bring a greater understanding of what tribulations many people have to bear.

The festive spirit is absent and the event itself is just another issue to get through. David joins us, glad to be with his brother and easing the load. The day is lightened by our young neighbours, the girls from Middle Hill who have spent quite a bit of time with him in recent months. Being educated at home as they grow older they become excellent waitresses, cash for them and a great help. He's bought small silver gifts for them and their eager chatter makes him smile. Dark clouds hang over the day, only lifting in late evening and in the barn last thing to give more hay to the horses one of the young cockerels is crowing in the moonlight, mistaking it for dawn.

January mornings bring small pleasures, early in the half light the wolf moon is still bright, low above Caradoc, its golden light illuminating the thin veil of surrounding cloud. The dogs set up a furious clamour at the gate and I rush to see what's there. But it's the moon they're barking at, startled because it seems so close.

Another day starts darkly but in the east where the sun is trying to rise there are golden streaks tangled with strands of silver lighting the sky over Wenlock Edge and blue slivers above, offering hope of a brighter day. I long to stay there and watch the climbing sun but must head indoors and by nine the golden hope is gone and the rain begins while I wonder what horrors the new year might bring. People rarely live happily ever after, except in fairy tales, and after all, what is happiness? The mere lack of unhappiness is perhaps a satisfactory state for existence.

The resident cock pheasant has arrived, calling near the cars, attracted by the bird feeders. I give him muesli from the Christmas hamper, unwanted because it contains nuts. His presence is a small nugget of joy. Much talk this week about Winston Churchill, fifty years ago when he died, with personal memories of his lying-in-state. The image returns of four troopers at each corner, silent and motionless, when the solemn peace of Westminster Hall is shattered as my school friend trips and knocks down the rope stand.

Black Sam is a constant companion for Beck, on his lap in the wheelchair or curled up against his legs on the bed. At night he's snuggled in the dog bed between Millie and Bryony but his fits are more frequent and he's obviously not well. He's also begun to sit on the worktop by the Aga, hugging the kettle and licking at the spout. Very unhygienic but we know it can't go on for long. He's been such a sweetie, now twenty-one, with us since he was three. He'll leave a huge hole when he goes.

The dogs listen to my tone of voice, assessing the mood, in no way to blame but a focus for my accumulated anger and frustration, trying to do everything too fast and making mistakes and taking it out on the dogs and even poor old Sam.

Nurse Suzanne is with us again, this time staying in Chaffinch. Expecting her any moment for breakfast I'm by the Aga with Sam on the mat at my feet when he begins to thrash about in the throes of another fit. When he's like this holding him seems to help and prevent injury. Kneeling beside him I keep his head up as he twists and shakes. The door opens and my guest comes in, exclaiming anxiously as she sees what's happening. At that precise moment the old cat shudders and is still, gone, dead in my hands. Apologies and embarrassment as she bursts into tears and there we are both sobbing on the floor.

Millie has watched all this, the death of her special friend and at evening we notice how she cuddles closer than usual to Bryony, missing the furry bundle usually asleep between them. Now there is only Tilly, Lyn's ancient tabby who came to us when she moved to Shrewsbury.

The weather is unhelpful, the month ends with a heavy fall of snow which delays the carers again and adds to his distress. Fortunately Suzanne leaves the day before the snow arrives in earnest. The carer situation isn't ideal as the company is short of staff and they are often late or only one arrives, when I have to step in. More heavy snow makes the hill difficult and some of the carers have no idea how to deal with such conditions. One of them drives off the concrete and gets stuck in the soft ground at the side. There's no choice but to get out there with a shovel and bags of grit to make it passable. Our wonderful neighbour, George, the same friend who came to the rescue years before, comes to help, though by now well in his eighties.

Sailing by

With the snow gone the snowdrops appear in profusion, making up for lost time, not long ago they were just tiny white dots in the grass and bare earth of the border. Held back by the frozen crust they've struggled to get through but beneath the white blanket they push up determinedly. Now the unexpected sun has hurried them into stronger life. For a few days it's almost balmy, so mild after the bitter cold. I'm not exactly a galanthophile but there's something about these gallant tiny flowers that never fails to lift the spirits in the depths of winter. The aconites are not far behind, bright yellow buttons scattered among the white, lifting their heads above the soil while the hellebores are already opening their buds. A robin in the feed room bobs about unperturbed and a wren has made a home among the old pipes and guttering at the back of the barn.

The jackdaws are noisy and quarrelsome in the ash tree with the hole in it, probably arguing over which pair would nest there and the crows are there too, harassing the smaller birds. When the carers leave Beck is in the wheelchair as usual by the Aga. Outside on the steps he built, another wren is busy among the moss cladding the stonework. It climbs vertically clinging to the emerald green bryophyte, seeking the insects which live behind the mossy shield. At my urging he moves the chair to the window to watch till the little bird moves on, a small pleasure in the daily boredom.

People come and go when they can make it up the hill, physiotherapists try to help but there's nothing anyone can do and now the condition is biting deep. It's hard to watch, hard on the sensibilities, he can't avoid groaning and gasping, all to do with the breathing. Much of the time he has muscle aches and a weird sensation of tingling and nothing helps it. Friends want to visit and some turn up without calling first but now he is on the ventilator all the time he doesn't want people to see him. Better they remember him as he was. He listens to Chris Woodhead on the radio, now quadriplegic with MND. His voice and breathing sound much better than Beck's and his courageous comments are inspiring.

For me there is growing panic and the realisation that he won't be here much longer and the ever present fear of coping when the time comes. Teasel spaniel comes into season and we have people waiting for puppies. If he is still here it will make a lot of extra work but it would cheer him and at least for a while take his mind off the impending end. And if he is gone it would be a focus for me and keep me busy in the emptiness.

The owner of the stud dog who Teasel has met before kindly brings him here and we arrange with the carers to stay longer so he's not left alone while we're out in the barn doing the deed. It all goes smoothly and doesn't take long but when I get back inside he is bad tempered, demanding to know why I've been so long. This isn't really him, disease and the drug are changing his character and I suppose when you know you're slowly dying you're entitled to be pretty pissed off.

Beck is a Valentines boy but his birthday is not a happy day. Tired and ill he's not especially pleased to see his family. They don't know what to say to him and anyway he can't talk much on the ventilator. Each morning he says he feels horrible and every day is a trial. Meals are difficult and whoever is helping must feed him with a spoon as he can only swallow food that is soft or nearly liquid, reminiscent of a helpless baby bird waiting with open beak for the parent to deliver some morsel. He won't take the protein drinks he has on prescription because he hates the flavours. This means it's hard to get enough calories into  him and after years of trying to control weight, it's now dropping rapidly.

He's on a whole cocktail of drugs, still the Riluzole, painkillers, stuff to protect his stomach from them, stuff to help him sleep and a morphine based liquid as an additional palliative. It's not easy for him to swallow it all and he's very reluctant to take the Riluzole which he reckons makes him itch. We sometimes forget it and we can't tell if it does any good.

He gets confused. Lawrence, a guest, comes in to use the wifi and Beck thinks he's one of the carers and starts talking about the commode. An embarrassing incident but they write a very kind email to me afterwards.

It's impossible for me to go anywhere without someone being with him. Apart from needing company we are afraid he might fall from the chair, now he's less able to keep himself steady.

The CCG have at last agreed to allow me five hours a fortnight, due to start on a Monday in two weeks.

Friends come to help, one posing a most perceptive question. 'Do you feel as if you're in a bubble?' That's a good way of putting it.

It's become difficult even to take the dogs out but when I'm released for a short while, I collect sticks for kindling. The ash trees scatter them, dry and brittle, ready to burn easily. It's a small atavistic pleasure, so basic, finding firewood as we always did, before we discovered how technology could handle our chores. Time and effort saved but does it really help us, or just let us avoid the physical activity we all need?

Beck has begun to say he wants it to be over, uncomfortable and irritable, staying in bed most of the time, connected almost constantly to the ventilator. Lynda Bellingham says in the book about her own cancer that a majority of people never talk about death and what happens afterwards. We talk about it probably too much, he's obsessed with the funeral, to the point I have to leave the room. Together we decide he should stop the Riluzole. It doesn't help and he thinks it makes him worse. He has become totally dependent in this slow dehumanisation and won't make even the smallest decision, telling them all to ask me. He hates the unsubtle descent from human to patient, the loss of dignity, made worse by eating problems. At least he can still swallow but nothing hard or crunchy.

He is stuck lying on his back or side because he can't turn himself. There is talk of a special piece of equipment which will turn him periodically but there's a waiting list of months. Angrily I say: 'We haven't got months.' So they pull strings and the thing arrives.

While the carers are with him I grab time to walk the dogs. There's frost in the valley and a vast mere of mist flooding through Apedale, creeping up to the trees on Wenlock Edge, dappled with sunlight glittering on bare, wet branches. At night I lie awake, trying to relax and sleep but every nerve is tense, listening for him. The slightest noise makes me jump, Bryony turning and fussing, Milly scratching and I find my body trembling and stomach churning — pure nerves, horrible.

March arrives with more heavy snow. The road is blocked and he's very ill. On the phone the doctor says it sounds like pneumonia. Beck, as the pharmacist, says we have the right antibiotics in his bedside drawer so we start him on those. His son is skiing in Switzerland and I get in touch to say he should come.

Eventually the doctor gets through the snow and confirms it's pneumonia but we've caught it in time. Maybe that's not such a good thing says the patient, ill and miserable. The nurse comes from Stoke again but it's a pointless journey and the MND coordinator is due but I call to tell her not to bother. Her secretary asks why she shouldn't come and gets the blunt truth — it's a waste of her time and we don't need the hassle.

The next week he's back on the antibiotics and not good. On the Thursday he says he might not be here in the morning and I know it can't go on like this for long. Contacting the vicar I say simply 'he's not so good' and by now she knows my understated communications.

It's Cheltenham Friday and I've just watched the horse I backed lose in the Gold Cup. Quietly she opens the sitting room door and peers in. Startled I say: 'Sorry, I didn't realise you were here.'

'I didn't want to disturb you,' she says. 'I've been with him a while, he's had the sacrament and seems more content.' Foolishly embarrassed I mumble thanks and she says to call her any time.

A couple from Stafford who've been before arrive for the weekend, self-catering in Red Kite and there's a young couple booked for Saturday night in Chaffinch. We discuss cancelling them but he says they're only here for one night and it's a bit late to cancel. In the morning he seems brighter and says he feels a bit better but stays in bed. The effort of being dressed and moved to the chair is just too much.

In the evening he's asleep by ten and after checking everything I'm in bed too but woken by the first notes of Sailing by on the radio. The shipping forecast — a boon for insomniacs — has just begun when the buzzer croaks on the beam. Scrambling from bed in the dark I press the wrong button and the damn thing won't stop, so I leave it and rush downstairs. He's struggling to remove the ventilator and I whip it away so he can speak. 'Oramorph?' I ask and he nods.

He manages to say: 'Hurry up!' but as I help him to swallow he starts to splutter and I fear he's choking. He turns his head to one side and I stare for what seems an endless moment before gasping and speaking his name. But it's over.

It's the Ides of March. A little less than two years after diagnosis.

There are no tears. The loss was long before the actual moment of death, now there is just numbness after so many wet eyes these last months. When I've covered his face I flop into the kitchen chair — the special armchair we bought early on so he could get up and down more easily — sitting and thinking calmly how to tackle what comes next. A call alerts my nephew but I leave the message to Shropdoc until morning.

The dilemma is what to do about the Chaffinch guests, a young couple from not far away here for a private night together. What to do? Pondering on this I take myself back to bed and eventually fall sleep.

By morning I've decided. I bolt the door to the sick room and do breakfast as if nothing has happened then get rid of them as soon as possible. First thing is to inform Shropdoc of the death and then call the undertaker, Fred the dead as he's known locally, stressing to both not to appear before ten o'clock.

Friends ask how I could do this, carry on with my husband dead in the back room. Some said 'how brave of you' but it wasn't bravery, it was simply the easiest and least stressful thing to do. The thought of telling a young couple that they must leave at once with no breakfast because my husband had died in the night was never an option. It would've upset them dreadfully, ruined their love break and made it more painful for me, shattering the veneer of calm I've carefully created. So they passed the closed door where he lay under the cover, dead in the home he loved, dying where he wanted to be, while they enjoyed their breakfast and departed, unaware of my tragedy while I waited for the doctor to certify death.

Perversely the extra hours of care granted me so I could get away start the next day and the girl turns up in the afternoon. But now there is no need and I have nothing for her to do. There must be something she says so I ask her to clean out the hens.

Strange happenings in the week of the funeral, ten days later. On the day before a psychotic pilot steers a plane into a peak in the Alps, inexplicable horror in an act of utter selfishness. Difficult to believe but human beings are always capable of evil, there is such a fine line between civilisation and chaos. It doesn't take much to trip the switch. Then Daniel contacts me from America wanting to stay here with some of his family but that's not possible.

On Beck's big day there's not much sleep for me, a wakeful night with the dogs restless. Outside the air is mild and in the half light an owl in mating mode is calling from the ash tree by the vegetable garden. The sky is clear and the constellations still just visible, promising a good day for it, drifting mist in the valley vanishes in the growing light. The birds are tuning up and beyond the barn the white cockerel is shouting his own dawn chorus. From the field below the cock pheasant, who comes to join the little birds for the wheat in the seed mix, is calling an answer and the wood pigeons who nest in the holly are canoodling on the Chaffinch roof ridge. Somewhere a vixen is screeching.

Sun and blue skies in a gorgeous Shropshire afternoon with the rooks in the churchyard calling loudly as they scramble to build in the horse chestnut trees. Before we leave the farm I walk to the top of the garden to his special seat to drink his health in the last of the Old Pulteney whisky we bought in Wick, on our trip through Caithness. With whisky and deep breaths I steel myself, determined not to weep. The hearse arrives and before the cortege moves off I glance up and spot two kites floating above the farm.

The family have decided they'll carry the coffin but don't realise how heavy it will be and it proceeds a bit lopsided up the aisle and then knocks with an unseemly lurch against one of the old brass oil lamps which hang there.

Afterwards someone tells me I looked furious. I was — but it boosted my determination to stay strong. He comes back out on the trolley.

They say it was a very personal send-off, the vicar reads something I've written about him and we listen to Rod Stewart and Elgar's morning song which he would understand even if nobody else does.

Outside the rooks are still calling as we bury him close to my father — there's a certain irony in that.

It seems apt that next morning they are reburying Richard the Third, the king in the car park. This probably much slandered monarch, whom I have always admired, is finally laid to decent rest in Leicester Cathedral. Shut away from noisy family I sit alone and absorb this oddly moving occasion, homage at last to one of history's most misunderstood characters.

When someone knows they're going to die it imparts a certain serenity or is it that the other person involved also knows and has the chance to accept it and be accustomed to dealing with it. The acceptance of death is so alien these days and we've lost the capacity to face it, it has become the unmentionable. People don't die any more, they pass away, pass or worst of all, pass over in awful euphemisms. And in the media they always 'sadly' pass away.

The wonderful Joan Bakewell did an excellent series on this issue. Death is the only certain thing in life, the fate we all face with the knowledge that we shall be no more.

Grief is a peculiar state, actually very physical, you think you're in control but you're not, making silly mistakes, leaving on the fire and lights and not locking the door — chaos all round but a strange sense of relief and a certain loneliness.

Friends and family ask the same question — 'What will you do now?' — as if my life must collapse into a turmoil of grief and indecision. What else would I do but carry on? And the truth is the grieving was done long before and all the tears were shed in the months before the end. There is nothing else to do and to leave this place with its memories, is unthinkable. All around are touches and features which he either built or thought of, so much of what we created here which others find so appealing.

All the stonework — the terrace wall, finished to great effect with the hefty stone balls, again found unwanted back in Yorkshire, Beck's balls, the subject of many jokes. I take a few days away thinking the change will help but always anxious to be back where at least there is a cocoon of comfort in everything we did together. In the weeks before he died I couldn't bear to hear any of the music we liked but now it's OK again. Strange how the mind brings black thoughts, forgetting all the good things, much deeper in than I realised, incredibly tired trying to hold it all together.

People come and go, taking away the equipment which made the last months of his life possible at home, the hoist, the turning apparatus, the wheelchairs but it's the bed going which rocks my hard won equilibrium. I close the front door quickly on the two guys carrying it out to the van, to hide the great welling of grief which momentarily overwhelms me. Better to be outside away from what is surprisingly painful. With the dogs in the top field the call of a curlew sounds forlorn passing somewhere close, the first of the year. Spring is evident everywhere, birds busy in the hedges and trees, in and out of the buildings, a wonderful diversion from the horrid task of sorting out Beck's stuff.

This process takes time and there's a reluctance to get rid of certain items, constantly finding things which jar the sensibilities. Such as a tape still on an old recorder, a tape of his voice, younger, revealing how much the illness had changed it. Strange to hear him as he used to be. And his old diaries high-lighting the deterioration in his handwriting. His wardrobe reveals strange secrets — marzipan chocolates and a little china, gemmed kingfisher in a box tucked away right at the back, a pretty egg-shaped soap holder, a set of tools for lobsters and several dyes, doubtless waiting to change the colour of some expedition clothing. And knapsacks and hold-alls full of expensive outdoor gear. Some of these he stored under the bed and I joked several times that they must be breeding under there.

The jackdaws are busy again, scattering wool and hair below the chimney as they drop bits in flight and the same cheeky pheasant spots me looking from the window. Sunshine highlights the full lustre of his plumage and the peacock eye feathers. When a bird lies dead you don't appreciate its beauty because the gleam has died. He may get shot next season or die on the road but he's having a great life now and he's survived to enjoy the summer and learn the ways of the world. Further up the slope the copper beech Beck planted has become a thing of beauty, especially in spring when its delicate pale bronze foliage is gilded by the sun.

With people in Kite and the house, I should go in to start breakfast, not linger out here too long staring at the valley seeking an answer that isn't there. The early morning stillness helps calm me and clarifies thought. The birds' chorus is finished and the only intrusion is the rattle of a green wood-pecker's hard working beak, rarely seen but frequently heard.

In the kitchen Teasel is busy suckling her day-old puppies and I've been up and down all night checking on them. She is a remarkably careful mother but there is always a danger that one tiny pup will creep under her and be suffocated. The birth was not without trauma as several of them came back-wards and one little bitch was tangled up on its way into the world, needing desperate help from me. By the time she's safely delivered she looks dead. For several minutes I struggle to save her, breathing into her mouth, tapping hard on her back to make her breathe and swinging her like a lamb. At last she gives a cough, her rib cage moving as she begins to shout. And I mean shout.

For the next hour she screams so much that I call the vet to ask if she could have brain damage through lack of oxygen. He says it's unusual in dogs. Finally she stops and when put to a teat begins sucking lustily. I say to myself out loud: 'I'm not keeping that one'. But it turns out that I do.

Our friends with the tortoises are here which is a comfort and they'll be in soon for their frizzled bacon, the way they like it. They weren't expecting to find puppies in the kitchen and are thrilled, so that at least worked out well.

Within a week Bryony has gone in a sudden horrible collapse, buried in the same hole as Sam, and Millie spaniel sinks into deep depression. The three mainstays of her life are all gone — Beck, Sam and Bryony.

Now she sleeps alone in the large dog bed, puzzled and lost without her close companions. She starts to hover near the puppy box and her gentle

sweet-tempered daughter takes no notice as Millie puts a tentative paw inside the box and reaches out to lick the nearest pup. Teasel watches but makes no move to deter her and when I look again Millie is curled up in the box with them all, topping and tailing the seven pups, in her element as granny.

This is very unusual behaviour as most bitches won't allow another dog anywhere near and can be savage but Teasel obviously has great trust in her mum and appears to welcome the help. As the puppies grow both bitches are involved and when I decide to keep one, the screamer, she develops a close relationship with granny.

Along with puppies April brings the consolation of swallows. Suddenly one morning a swallow is there in the yard, chattering from the wire and by tea time another has landed, two days earlier than last year. Their insouciance fascinates, arriving from wherever, looking down at me so casually, cleaning their wings and flicking their streamer tails, as if they've never been to Africa and back since last seen. They find their way unerringly to the spot where they were born.

The mess they sometimes drop on the washing is always forgiven. With deep blue gleaming backs and charming chestnut bibs, their busy chatter and constant activity transforms the place and I can't be lonely while they flash across the yard or overhead like anchors in the sky.

Once the puppies start weaning at three weeks it's four meals a day and plenty to keep me occupied with more guests here as the spring moves on. The pups, outside now in the stable, are growing fast and Teasel has been hunting and brings back baby rabbits for them. Gruesome but indicative of basic wild instincts in our canine friends.

On the shortest night of the year I want to be outside as long as possible. The owls are noisy, calling each other, with youngsters close by in the ash tree, so I name the puppy Tawny. She is amazing. At just nine weeks she already knows so much, in a way like a human child, building up knowledge as everything is explored and added to the fund of experience.

In the morning the dogs are dew-wet from the long summer grass. While they run over the fields the swallows dash around us in swooping flights, the dogs rushing back and forth in hot pursuit, deluded into thinking they might catch one. The birds appear to be playing but they're following the movement which flushes insects from the grass.

In full summer the swallows are madly active in their insect hunt, in and out of the open stable door to drop flies and other bugs into the ever open yellow beaks. The fledglings leave the nests but linger in the buildings, perching on the roof beams or on the length of timber which once held a hook for tack cleaning. Or they sway on the wires while their parents feed them on the wing like aircraft refuelling in mid-air. Evie the Gordon stares fascinated as the youngsters fly over her head.

Two jackdaws perch side-by-side among the topmost leaves of the plum tree, like two old ladies looking on at a dance and swifts are hunting high in the air. A long grey cloud hangs above the Lawley, trailing like smoke from its summit. Friends keep asking me to visit but I feel a strange reluctance to leave here, as if a spell is holding me which I can't break.

A Canadian couple come for three nights in Chaffinch entranced by the place and the puppies. They found us on TripAdvisor and I mention the awful review which induces laughter from both. They'd seen it and read between the lines: very reassuring for the future.

Soon after this the girl from Stuttgart returns for a three day visit. She found us originally by walking past on a previous trip to the hills, surprised and kind to find me now alone. Helen and Paul are in Kite for their usual two days with Bracken, Teasel's pup from her first litter. When they leave after long walks on the Long Mynd they take with them a new puppy, Willow.

September is busy and beautiful, a time of bright mornings and chilly nights, the sun in splendour at both ends of the day. With dogs around me I linger by Beck's seat, gazing at his view towards Ludlow.

A whisper of breeze strokes my bare arm but the turbine in the valley is still, its arms horizontal with not a breath of wind to turn it. I wonder how could I ever leave this landscape which never fails to help and bring some element of joy.

Out in the stable Dolly waits while I wonder what to do with her; keep her as a toy for fun or advertise and sever the last link with illness. Perhaps she might pass as a runabout on the land but that's not what she's made for and she couldn't carry bales of hay.

Eventually I advertise on line, startled by a very prompt reply from a guy in Sussex newly diagnosed with Parkinson's disease. He's taken the advice of his consultant to look for secondhand and says he wants it to get to Waitrose and the pub. I tell him all about it and we settle on a price not much less than we paid.

He arranges collection in a very big lorry struggling up the hill. I drive the Breeze reluctantly onto the lift and watch them strap it in, staring as the roller door comes down. Now it's sold I don't want to part with it. My eyes follow the vehicle until it disappears, ridiculous tears wetting my face.

After

Life goes on they say. Arriving at a bleak crossroads there's a simple choice, give up or get on with it. My way is to get on with it and swept into an increasingly busy year there isn't much time to mope. Having guests around gives little chance, the necessity to make an effort is good and the majority of people who come are interesting. At first I make a pretence of not being here on my own, adopting the royal 'we'.

The fact of recent bereavement is not usually mentioned as it's not easy to share grief with strangers but sometimes a conversation becomes more personal, often when someone speaks of their own loss. They always say instinctively 'I'm so sorry' which is quite unnecessary but the situation can make them uncomfortable, feeling they must say something and it's the familiar words we all slip into. But people generally are very kind.

Late April brings a blackthorn winter, bright sun but bitterly cold as the hedges show the small white blossom among the thorns. It starts to snow heavily as I begin to hang out the washing, defeated by a howling wind which thrashes down the daffodils with an icy mix of hail and snow.

From the window during breakfast I pause to watch a small charm of goldfinches in the swaying slender branches of the silver birch. On the other side the usual cheeky robin is on the wall watching the ancient skinny cat, only a couple of feet away. Head on one side, he waits till she's finished then nips down to pinch the leftovers. He seems to like being close to the house, in the porch or on the steps, showing little fear of me. Another time, in picture card style, he's on the fork handle in the border.

On the hill the rainy days have brought a flush of growth and around the sycamore tree a miniature forest has popped up as the host of winged seeds from autumn thrust up towards the light. They will struggle once the grass grows and sheep will nip them off as they forage, though they contain a toxin which can affect horses and other livestock.

With maturity our eyes seem more open, seeing things hitherto unnoticed, the joy in small things, insignificant cameos which create the beauty around us. It's too easy to go about looking but rarely seeing.

A strip of dry bracken on the distant hillside, picked out in gold by the brilliance of a moon at dawn; or a patch on a field where the sunlight peering through clouds is shining on a particular spot, turning the new growth of corn a paler green.

As spring turns to summer there are days when morning mist touches the valley slopes with whispering threads, leaving just a trail of mist as if the hedgerow trees are smouldering. Clouds are banked up behind the Wrekin and through half closed eyes they appear as another range of hills in the distance and then with white cotton cumulus it could be a scene from the Himalayas. Within minutes the sky clears, as blue as the Mediterranean with flat bottomed cirrus floating like barges tethered in the air.

The radio brings news that a famous MND victim has died. Chris Woodhead, who we heard speak so eloquently to Michael Buerk about fortitude and stoicism, virtues barely understood by many but something you come to know when touched by death.

Among the drowsy sounds of summer it's time to relish the evening sun from the terrace, as it throws long shadows across the green fields below Caradoc; mesmerised by wine into good memories. Beck seems nearest when I'm there — picturing him perched on the stone capping on top of the Pont du Gard, where we were appalled to watch two small children running along the aqueduct high above the river.

Small stalls sell dark red wine under the olive trees and a naked young man exhibits in the river, where we swam among shoals of trout. All changed now, it's a World Heritage Site, the unique atmosphere lost for ever. Or the heart in mouth moment when he fell off over a wall out hunting, leaving a large dent in his silk top hat.

And when I look across at the Lawley it recalls the white Christmas it snowed after breakfast and we decided to walk across the valley to the crow, the weathervane on its peak. It's much steeper than it looks and already slippery with the increasing depth of snow making me resort to hands and knees. We follow the undulating crest and arrive home tired but gratified, greeted as the door opens by the delicious aroma of roasting goose in the Aga.

Or High Force enrobed in ice, the falls in Teesdale painted by Turner during the Napoleonic Wars, one of our 'Great pictures we never took'. We trudged up to the waterfall on a cold February day, camera in the car. A long walk but worth it to see the cataract frozen from top to bottom in all its plunging glory, white spray and yellow water all set like glass.

A wasp is exploring the summerhouse, buzzing lazily and a cheeky chaffinch comes to look at me, unbothered by my presence. A bumblebee feeds on the shallow trough of sedum in an avid hunt for nectar among the tiny flowers, its body bright with a band of gold and an orange bottom. It moves to the cotoneaster hedge, home to blackbird nests each year.

When the speckled blue eggs have hatched and both parents are busy feeding chicks the cock bird uses one of the ornamental bowls as a launching pad each time he returns with a morsel. He lands on the pot, glances towards the house, then darts into the thicket with his delivery. The hen bird makes her approach the other way, downhill across the grass.

The warmth keeps me out there as long as possible and in the crepuscular light just before midsummer, the last of the sun filters through a floss of red cloud. As it fades into dark two bats are abroad, missing my head by inches and a tawny owl calls constantly to its mate. Seven years ago we were frantically preparing for the big party.

The bird killing season is here— not the shooting season but the unintended cull of baby songbirds, the downside of this avian paradise. Birds in every bush, fluttering, cheeping, gathering material for their nests, oblivious of anything but tackling the process of reproduction. It's fascinating and wonderful to see but we have to watch in case the dogs find a site. A newly fledged youngster on the ground is helpless until it finds its wing power. Planting a new rosemary bush I realise the nest is in the bank of cotoneaster. Blackbirds seem particularly unaware of safety, often building too near the ground or in precarious places like bonfire piles. A jackdaw has already found the spot and the last egg, blue and mottled brown, lies broken on the path below. But two days on a young blackbird is fluttering against the cottage wall, trying to land but then flies strongly onto the gate and into the holly. One at least has survived.

Jackdaws, crows and magpies, all take songbird nestlings to feed their own. When a hedge is badly cut, left flat like a dinner table, the corvids can reach in with their strong beaks to pull a baby from the nest. Or tiny pink corpses on the ground, with big grey unopened eyes, sparrows mostly, casualties who've fallen or been pushed from nests under the eaves.

A wren is busy around the stables, in among the pots of growing veg, but her speedy flight makes her hard to follow. Soon youngsters are flitting close to the ground from their nest in the middle loose box. Outside in the dark with Millie, I'm startled by the sound of young owls in conversation. Not the classic sound of adult birds responding to each other and it's good to know they've reared a brood this year. I pause and listen to their juvenile chatter before they fly further up the field, their calls gradually fading into the night. Sometimes the yard light catches a flash of pale wings as an owl whips over the stable roof. There are plenty around but in the winter of the owl survey they seemed scarce. Only one call a week was needed but in several weeks I drew a blank — perhaps they knew we were checking up on them.

A small bird is working busily up on the grass but at the distance I can't be sure what it's about. The glasses reveal a goldfinch feasting on a dandelion seed head, its sphere of fluffy parachutes just at the right height to reach. Its beak delicately plucks a tiny seed from the base of each parachute as if making a wish.

Like thistles, teasels and nettles, dandelions have a lot going for them and they pop up all over the farm as a vital source of food for wild things. The place has shown us many lessons over the years and manicured grass is no longer a priority. Living here has brought an understanding in its simplest form of the interaction we have with the natural world and how the actions of each individual impinge on our abused planet. It's sad there's such a gap and lack of understanding between the urban and decreasing rural population. Our roots are in the land and many of the best things in life are here, small, simple pleasures which, when all the contrived delights of modern society are found wanting, reveal the true value of these old realities

Where once we would have culled the golden heads among the grass now we appreciate the diversity and leave rough places for birds and insects. Dandelion leaves are picked for hens and tortoise guests. The plant is good for humans too, with medicinal uses, the flowers make great wine and young leaves are good in salads. Disliked by keen gardeners it will thrive in difficult conditions so has become a symbol of survival and of wishes coming true which is why its fluffy heads have been blown hopefully over the centuries.

There was a time when we would've collected any dead wood for the fire but now some logs are left to rot, making food and habitat for the many tiny beings unnoticed in the ground. When tidying the garden I'm reluctant to destroy a living plant because it's in the wrong place. There's always the urge to find somewhere else to give it a chance to live.

In the early years we did battle annually with stinging nettles but now there are plenty around, feeding the insects and in spring their young tips make a great substitute for spinach. Friends who'd spent time in America, with marked Stateside values, were very discomfited one evening after complimenting us on the cheese and spinach tarts they'd enjoyed as a starter. When told it was cheese and nettle they were horrified. But they should only be picked well away from traffic or other pollutants, especially if there is a male dog in the family. But they have a high nutritional value and make an excellent tea for a traditional spring tonic.

The same with thistles, entranced by them at first as part of the magic here, then for a long time finding them a nuisance, wanting to be rid of them, until time taught us to appreciate their benefits. Once you've seen how the goldfinches are drawn to the seeds, you realise how you deprive so many creatures by cutting them down or worse, using poison. Nectar and pollen are vital food sources for bees, butterflies and other pollinators and songbirds love them and also gather thistledown for their nests. In the past people used milk thistle for liver disorders and gallbladder problems.

Richard arrives for another stay in Kite, still seeking a niche in life. We talk about his Asperger's. I can't understand why anyone would find it hard to employ him because he seems pretty much like most people I know and he says: 'Yes, but you're calm.' Which makes me laugh thinking about a young relative imitating my far from calm behaviour. Strangely over the years other people have remarked on the atmosphere here which apparently conveys an illusion of calm and relaxation, which is totally crackers because I'm so often anything but. Roger the vet said long ago about the stud work that it was a good place because we were so relaxed with the horses.

This gentle guy seems to feel comfortable and safe here. Naturally asking about Beck, he's saddened by the news and reminds me of the first time he came when he tried to get a meal at the pub at five to nine and they'd stopped serving food. He came back hungry and Beck made him cheese and pickle sandwiches. I'd forgotten that. He comes again the next year for an interview at Harper Adams University, desperate for a job doing something on the land but is turned down yet again. It's sad that a bright intelligent guy like him can't find fulfilment.

He's keen to watch the birds, especially the starlings. There are more about this year, often perched on the wires in line like the swallows. It's good to see them because, despite all the wonderful shots of vast swathes of them in the sky, the native population is declining. Their cheeky bright bodies are incredibly synchronised, wheeling across the dusky sky looking for their roost. Some choose the golden yew we brought from Yorkshire, dropping as one into its welcoming cover or landing in the bay tree to upset the sparrows.

On one of his walks round the village Richard reports watching young wagtails dipping in and out of the ford, their tails bobbing as they frolic in the water.

The late summer days are hot as ten ravens perform acrobatics over the valley, somersaulting on the thermals, calling clear in the still air. Unusual to see so many together in a family outing. Another day I look up, alerted by the harsh anxious cries of a pair chasing away a kite. Young kites play here for two days, in and around the farm and just over the hedge in front of the house, twisting and turning, gambolling in the light wind. Their tipping tails in the sun flash red. I'm transfixed by their beauty and waste long minutes watching. It's hard not to think about Beck, how thrilled he would've been after waiting so long to see them here.

On another sultry evening we're in the summerhouse for a pre supper drink. My friend from Edinburgh relishes the valley prospect, set with golden fields after harvest, watching a flock of starlings descend on the fresh cut cornfields.

From beyond the Battlestones wind driven black cumulonimbus crowds in fast, towering up the sky, clouds tumbling in on themselves with the pressure. The day darkens and heavy drops are spattering on the flagstones as we catch the first rumble of thunder on its way. Deciding to make a move we collect our glasses but with a roar the rain arrives as if a bucket's been emptied.

We're trapped for an hour watching it fall in rods with lightning all around and thunder crashing without interval right overhead. It's magnificent to watch, feeling safe in the wooden building though hunger pangs are kicking in. In a brief lull we make a dash to the house.

While we eat a late meal at the kitchen table lightning still plays over the Lawley. It lingers above the hill, flashing and banging for an hour and a half, with the noise of howling wind and thunder crashing in a continuous rumble, unlike any storm we've seen before. The noise is fantastic, overwhelming, before it moves north, though we still see constant flashes in the distance.

The year moves on in its diurnal course, the seasons pass and the holly trees are thick with green berries, some already touched with colour. September is still glorious but the stables are suddenly empty of swallows and I fear they have left early to head south.

They leave that sinking sense of oncoming winter which always hits when they go, the last remnant of summer. But two girls with horses staying in the twin room are using the stables and they find swallows flitting in and out over the horses' heads, youngsters from a second brood. They are still here as the month ends with a series of incredible sunsets and a huge golden harvest moon. Two weeks later there are a pair chasing insects in the top field, maybe on their way from somewhere further north.

Round the side of the house en route to let out the hens I disturb a flurry of small birds busy on the berries. A gang of long tailed tits, tails flicking in agitation. My intrusion sends them on their way, a pity because usually we only see them in hard weather.

At evening the horses come down into the paddock looking for a sweeter bite, ambling into the barn to see what's happening, early bats flying over their heads and out low across the grass. The warm air seems to induce excited activity as they whisk about in a hunting frenzy. One whips past my head like a swallow but they have really gone now on the long journey south. Imagining them traversing land and sea, I wonder how many will return in spring. Always one or two arrive ahead of the rest to perch chattering on the wire looking down as if they had never been away.

Two couples come with a car and motorbikes, a bulldog and a Jack Russell. They go off mid morning to a biker event but watching the racing in the early afternoon I hear scratching and other noises in the house.
Spaniel puppy Tingle is only four months old, born three days before the Brexit referendum and she gets the blame. But the noises persist and come from upstairs.

Sure enough, when I open the Nuthatch door the little terrier is scrabbling to come out. Very much annoyed, when I check Chaffinch, the bulldog greets me happily from his position on the bed. This is a total no no, our website is explicit that dogs must not be left unattended in the rooms. Several phone calls to the owners' number bring no response.

Adding insult to injury these guests query the price at pay time. It seems they'd found an advert several years out of date. This kind of problem is unusual because the majority of our visitors are sensible and considerate and a pleasure to entertain.

Next day a scout master arrives with his family for an annual gathering at a local farm. He's spending the night under canvas but his wife and daughter have opted for home comforts. When they return from dining al fresco with the campers they call me to look at the strange sky where a long narrow cloud pointed like a spear moves across the full moon, blurring the brightness and smudging the moon's face until the cloud slowly disintegrates.

Earlier the sunset lit up tier upon tier of cumulus, all edged with gold. A clouded sky creates the best sunsets with changing patterns that catch brilliant tints and rim it all with radiance.

Black birds gather in a flock at dusk. Rooks, crows and jackdaws sweep from tree to tree like a cloud of gnats against the grey sky, the raucous cries sounding in the evening gloom as if they're summoned to a meeting. The throng includes the raven family which have bred especially well this year although the patriarch has been found dead. One of the originals tagged when they first appeared here, he was probably eighteen years old or more.

The ravens came after us and it was a triumph and joy the first time we saw them soaring overhead. Some seem anxious, agitated, flying lower in circuits back to the Scots pines in Motts Plantation where they have nested for more than twenty years. Birds with an aura of mystery, they wheel together, calling their harsh kronk. The sound of their wide beating wings comes clearly through the cool air.

In the middle of a Monday morning, the anniversary of the Great Storm of 1987, a weird sun hangs overhead, deep red like sunset, dodging behind clouds chased by a rising wind, which seems to come and go. The sluggish turbine in the valley just manages to lift itself over the vertical then picks up speed as it turns to find the wind.   It's the tail end of hurricane Ophelia with gusts of up to 90 mph causing severe damage in western Ireland where three people are killed by falling trees. The worst hurricane to hit Ireland for fifty years, its passing creates a pink haze around the sun projecting a strange light onto windows. High above us a procession of gulls passes over, driven inland by rough weather at the coast.

The mild days of November fade into storms and heavy rain which bring a rush of falling leaves swirling and whirling in a mad dance as the wind chases them into piles. Oak, beech, ash, sycamore, all blowing together with the ubiquitous holly until they land in a neat pile, usually at the front door. If you're quick, the wind does the work and they can be gathered up with the same two boards my father used. Some whirl at head height to be carried away down the lane. In the fierce wind a raven flies low over the garden, struggling to make headway in the gusts. A scream makes me break off from feeding the dogs — maybe an angry woodpecker but then a sparrowhawk appears, calling in fear or fury, chased by two crows.

The strange year drifts to an end in mild, wet weather, bulbs already shooting but mud everywhere, the dogs filthy every day and a longing for the respite of frozen ground. Millie lies on the carpet staring into the fire, watching the glowing logs subside. Kneeling down to stroke her ears I whisper: 'You're missing him I know, same as me.'

At the 3am blackspot I'm thinking about death and the trouble with dying because you don't get to see what happens next in the world. Another day of terror, this time in Paris and more statistics on climate change and I wonder if the world will ever unite enough to save the earth. The United Nations is a powerless talking shop which never achieves anything when it really matters, always too late when the slaughter has already happened, as in Rwanda, Bosnia and the Middle East. We can only watch to see how it all works out. That was why Beck wanted to stay long enough to find out how the Scots voted. He cared about it.

A sunny afternoon just before the solstice, the sky a perfect blue and it's ten degrees at dusk. Dawn next day paints the eastern horizon with a deep crimson wash — a perfect shepherd's warning. The grass in December has never been so green or copious and there's no need for a coat outdoors.

Taken for granted

The idea of running a bed and breakfast had loitered in my head from the early days. Some businesses probably launch with a big splash, plunging in at the deep end but you could say we tiptoed in at the shallow end, 'seeing how it goes.' But for several years before Beck's illness the realities of paying guests had become apparent and whereas at the start we would take more or less any booking, it became obvious that single nights can be a problem. At weekends in the summer months a one nighter means you might turn away people wanting three or more days.

Now I understand the difficulties I found in my youth alone on a Sunday evening in Scotland. Door after door was opened and closed with 'Sorry, we've nothing available.' Sometimes you feel mean turning people away when they sound desperate but needs must. It's not so bad mid-week or out of season and we always try to help where possible.

The single night issue is particularly difficult with weddings and now we only take bookings for two nights. Guests tend to arrive on a high for what they consider to be the most important event ever. But for me, when you've done the wedding page on a local evening paper you have a more cynical view of the happy couple — girl in a white dress, usually, with a grinning fella attached.

A London family booked several rooms and effectively took over the place when their son married a local farmer's daughter at a swish affair. What they hadn't mentioned before the party arrived, with a very young child in tow, was that they'd booked a local baby sitter. They informed us that the girl would use the small sitting room and the kitchen as required. The imposition in itself was not an issue, it was the arrogance of not asking if this would be acceptable and the patronising attitude towards myself and other local people involved.

At breakfast next day they were complaining about the girl who had gone home very tired on their return in the early hours with the baby seat still in her car. After listening to these unfair comments for some time I said it was surely up to them to make sure they had it before she left. Startled glances greeted my intervention but the look on my face forestalled any comeback. That weekend made me wary in future.

On the other hand some wedding parties bring interesting people who are a pleasure to meet and the two night rule means there is often time to chat and maybe share a drink or two. When a family from Scotland arrived for a cousin's wedding at Wilderhope Manor, the two sons spent the Friday evening practising their chords for the Highland music they would be playing next day.

Before they left for the party — all three men fully kilted — one stood on the cottage steps to send the stirring notes from his Great Highland bagpipes ringing across the valley. These magnificent pipes, at least a hundred hears old, were surprisingly heavy to handle and playing them successfully calls for considerable human fitness.

A winter wedding ended with the lane blocked when a coach was hired to distribute guests back to where they were staying. Bad weather was forecast and the firm's owner, who knew the hill, had instructed the driver not to attempt the slope if snow arrived. Which it did, late in the evening.

Our guests were dropped off and we heard the coach depart. Beck was due to read the lesson in church next day and duly set off in the car to return in five minutes to report the coach's front end stuck in the ditch. The driver had found it impossible to turn because of the snow and set off to reverse down the hill, a difficult manoeuvre in the dark.

It snowed enough to cover the hills, the sun bright on the only section of the Long Mynd visible from here, between Wilstone and Caradoc. Through binoculars we watched the dark figure of a lone skier gliding swiftly downhill, sharp against the white.

With a steep road the possibility of snow at the wrong time is always a concern when people book in the cold months. But most are very flexible, arriving in suitable vehicles though sometimes cars are abandoned at the bottom, the journey completed on foot. One couple had friends not far away and simply commandeered their Land Rover to get here.

The temperature varies greatly and can drop within a mile from 1.5 to -0.5. Cold hangs in the hollows and the road to Stretton shows black tracks through the frost. The dark leafless trees stand stark against the pale land. After a bright day the winter sun sinking from sight still shines a rosy glow all along Wenlock Edge and the farther slopes.

Another beast from the east brought a bitter February with the temperature down at -9. An older couple had taken the cottage for a week and coped well with their four wheel drive but half way through the week the snow set in with a vengeance.

As I returned from town it was heavier and starting to settle and within half an hour the ground was white and deepening, thick underfoot. Indoors the north facing windows were opaque, with goose feather flakes clinging to the glass. I've called them that since childhood, big fluffy flakes like the soft white down from a goose's breast which float down silently piling on each other to make the lane impassable. We were all marooned for two days.

The couple seemed cheerful and unperturbed when I went across to check they had all they needed. But with books and DVDs they said they had enjoyed it. Husband Peter remarked that it said a lot for their marriage that they got through the two days still on good terms.

The snow lingers, frozen drifts lying against the hedges, eighteen days after the onslaught, though the water butts have begun to thaw. The fields have never looked so brown and tired and the daffodils are still only in bud. It's as if the land is holding its breath, desperate for a touch of warmth in the soil to launch the green flush of new growth.

The late spring seems more ominous because until we see the longed-for first leaves we won't know if the ash trees are still healthy. This is a concern each spring with the ever encroaching prospect of ash dieback. The ancient specimens that border the fields could be approaching their double century if they were planted when the land was first enclosed in the 1840s.

Another mystery in May is the laburnum trees flashing bright yellow blooms in the hedgerow on the way up to Wilstone Hill. We always thought it strange they should be there where livestock graze as they're poisonous to humans and animals, especially the seed pods which contain the toxin cytosine and could easily be eaten on the ground.

Were they planted there deliberately or did the pods arrive by chance on the wind or brought by a bird? We have never found anyone who knows the answer.

The cottage proved an excellent investment. It seems to strike a chord with people who enjoy the ambience of its peace and location and the idea of footpaths directly from the door. It has collected a fan club of regulars who come at varying times in any year.

It's very rewarding to see people sitting in the sun, enjoying the place and the panorama of valley and hills.

Being a private road we get very little passing trade but walkers striding by often come to the door to ask for details and go off with a card in their pocket. Some time later, often years, there might be a call or an email saying something like 'we walked past you once — or several times — and always said we'd like to stay.' Fortunately the place is very self-selecting and draws mainly those who appreciate what we do.

Offering advice to others isn't always easy. People have their own ideas but many of our guests are not young and daring so I have learned to caution drivers about one descent from the Long Mynd which can be a shock for the unwary.

The valley between the Mynd and the Stiperstones is beautiful, especially in spring and the road to the right takes you down a glorious winding scenic route. At different times of year you might spot young foals among the wild ponies or maybe a stallion keeping watch. Turn left for the glider station and the direct route to Asterton and you're soon on a steep and narrow road.

Probably built by the Romans straight up the hillside with no barriers or passing places, it's not for the faint hearted. The sheer drop on the right demands a bit of steel in the guts. The one small tree on the scarp has been known to save the occupants of a car which went over the edge, or so we were told — though that could have been apocryphal.

New to the Mynd, we used the road several times while exploring and when on a frosty, moonlit New Year's Eve we were invited to a party at Wentnor we took the shortest route without a thought. A few hundred yards down the hill we hit the first patch of ice, skidding close to the edge. A very nasty stomach-churning moment but there was no way we fancied reversing uphill in the dark.

A slow crawl in low gear took us safely to the bottom but we took the long way home via Horderley. Now I stress the importance of not taking the wrong road at the signpost.

Some drivers also avoid the Burway, the 'main' road across from Church Stretton, especially if they glance down into Carding Mill Valley from one of the bends.

When Beck's mother lived with us and was still able to appreciate such things, we took her on an August weekend up to the Mynd to see the views. Coming back down the Burway we hit a traffic jam, backed right up to the top, caused by a woman who froze on the bend, freaked out by being so close to the drop. Eventually she was persuaded to get out and let someone else take the wheel and move the car.

But guests are generally glad of information, particularly if they're beer drinkers eager to sample some of the produce from several local breweries.

What to charge has always been difficult especially in the early days when bathrooms were an issue but we've always been on a par or slightly below some in the area.

One guy called to ask about rooms but when told the price he said 'that's dear for Shropshire' and began trying to negotiate a cheaper rate. When told the price was as stated he said: 'I'll leave it then.'

'That's fine,' I said. Next day he rang back to ask if a room was still available, which it was. I asked why he thought Shropshire should be a cheap area to stay and he mumbled something about being out of date.

'I expect you take the view for granted,' is a regular comment from guests. No, the landscape offers never-ending fascination. Subtle aspects bring an ongoing source of interest, changing from day to day, different throughout the year and the accompanying weather patterns impinge enormously on daily life.

Most visitors come because of where we are but there are some who don't understand, asking how we stand the quietness, 'don't you miss the buzz of a town and people?' The answer to that again is an emphatic no.

Humans vary greatly in their behaviour the more affluent they appear — or pretentious — the more they are inclined to take liberties. The rooms are provided with a range of toiletries and drinks facilities and it's amusing to note the ones who clear everything to take away, sometimes including towels. When people arrive you can be instantly at ease with them, on the same wavelength, but with others conversation is forced and stilted.

Sometimes you take to people and sometimes you can't; with a pair from the London area who'd booked Chaffinch the female partner was a fussy little woman. She seemed not to appreciate the landscape or the ambience. Her husband had spotted the crags on Wilstone as he parked the car and asked how long it would take to walk up there, keen to make the most of a lovely evening . Sitting out in the hot evening I could see two figures outlined on the skyline near the rocks, one quite tall and the other smaller, slightly bent.

When they came back she sat outside the room engrossed with her laptop. She ignored me as I said I'd seen them on top of the hill and asked if she'd enjoyed the view. I persisted, saying: 'It's worth the effort isn't it?'

Her only reply was 'there's a lot of sheep muck about up there.' Never mind the view! Obviously not a lover of the countryside or did she expect the paths to be regularly swept?

This same lady laid the towels out on the lawn to dry before I could get in to change them. On the morning they left I was astounded to see frilly panties and other items dangling from the holly trees and red valerian opposite the Chaffinch door, looking the epitome of a campsite. Not what you expect from middle-class people from the south of England. Reminiscent of a previous guest who also liked to drape various items of clothing over the vegetation, perhaps a throwback to distant times when no washing line was available. She was an elderly woman who came with an attractive young man from Antigua. She was clearly very proud of her Jewish heritage and used every opportunity to talk about her background throughout the week-long stay.

I came home to find the shrubs in the border and the tables and chairs in front of Chaffinch festooned with washing, including some very snazzy underwear. Not happy with her approach to laundry I offered to do a machine wash for her. She had an inordinate amount of washing which she hung on the line in a very particular manner.

A week is a long time with a guest who ignores the rules and she thought nothing of bursting into the sitting room to find me on some pretext. She made several difficulties about breakfast and tried to inveigle her way in to join the couple staying in Kite, knocking on the door to introduce herself and explain her very strange theories about bananas.

She showed no interest in the wildlife or landscape and I was puzzled why she had chosen to come here. But others are more observant and one guy drew my attention on a wet summer morning to the snails copulating on the wall top, sheltered beneath the thick leaves and crimson blooms of sedum. They stick together for a long time; being hermaphrodite both snails transfer sperm and the same pair may be at it for hours. They don't actually need to mate as they can fertilise themselves but these two looked to be enjoying it.

Snails are common in the garden, it's amazing how well they breed here. Clusters of their eggs appear hidden in pots of compost. Or turn over a terracotta tile that might be shielding clematis roots from the sun to reveal a snail nursery. Maybe half a dozen tiny snails attached, along with several fully grown. I pop them over the wall into the long grass, knowing they'll make their way back unless a blackbird or thrush finds them first.

After a night of rain, warm gentle rain which soothes the land, I notice a snail crawling across the newly painted table outside Chaffinch. Picking it up for inspection as its fully extended horns twitch towards me I'm surprised by the length of its tail and realise how large the actual body is compared to the size of the shell and how much volume is packed into that small space.

On a cloudy May morning there's frantic feathered activity all around and I watch a kite approaching from Motts Plantation. A raven is flying the other way and the kite veers away clear of the raven's passage, eager to avoid confrontation. Right overhead, in another flurry of angry wings a sparrowhawk is being mobbed and driven off by a cluster of swallows who succeed in protecting their nest territory in the yard. The agile birds are more than a match for the intruding hawk but later in the morning, from the window I catch another glimpse of him or her sitting on the hedge, waiting patiently for an unwary songbird. The crab apple is notably empty for some while. These elegant long tailed raptors will have a nest of their own not far away, a constant threat to the smaller species. Meanwhile a lone jackdaw calls repeatedly from the purple maple, with short sharp anxious cries like stone striking stone, maybe seeking a missing mate.

On the way to Stone Acton a heron lifts lazily over the hedge, trailing its long legs and peering down as it rises ahead of me, probably hunting along the stream or the neighbours' pond. Up the hill a large jack hare lies dead in the road, his ginger tinted coat clean but for the obscene mess where he's been hit behind. A large startled eye still looks bright in death. It's sad to see him like that and I move him to a grassy spot beneath the hedge. But at least it means there are hares about.

The sun comes out later then clouds bring on a fine rain and soon a rainbow appears as a complete arc across the valley. Its full depth of colour is clear and brilliant, a second bow in mirror image behind. The clouds close down and the threatened rain arrives in a torrential downpour with a gale of wind.

The pattern of this time is sunny mornings, which means getting on with anything you want to do outdoors, like hanging out the vital washing, while watching the bank of clouds roll in from Wales. With luck the washing will dry before the first drop falls. Attention to detail is an important point in the accommodation game, that last minute check to ensure all is as it should be for fresh arrivals.

Cloudscapes are as fascinating as the land beneath. On some clear days of intense blue the clouds stack up in odd formations, separate, climbing like tall white pillars into the sky with bases so flat they resemble decanters on a ship, designed to ride the rolling sea.

On unsettled days this solid base sees misty wafts spiral upwards in a mass of white and grey, drawing down the rainclouds. Sunshine picks out every fringe, so bright it's hard to believe rain is on its way; while the wind increases to chase cloud shadows fast across the fields. Soon a black mass rolls in from the west over Wilstone. One moment the sun is shining, the next fierce drops bounce off the ground. The heavy shower lasts only moments before the sun returns and the tumbling mass moves towards Much Wenlock. To the north east the Wrekin is obscured and dark fingers droop towards the valley where it's still raining.

The wagtail parents, a constant presence in spring, are on their second

brood, plus several youngsters from the first lot. Pale and less defined in colour than adults, they appear hesitant, taking long looks at me as they scurry across the ground before deciding to retreat. The parents are busy, back on the apex of the stable roof and in the barn, hurrying back and forth with full beaks of food for the new chicks. They chirp in annoyance as I pursue the Monday morning dash, tails wagging with impatience until my back is turned and they dart into the secret site of their nest under the flutes. It must be very hot in summer but they use the same site each year.

We put up a special open-fronted box for them under the overhang but it has been ignored for years. If I don't move they fly off in disgust, a wavering flight dipping and rising over the barn, entrancing as they hop around in the paddock grass seeking insects.

A very small bird is on the sill outside peering into the kitchen, staring through the glass in confusion. It turns to look at me but makes no effort to fly away, another fledgling wren. It hesitates then takes off heading for the shelter of the holly tree which means it can fly and will hopefully survive. Another wren, maybe its parent, is on the round conifer, singing its heart out with wide open beak.

While I'm shutting in the hens for the night the cockerel is diverted and suddenly rushes up onto the hay. He's spotted a missing hen outside on the bank and clucks to her imperiously. As she makes her way round to the gate he hurries after her on his side of the wall and rushes to wait by the wicket. Determination in every feather, he struts up-and-down impatiently as she looks for the way through. When her head and neck are his side of the fence he gives her a few encouraging pecks, hollowing his wings as if to tread her. When she's through he circles her in satisfaction before chasing her into the shed; a true shepherd to his little flock, much like his father, protective and self-important.

A couple from Staffordshire have booked for two nights to avoid their son's raucous mid-summer party next door. They arrive with the guide dog they're training, a lovely nine months old black Labrador. He comes in with them for breakfast to sit by their side at the table with perfect patience, awaiting his own breakfast which is eventually given to him on the floor. Already very fond of him, they're waiting for his assessment as a possible future stud dog. If he meets the strict requirements he will stay with them permanently.

The diary is well filled until winter, enough to keep me busy, plus some early bookings for next year.

Hiatus

Then everything stops. A spiky microscopic organism brings the world to a standstill. And soon the sinister word 'lockdown' is whispered everywhere. Surely that can't be, I keep saying, lockdown is something they do in prisons, surely we aren't about to turn our country — no, much of the world, into a prison.

But yes we did. Exactly that, in a climate of fear created by politicians and so-called experts. But it seemed to me the worst thing was that most people, the public, obeyed like sheep, as if they were citizens of a police state such as China itself, where the whole thing apparently began. For a while Britain did turn into a police state, with a confusing array of restrictions, regulations and directions.

Elderly people having a cup of tea in the garden with a friend were arrested, neighbours told tales of illegal meetings. Worst of all, old people were shut away with no right of choice about seeing their loved ones.

It's hard to believe that the public accepted it and meekly did as they were told. Encouraged by government they stood outside their homes each Thursday evening to clap in support of the NHS, like a new religion. The NHS certainly deserved support but proper planning for such an event would have made more sense.

The restriction of personal liberty was unprecedented and the price was very high, too high, bringing collateral damage that we are still assessing. Damage to mental health with all other illness apparently disregarded, along with increased aggression against women and small children in the home. All normal considerations abandoned.

Alarming rumours and reports had begun to circulate about a dangerous new virus emanating from the Far East, of people becoming ill and a growing toll of death; stories from before the previous Christmas of people hit by flu like they'd never known before.

Anxiety increased as illness and a tide of panic encroached on Europe and Britain. But still the big events of spring, the Cheltenham racing festival and Crufts dog show went ahead as planned. The latter with a sizeable contingent of competitors and their dogs from all across the world.

Even before the lockdown began that spring and the situation was labelled a pandemic, both phone and email were busy with guests cancelling their bookings, some genuinely frightened, most just being cautious and postponing their stay till later in the year. But before long it was actually illegal to do any business at all. The diary shows page after page with either no entries or bookings with a line struck through as cancelled. But a litter of spaniels had arrived in January and prospective owners were able to visit to choose their puppies which were away to new homes just as the crisis hit.

The introduction of the two metre social distancing rule seemed sensible, especially to someone who can't stand crowds and the initial edict was no gatherings of more than two and no travelling. Talk began about masks and I recalled seeing them used routinely in far off countries, nose and mouth covered mainly to fend off wind-driven dust from the desert. But in Britain? Soon we were all obliged to cover our faces, moving from lockdown to lockdown, then to ridiculous tiers, removing all freedom of choice. Everyone wore masks, people were scared and some have never regained confidence enough to live normally.

But the enforced cessation of activity brings its own compensation with sunny days and new life all around, making it hard to believe what's going on in the world, the madness of it all. Now more than ever I count my blessings for living here, out with the dogs and nobody to bother me, happy with my own company. For ever thankful also to be lucky that an operation to free a trapped nerve in my elbow was moved back a month from its scheduled date — the day lockdown began. The op would almost certainly have been delayed and the nerve in my right arm damaged beyond help.

As the first phase shuts down our darkening world March goes out like a lamb with unseasonable heat, the sun blazing on crowds of celandines which paint the verges and banks with a gloss of gold. These small flowers emerge from the earth as if in instant bloom before the grass is long enough to overshadow them. They're a joy on a sunny morning and from the sky I catch the increasingly rare sound of a curlew flying over. A pair of yellowhammers are suddenly very visible in the tree, a gorgeous bird now seen here more often. They must be nesting close by, resplendent in their spring attire, brilliant yellow heads and breasts behind the stripes.

With delight I find a pair of redstarts are nesting on the steel beam in the barn, the richly attired male is easy to spot with his grey chest and white dabbed head; he seems to perch a lot while his plainer wife does all the work. But both are unmistakable with their long red tails. Usually they build in the hedge near the cottage but this new site is ideal to watch them. The spotted flycatcher is back in the sheep house sharing with two wood pigeon couples. They drink from the stone bird bath with more than their usual nonchalance but the usual tiny tragedies still occur.

The stillness is uncanny, as if the very earth is holding its breath, no whisper of wind, the turbine in the valley unmoving, hardly a vehicle on the lane, no traffic, only the distant sound of a tractor. A necessary visit to the vet in Ludlow finds the A49 almost totally empty of traffic. What bliss. The sky seems especially blue, cloudless, unmarked by vapour trails but the birdsong is suddenly loud in this unexpected peace. Evening brings the lightest breeze rustling the trees and in the clear nights the stars seemed to shine much brighter. And dry, so dry, with no sign of April showers.

But this idyll brings an awful sense of guilt because life goes on here more or less as normal and I find myself enjoying it while out there people are dying in increasingly alarming numbers. My thoughts are frequently on those trapped in high-rise buildings for whom it must be appalling without even the consolation of a garden, however small.

David Hockney talks on the radio after posting his wonderful pictures of daffodils in Normandy in an effort to cheer all those behind locked indoors. One is called 'they can't cancel the spring.' We've all become too far removed from the natural world, he says, lost that fundamental contact which makes us what we are, though being restricted brings greater awareness of the reality around us. The question is whether we've left it too late, perhaps new generations will be better inclined to look after our planet. Guests in my kitchen rarely mention or even notice the epigram on the wall from J B Priestly which sums it up: 'The Earth is nobler than the world we built upon it.'

One of the few positives during the initial lockdown is a sudden realisation for many people of the simple pleasures that a garden or even window boxes or pots on the doorstep can bring. At one point it was impossible to buy seeds, either for flowers or vegetables, all snapped up in this new enthusiasm. When visitors came again most were keen to take home any produce, not least the mushrooms.

For me the vegetable garden has always been therapeutic, from when Ken first ploughed the corner of the field, creating great ribs of upturned soil and stone which at the beginning looked a herculean task. But piles of beautifully friable rotted horse manure mixed with the light soil made it work. Merely handling the plants and the soil itself is a joy, out in fresh air among the raw earth which creates everything.

Take the mystery of a carrot seed, as light as air, germinating into green feathery leaf and eventually that magical orange root. Picked young, wiped briefly on dewy grass and eaten at once, the taste is wonderful. Instinct says this is all good for us but science now shows that contact with soil is actually beneficial to our gut microbiome. When the black cloud of depression or loneliness descends, just half an hour spent turning the earth or tying up plants that need support — perhaps a raspberry cane or a floppy broad bean — the physical proximity to this most basic life form lifts the spirit. Sometimes a robin waits nearby to watch for any treats uncovered by my efforts.

April brings back the swallows in good time though not so many as in the early years when often a dozen or more pairs were busy here. But a bonus is the Super Pink Moon, the biggest super moon of the year, ironic as it appears at dusk in such beauty as if to bless its benighted planet. Called pink, not for its colour but through association with early wild flowers such as the native phlox, also know as moss pink. It climbs the sky like a shining beacon of hope in the growing darkness. Wrapped in a rug I stay out despite the chill to watch as its brilliant light eclipses the stars behind it.

It's almost as spectacular as the autumn Super Moon four years earlier which was very special because on that particular night the moon was the closest to the Earth it had been since 1948, a third brighter than a normal full moon. We were fortunate to see it rise despite the clouds moving fast high overhead. At dusk we watched a growing glimmer as it first appeared in the fading light, a spectacular gilded disc lifting clear of the horizon. Gradually the whole orb was visible, more like a setting sun, tinting the surrounding cloud. Then a skein of stratus flattened the circle and moved to sit like a bandana on its brow. It rose surprisingly fast through the wispy strands until it vanished into darkness with only a pallid glow revealing its position. All evening it was a ghostly presence, vanishing and reappearing but for seconds at a time the pale shape gave a surprising amount of light.

The VE Day anniversary comes round again — 75 years ago this time — but what should be a national celebration turns into muted, clandestine gatherings of no more than six people, according to the latest regulation. In the village neighbours cluster outdoors in the lane to make the most of the heat and share a few bottles of wine, their chairs on chalk marks placed carefully two metres apart. Stunned by surprise they watch the arrival of a police squad car checking information received about an unlawful gathering.

All through the month dry, hot days follow one after the other, frustrating with no guests here to enjoy it. The lack of rain becomes a concern as the fields turn brown and the fresh spring grass is burning off, made worse by hot wild winds. Kites circle low over the farm, in search of carrion, missing their usual feast from the silage making.

Knowing nothing of the world's problems the dogs enjoy the sunny days regardless, racing across the paddock towards three young crows sitting on the fence like the witches in Macbeth. An easy perch for them, not far from their nest in the big alder tree which rises tall on the bank, its roots fed by the boggy patch below where springs meet on their way downhill. A patch that's useless but wonderful, an untidy mess of fallen branches, bluebells and marsh marigolds transported from Wiltshire, a haven for all the wild creatures. Taken for granted, over the years we never looked at them as individual trees.

The youngsters hop, one foot to the other, fluttering anxiously as the dogs approach and fly clumsily to the next fence where they cling to the wire. When the dogs are back with me they return to the greater comfort of the wooden rail. They practise new-learned flight, wheeling and soaring with their parents. Perhaps they roost all night on the paddock rails, I've seen them perched there in the crepuscular light of dusk.

At evening it's the white bob scuts of rabbits disappearing through the grass which attract the dogs, making a run for the fence after enjoying the clover which has established itself increasingly over the years. They soon return once the dogs are gone. Around the fields, they're eager for new scents in the cooling air, maybe of badgers already abroad in the half light.

Like humans the rabbit population has been hit by a virus. Viral haemor-rhagic disease is affecting them badly on top of myxomatosis, a cruel disease which seems to recur every few years and cuts the numbers for a while. While we might curse them sometimes for nibbling the leaves of young plants or raiding the veg garden, their role in the food chain is vital and their demise would be a huge loss to the predators who depend on them.

Above all, it's good to see them, charming to watch and another attraction for visitors. They seem vibrantly abundant, encroaching ever nearer the house, boldly busy in the top hedge under the wild plums, trimmed white with blossom, or chasing each other across the grass. Even the pub menu has rabbit hotpot for a while. Guests love to see them and from the windows watch them enjoying our neighbour's mini orchard. New extensive burrows have been excavated among the roots of the hawthorn hedge between the fields. Two or three of them will chase each other, care free and heedless of who might be watching.

It sometimes feels as if we're under siege from them but more so by moles whose earthworks sprout in lines across the field and the lawn. It's probably coincidence but in this year of human disaster they are doing particularly well and the dry weather suits them.

In the steep field below, once quartered by a barn owl seeking voles and mice, the line of ancient gnarled hawthorns is broken by a holly tree, where a pair of magpies nest. They are busily pecking something on the ground while two large healthy rabbits chase each other through the tussocks of tired grass. Down the lane the great stand of wild honeysuckle is in full flower, falling from its host tree like a waterfall, its scent filling the evening air as you pass.

The sky is dappled with patterned cirrocumulus clouds flushed pink with the sunset, its sinking rays creating an effect like abalone shell, the undulating ripples of a classic mackerel sky, caused by high altitude waves in the atmosphere. It hopefully means a change in the weather and the chance of rain. Sure enough the morning dawns wet and grey with mist covering the valley and a steady but welcome rain falling all day.

After two months of nothing eventually we're allowed to accept self-catering guests but no bed and breakfast. The extra work involved is considerable, wiping every conceivable surface that a human hand might touch takes a lot of time. Handles on doors and cupboards, light switches and worktops, all cleaned with bleach solution.

It seemed at the time and still does to make very little sense, and I, like many, have never believed the wretched bug could live for any length of time on a smooth surface. But diligently we did it all and to make doubly sure left a gap of twenty-four hours between visitors.

The ongoing crisis brought many elements of farce, not least the 'We're good to go' logos promoted by the tourist industry proclaiming with a large green tick that 'processes are in place to maintain cleanliness and aid social/ physical distancing'.

Which was totally meaningless since it was merely a box ticking exercise, self-certified, with no external form of checking. These were plastered all over websites. At least by then there was the expectation of a vaccine break-through for everyone.

Among the first visitors we welcomed back were a Black Country couple who'd booked a weekend in the spring. They arrived with Finn, one of our spaniel puppies, born in the January before all hell broke loose. The weather was good for walking but on the second afternoon when they returned ready for a cup of tea they found the taps had run dry.

Of course this caused a panic of activity to find the cause. There was no water in the house but the neighbours below still had some so the guests were supplied with containers of water to keep them going. But before long that well was also dry. Next it's check the reservoir, if it's empty there must be a mighty leak somewhere. But no, the reservoir is full to the brim which is an even greater puzzle. Over the years at North Hill no water in the taps means an empty reservoir. The only possible explanation was a blocked outlet which meant emptying the whole thing to investigate.

While I'm agonising at the thought of bailing it out with buckets and a rope neighbour Nick is on the phone to hire a pump. After a few hiccups in getting it to work the job is done in short order and clean water is soon gushing out over the hillside. Claustrophobia rigidly under control I go down the ladder to investigate and scoop out the water which the pipe can't get. Once uncovered, the problem with the outlet pipe is revealed — its metal filter is covered with sandy silt brought up from the borehole.

This has never happened before and we could only conclude that because of such low usage in recent months there was insufficient movement to keep it clear. Covid had stranded the neighbours in South Africa until late spring so there was only me using the water.

In July we can start taking guests for b&b and the diary is pleasingly full. The week before the warm, sunny August Bank Holiday brings a host of last minute enquiries including a London family who want a double and a twin. The twin was out of action with a leak in the roof valley discovered during the mid-month thunder storms and torrential rain which had stained the wall. When I explained it was unavailable the guy was unperturbed and insistent, saying: 'Don't worry about that, it's not going to rain'.

He was right about the weather. He and his Estonian wife were delighted with the scenery and enjoyed the weekend taking long walks with their sweet Cocker Spaniel.

At that stage we were operating with great caution, with the double doors in the dining room open to let in fresh air. That Sunday was memorable with a family of four in the dining room and two small tables in the sitting room to accommodate eight people with social distancing, which would have been very trying without the help of my young waitress and something I decided we would never do again.

It became a scramble then to fit in all the people cancelled from spring plus the new business from people eager to get away for a break after all the restrictions. But it wasn't long before more rules were introduced just as a couple arrived from eastern England with a young Gordon Setter, Florence, or Flo, one among so many dogs who had suffered during the lockdown. It was a bad time for young puppies and their owners, so difficult to get them properly socialised. But Flo was a little sweetheart and benefited from mixing with our dogs. They won their two-day stay in Red Kite Cottage in the draw at our breed rehoming society's open day and tacked on two more days. The cottage has proved a happy getaway for them and all three have become friends.

Just after them came guests from Surrey collecting their daughter from a camping expedition, along with another Cocker Spaniel. They were very taken with the Springers, especially Tansy, saying as people often do, let them know if she has any puppies. And they meant it. We went north for a mating despite the risk of going into a higher tier area and they had the best dog in the litter born the following February. This was a puppy who at birth had a lot of white coat — the liver colouring becomes more dominant as the puppy grows — and was disregarded on account of this. But it's not colour but character that's important in a dog and this little lad had it in abundance. Herbie turned out to be quite a star.

In the eastern sky of a dark October dawn a golden light outlines choppy shadows on the horizon as the sun wins a race with dark cloud encroaching from the Atlantic. Somewhere a restless rook is speaking softly. Soon the weather clamps down as the rain begins. It looks like setting in for the day but within half an hour a rosy tinge appears above Caradoc and the sky clears into blue.

The cancellations begin again when the 'three tier system' and the 'rule of six' are imposed and then Guy Fawkes' Night introduced a second national lockdown. Non-essential shops were closed and people were prohibited from meeting those not in their 'support bubble' indoors but they could go outside to meet someone not in their bubble. As the temperature drops nearly to the bottom on the barometer higher tiers and tighter rules mean that after all the hype about preserving the festivities the gallant Boris effectively cancels

Christmas. Yet more restrictions follow plus the confusion of different tiers around the country and the arrival of new variants of the accursed bug.

Several guests over the years have become regulars but as they get older with more health problems, they stop coming. You have to assume the worst or at least that they can no longer make independent journeys. You can't ring them or send an email to ask if they're still alive.

It's sad when you think they've gone and you don't know what happened to them. One couple, who found the cottage a perfect refuge from their very stressful working lives in caring, had booked it for a second Christmas but close to the date were forced to cancel. A new year email brought no response and we heard no more from them. Neither was in the best of health and it's possible one or both succumbed to the virus.

Hail in May

In the second year of the virus early spring comes in with a gentle kiss, a sharp increase in temperature and brilliant sunshine to lift the spirits as we come to the end of yet another national lockdown. Beyond the window a wary hen pheasant creeps up the lane to feast on the fallen seeds from the feeders. A cock pheasant, maybe her mate, flutters in from the road to join her and for a few moments they feed together, gobbling in haste. Lolloping past them on the concrete comes a rabbit, nonchalantly watching them as it passes, to disappear under the conifer and carry on casually across the lane, through the hedge and away down the field. But three's a crowd and when another cock appears the party's over and they take off in a turbulent squabbling flight. But they have survived the winter and it's noticeable how many more are around, having escaped the ritual gunfire, due to the restrictions on shooting. Above them in the tree sparrows are enjoying a spree with the fat balls and two collared doves wait snuggled together on the fence.

April turns so cold and dry the grass is struggling to get through and with little moisture the land has dried up totally. Dawn comes alive with rose charged fingers of light above the frosted ground under a pale blue firmament crossed by aircraft trails marking the world's return to busy uncaring life. April's showers seem a thing of the past. My father always laughed at my early attempts to grow vegetables, saying 'you don't water in April' — but you do if it doesn't rain. Everywhere is parched and out on the verge several sparrows are dancing in the dust. Despite the cold the swallows come, moving straight in to begin renovating their old nests in the stables. They struggle to find fresh mud for patching so we create a puddle in the paddock to help them. Somewhere nearby a pair of green woodpeckers must be planning a nest, rarely seen but marked by their repeated laughing yaffle. In the fields the dew is heavy and darker trails show where rabbits have passed.

But the jet stream moves and May is more like March, coming in with a fury that takes us all by surprise. The spring greenery is sharp, sparkling, against the dense darkness of the storm clouds bringing hail, heavy rain and showers more like April.

After one of the driest and coldest Aprils on record, with deep frosts, the days of torrential rain and gales buffeting the country make everyone cry out for proper spring warmth. The high-pressure vanishes as gales and squalls rush in from the Atlantic, in keeping with the national mood.

The wind rips young tender leaves from trees and hedges and Caer Caradoc is white, one day with snow, another with hail, more like February, spitting hard on the skin if you're caught in it, leaving puffs of white in corners and against tree trunks.

Vicious winds thrash the trees, like musicians dancing to a crazy beat and the yellow tulips in the pots are spoiled, ripped out, pathetic on the ground. Blossom is everywhere, late on the scene after the early chill; hawthorn, apple, plum and on the dark wild bullaces but the rough winds scatter the blossom like confetti on the grass and you wonder if the flowers have had time to set before they are torn away and whether there'll be fruit in autumn.

We had plenty of warning. The meteorologists are pretty accurate these days on their short-term forecasts but it was possibly a day early. The worst of the storm came during the night, leaving the yard a mess of flying buckets, watering cans and plastic flowerpots strewn everywhere.

The nuthatches defy the wind, flitting from the hedge to grab a peanut, their blue-grey backs bright in the tree, flashing their peachy breasts as they run down the trunk. Competing birds hang on grimly to the feeders as the branches of the little tree rock in the wind but nothing deters them from their food.

It's one of those storms that comes and goes quickly, throwing down torrential almost horizontal rain, clouds moving fast overhead, driven east by the force of the wind. Next minute a blessed hush as the sun comes out and suddenly it's too warm in waterproofs. In the stormy atmosphere a tentative pale rainbow appears but it's quickly gone, dissipating into cloud.

We move into the so-called roadmap out of lockdown, supposedly in four steps taking up half the year, trying to judge the best way to handle bookings, keeping people well apart or accepting only self-catering guests. Plenty more cancellations and bookings moved to later in the year. The weather seems to emphasise the national depression. The lockdown ending is delayed by four weeks to allow more people to receive their first dose of vaccine.

Bluebells appear quietly, hesitant in this climate, among the grass along the verges and in the woods where they lay a misted carpet of blue beneath the trees. Often passed unseen, violets grow hidden by grass or by a mossy stone, delicate, sweet flowers so small you hardly see them 'half hidden from the eye' as Wordsworth put. it. Soon the meadowsweet is decorating the hedges with creamy sprays of blossom, luscious after the rain.

Screams overhead from a furious crow mobbing a buzzard, moving fast over the house as it tries to dodge the black bird's attack. The buzzard heads east pursued by the crow, into the path of the angry mate and together they press their raucous assault on the intruder. The raptor tumbles and turns, its pale under feathers catching the sun. The crows persist in the chase until it flies away, eventually turning back towards the hills but well away from the crows' nest.

Frantic birds are catching up all around the farm, the great tits are back in the barn in the same hole in the wooden panelling, made long ago by an angry mare repelling Cloud's amorous advances. The dogs know the nest is there, shoving their noses close to sniff the activity inside. You can just see the huddled chicks. As they grow their hunger calls are more insistent with the adults on a constant cycle, diving back every few minutes with a cache of insects for hungry throats — aphids, spiders, small beetles, caterpillars, bugs and other juicy insects, all full of protein.

Two kites are circling directly overhead, especially thrilling because after waiting so long a pair are nesting only a short distance away down the lane.

But the rain has done its job and the sodden days create a flush of lush grass, almost too much to keep on top of. So much growth that it's given the farmers a third cut of silage or hay from thick tall grass. Everywhere tractors and machinery are rushing from place to place while the sun shines, with balers, tedders and piled trailers. Stripped fields are littered with black wrapped bales of haylage or netted rounds of hay.

The chestnut tree brings feelings of regret, a constant reproach each time I pass it, decked for spring with its candles of pink florets. This lovely tree has grown tall, its canopy spread wide at the base but its shapely crown shows. disarray, decayed and ripped out by storms. Vicious winds in this unseasonal May have torn down one of the lower branches, crushing the bough below. It trails the ground, its new leaves and flowers upright on the grass. Beck didn't know how far the ruin had progressed. Horses and sheep have damaged its protective fence, chewing the bark almost completely round. Now there's only a narrow vertical strip lifting life-giving water to its branches. Dying by degrees, its original splendid form is lopsided, though new leaves mask the injury. From one angle it looks magnificent but from another the tell-tale signs are all too apparent.

Before long neighbour Phil will be making hay and it seems sensible to take a load, not knowing if the old horse Sonny will still be here for winter. So I'm busy tidying the last few old bales ready for the new crop. Lugging one bale aside I find something unpleasant — or so it seems — trapped between two bales on the floor, looking like a curd of pus. Something hissing with life, like a fermentation. Thinking it's something dead causing a feeding frenzy for a host of bluebottles I back away to find a fork.

As the offensive thing is lifted onto the bale there's an eruption of agitated life and I realise the fizzing is actually the buzzing of many bees and the sub-stance is thick pale golden honey. They're angry and I'm the object of their fury. Calling the dogs away from the cloud of frantic insects I retreat to seek advice from the nearest authority on bees. Jane and Phil duly arrive with the bee suit, amused at my concern. Their nonchalance is reassuring, explaining that these are white tailed bumblebees which would soon vacate the barn once their breeding activity is over. We replace the bales and cover the site with a sheet of plywood to be given a wide berth for the next few weeks.

Swarms sometimes create a home in chimneys, causing great alarm among those who don't know how to deal with them. Jane's have swarmed three times this spring, once in the hedge on the lane side which she managed to capture. Another time around twenty thousand bees form a dark intense gathering on the thick trunk of an apple tree. These are impossible to capture because the tree is too thick to be shaken to collect them. Mending fences another day in the back field we hear loud buzzing from a seething mass hanging not far from us against the hedge. I've often considered beekeeping but concluded that my plate is already full enough.

Jane shows me a hayrack planter on an outside wall, left in last year's disarray because it's been the roosting place for a gang of wrens. It's full of holes, either mice or maybe insects but she saw seven wrens issuing out one morning so has left it unplanted for the spring.

The heat is ideal for hay making and the long days produce a delicious crop, green and dry, its smell filling the barn and yard with that deliciously evocative scent of dried grass. Along with wood smoke and petrichor — the smell of rain on dry earth — the fragrance of fresh hay is a dose of instant nostalgia. Swifts fly high above, feeding on the wing and the yard is full of young swallows watching from the wire.

As the heat persists we look for the relief of rain but in Europe it arrives with destructive force bringing deadly floods and havoc to unprepared towns and villages.

Summer brings plenty of enquiries and the diary is filling fast. Good in one way to bring welcome business but it also brings plenty of work with bed making and ironing, not to mention the breakfasts. Fortunately the girls take turns at waitress duty.

One bonus among the Covid advice was the recommendation to stop bed making for guests during their stay — usually a definite requirement for what is known as 'serviced accommodation.' That has always been one of the downsides of doing b&b along with the occasional people who are not as careful as they might be or don't appreciate their surroundings.

A couple from the west country book a few nights on a round of family visits. The. husband, a farmer, has recently been diagnosed with Parkinson's disease and struggles with walking. They are upstairs in Nuthatch and come with a dog and a huge suitcase which is difficult for his wife. Other guests help her and when they leave I suggest she buys two smaller ones.

This busy period brings some amusement as I spot the husband from Chaffinch scrabbling around his car. I watch a moment before going out to offer help and find him trying to clear up the shattered remnants of his rear window. A brush and pan solve the easy bit but they leave in the morning.

He's been busy on the phone but can't get anyone to come out till the next day or later. It turns out he backed into the letterbox on the wall. I'm puzzled how he managed to do that as it's hung there unscathed for a very long time.

He explains that the sensors on his car are at a lower level. I resist asking why he didn't look in his mirror or glance behind through the window. At that moment his wife and I make eye contact and I turn away to hide a smile. She moves towards me, also trying not to smile and whispers: 'Thank God I wasn't driving.'

He says: 'I need some sort of sheeting to cover it.'

Always one who tends to the 'that might come in useful some time' school of thought I hurry away. The poor guy's face lights up as I return with a large section of heavy duty polythene sheeting, the wrapping from a new mattress. That and a roll of gaffer tape make a good repair which should get them home to Buckinghamshire.

He must've hit it pretty hard to shatter the window so completely — but there isn't a mark on the letterbox.

A campanologist arrives with his new partner, both widowed. Unaware of his interest in bells, I explain that the pub no longer serves food on Tuesdays. They're disappointed until I say it opens at nine for the bell ringers after their weekly practice session. His face wreathed in smiles, he explains that he's a recent convert to ringing and wonders if they might drop in at the church to watch and listen. Given the okay after a quick call to the tower captain their evening programme is decided.

Next morning they're both full of it. They were given a warm welcome as the team was several ringers short and he was asked to ring with them and join the convivial session afterwards in the pub.

Breakfast chat with another guest reveals her as the author of a children's book about insects. Its fascinating insights into these tiny lives include the fact that earwigs incubate their eggs. Since then I've looked on these small neighbours with new respect, along with wood lice and silverfish.

My early morning inspection in the mist reveals two sets of bright lights shining through the gloom where early bird farmers are working in tandem on the slopes across the valley. With two tractors on the job it doesn't take long to clear the field and replant it, maybe with winter corn.

This activity, with half a day's work done before breakfast, is a different patch from the one that caught a guest's eye the other morning when the large yellow harvesters were busy lifting fodder beet, rapidly turning the green field into bare brown earth.

The next day they're at it again before daybreak, headlights tracing the line of work and by the time I'm out of bed watching as the light grows, half the field is ploughed. Next they're hedge-cutting, this time around the edges of a crop of feed turnips, growing thick and lush. In due course sheep or maybe finishing lambs will be turned out to graze them down. First the green energy-rich tops, then they'll eat the roots out of the soil, giving rise to the notion that the poor sheep have nothing to eat but mud.

A lone female guest sets off for a day in Shrewsbury but then we notice her red car halfway down the lane parked in front of another vehicle. She wanders back up to tell us the road is blocked by a fallen tree. But no panic as our neighbour is there with a chainsaw and soon has the sad remains of a hawthorn piled at the side of the road. She walked down around the corner to watch the clearing job — an added entertainment; all the joys of country life.

The wind hadn't seemed that strong but the aged tree must have met its nemesis since breakfast as the road was open less than an hour before. It was thickly entwined with ivy, wound round and round the trunk and hanging heavily in the top branches; long established with heavy clusters of berries strangling and weakening the tree. Ivy doesn't produce berries until it gets as far up the tree as it can go and then starts to fruit, in this case just too much for the tree to take.

Later she returns from her hill walk to report a flock of linnets flitting about the gorse on the way to Wilstone Hill. The wagtails are busy again around the yard, watching from their favourite site on the stable roof, youngsters around from the second brood. One is on the wall as I approach. It doesn't fly off but turns its head to examine me as if uncertain what I am. Rather than fly stead it hops down to the ground and scuttles away on foot.

Deterred by our narrow lanes guests from north Yorkshire decide to walk down for supper in the autumn dark. No need for a torch as their way was lit by the growing light of a gibbous moon. Hoping to see rabbits or maybe a badger they're disappointed. Any wild creatures were probably long gone, disturbed by the approach of humans on foot. Certainly they alarmed the wood pigeons roosting above which exploded in a cloud from every tree they passed, one after another all the way down.

Two fat pigeons waddle past the window and when the hens get their evening ration of corn the little grey-brown Dunnock nips down off a beam to join them. Sometimes a robin takes its place.

Apples lie in heaps where the Bramley and the Cox drop their fruit to roll into the grass, a fresh supply brought down by last night's wind. Collected by the bucketful they're enjoyed by horses, dogs and hens. The rest are left for the birds, especially the blackbirds who'll clear them away before the spring grass emerges. As I cook breakfast a squirrel is there munching contentedly on a large cooking apple and a fat cock pheasant is feasting on the fallen hawthorn berries.

Glancing casually towards the Wrekin I realise there's something missing, the tall chimney marking Ironbridge power station. Always there, peeping above the surrounding landscape. A major local news event when they blew it up, along with the cooling towers — and I missed it.

In this northerly group of islands enveloped so often in swirling cloud, the weather is a constant fascination and in the countryside it assumes greater significance, a never ceasing topic of conversation whether extreme heat or cold. Clouds especially do much to dictate the character of place and people. The hills here affect the weather which can be totally different within a couple of miles. One summer day we were in Church Stretton with hay rowed up at home ready to bale. The heavens opened for torrential rain which went on for half an hour, heavy enough to ruin the crop. But we came over the hill from Stone Acton into bright sunshine and no suggestion of rain. The hay was baled and in the barn by evening.

It turns exceptionally mild and we wonder if this is another manifestation of climate change. The dawn comes up golden, peeping gradually above a bank of deep grey cloud. The light is especially clear behind the skeletons of leafless trees and the rocky outcrops on Caradoc, an effect which seems to bring them closer. At mid morning the clouds roll in bringing showers more reminiscent of April.

The grass is still growing and the horses' dung is a vivid green and sloppy as spring. Birds fly high above in large flocks, some of the first migrants from the north arriving to feast on the autumn berries.

The fieldfares linger, landing in the swaying branches of the silver birches. The leaves are golden before the fall and the birds are easy to see as they decide where to go next. Flying in on the wind they flock here to break the journey, then on a sudden impulse launch into flight together. These members of the thrush family are drawn to the crab apples, along with holly berries, rose hips and hawthorn. They soon strip the branches. Any time soon we'll be seeing migrant robins to boost our native population, arriving from northern Europe for the winter.

Over the hill in Nant valley flocks of Bramblings have landed, thousands of them, distinctive in flight with their brilliant white rumps and pretty autumn colours, visitors from Scandinavia and Russia where the cold will be hiding the seeds which are their main diet. Our milder winters keep them fed and they particularly love beech mast in the woodlands. Because it's winter when they come we don't hear their song in the same way as their cousin the chaffinch but it's said they develop regional dialects, singing a different tune in different parts of the country.

Flowers are blooming out of season. The pretty pink diascia in the Chaffinch window box which a few weeks ago was looking tired and ready for cutting back has bloomed again in a fresh show. The roses are flourishing and on the terrace the marjoram is showing tiny white flowers. The rock fumewort or corydalis has come back into flower. It's an amazing plant which appears to grow on nothing, clinging to a roof or stone walls. Pretty scalloped leaves and yellow flowers hang in clumps around Chaffinch, concealing an ugly stump.

Valerian too has a new offering of bright colours. The leaves were slow to turn, the oaks only now developing a cloak of copper gold, bright in the autumn sunshine but the first harsh frost will bring them whispering to earth. The temperature is amazing, not just mild but actually warm and pleasant despite the grey clouds driven by a brisk wind, too strong for bonfires.

But the new week starts with bitter cold, an icy wind and dawn a threatening red. The cold on the hill is so biting that ears and face feel like ice, and the cloudless sky presages a deep frost. Before the sun is up there's frost in the village and up here a silver tinge on the grass with a mist creeping along the valley, lapping the base of Caradoc.

After the cold a massive storm named Arwen inflicts enormous damage over swathes of Scotland and north east England, leaving thousands without power and millions of trees destroyed or damaged. The noise of the wind thrashing round the house makes it hard to sleep.

During breakfast guests exchange night time experiences, the howling of the wind and roof tiles rattling in succession like piano keys as the gusts lift them. Both cottage and house appear to have escaped unscathed but the front of the summerhouse has blown out and panels of corrugated sheeting have been ripped from a couple of shed roofs and two trees are down in the top field. One of the old ash trees on the lane side has shed a huge branch, luckily into the field or it would have completely blocked the road. It can stay where it is for now and make firewood in the new year. Another such storm years before came out of the west, mostly missing us, sheltered by the bulk of the hill. Whistling straight along the valley, it picked up the neighbour's corrugated iron shed and dumped it on top of his Porsche parked outside. It lifted a greenhouse further down the hill, right over the stable block, to drop it in the road, and uprooted a conifer near the house.

The aftermath is shattered glass, leaves everywhere and plants in the borders and on the terrace seared by the storm's ferocity. The late flowering fuchsia, still in full bloom, is stripped bare of flowers and foliage. The naked stems remain, stark and trembling. The sheep paths are covered with gorse needles making a soft mat underfoot.

Recently we cut out the dead wood in the tree line above the bank field and finally got rid of the ancient and twisted elder which had strangled a hawthorn for years. They were entangled like lovers but when we pulled away the rotten wood a few tentative twigs and green leaves showed it wasn't entirely dead. Now the storm has brought the hawthorn down. They held each other firm against the elements for so long but with the elder gone the hawthorn couldn't stand alone.

The crabapple shakes wildly, its branches bending before the blast, more of its red fruits ripped away. Despite the elemental fury the bright blue flash of a jay's wing catches the eye, the bird clinging to a branch, pecking at the ripe fruit. An unusual sight, such shy and wary birds are normally only seen near the house in severe conditions when hunger overcomes their timidity.

It keeps coming back, out there all day among the branches or feasting on the ground. But there are actually two of them, working together, so busy they can't be eating them all. Flitting from the hedge to grab more, collecting those fallen in the road but returning so quickly it's obvious they're storing them, probably just under the hedge in the deep leaf litter. They become more bold, though still wary of movement in the house which launches them into flight.

These striking birds trigger memories of finding a jay wing feather in the garden, kept for years among childhood treasures. A blackbird is busy in the tree and picking up fallen crabapples on the ground, clearing the concrete where they've been squashed by wheels. Its sharp yellow beak is smeared with pulp. Below him two robins fight fiercely over one apple. Two brace of pheasants march up the field in the afternoon, probably from the shoot at Stone Acton, as if they know they'll stay alive by staying this side of the hill.

Sunburst

The virus years run together in memory, difficult to distinguish one month from another but the weather as a character is hard to pin down and still seems to be doing the wrong thing at the wrong time. April showers move to May but rain is soon forgotten through scorching July days and persistent grey cloud in August. Erratic weather patterns point to climate change and the lingering threat of hovers in the background.

If it didn't come from bats or even the poor crucified pangolin then surely we've brought it on ourselves for the disregard and abuse we've inflicted on nature. We're bound to face more pandemics because we've destroyed so much natural habitat for the wild ones, bringing animals into ever closer contact with humans. Disease is a natural consequence of what we've done to the Earth. Was this nature's attempt at payback? In this grossly over populated world we've created, the creature with the finest brain, us, is the only animal which destroys its own environment.

More likely the cause was human meddling and the debate will continue for years — until the next time. Perhaps we shall be left with a healthier population and even learn a better way of living. We can only hope to have learned from the crisis. The world and nature improved so much when all was quiet and we weren't impinging on it with our perpetual search for 'growth'. Some time there must be a limit when we learn to be satisfied.

Breakfast radio catches my attention, always drawn to any mention of research into MND. A professor at Sheffield University has led clinical trials into a new drug with unprecedented results showing it could slow the progress of the disease in certain patients, and even improve symptoms for some. The research isolated a gene which was found to cause MND. It includes an enzyme found in all living cells which acts as an antioxidant to reduce reactive oxygen species that would otherwise cause damage.

About two per cent of people with MND have this mutation which causes the enzyme itself to poison their cells. A spark of hope, but despite these small steps to date there is no cure for this cruel disease and only minimal treatments to ease the symptoms.

But 'back to normal' is the catchphrase and with travel restrictions lifted everyone is anxious to be out and about. Many still prefer to stay in the UK, which is excellent for business and Easter is the busiest for years, including the blackberry pickers, enjoying their return.

Despite the bitter cold and flurries of snow after Easter the trees display pale foliage, the delicate green which prompted me originally to paint the garden furniture with the well-named Spring Greenery. Beyond the paddock the copper beech leaves are a pale bronze when they first break from the bud. Evening stillness accentuates sounds, the bellowing of cattle in the valley calling their newborn calves, the cackling of pheasants and the haunting voices of wild geese, hoping to nest on the pond down the hill. The messy Canadas are discouraged from breeding as they deter other species from nesting. But the sound and the sight of them in flight is uncannily romantic.

Sparrows are everywhere, under the eaves, in the bay tree and the whitebeam and all the hedges. One balances on the wire with a feather in its beak obviously intent on building somewhere close. Unconcerned by the comings and goings of humans and dogs, as I scatter seed on the wall tops or the mounting block, at least one of them is already pecking eagerly as I walk away. The bubbling cry of a curlew makes me look sharply skywards to see it disappear away over the top field. The curlews have bred around here over the years but are increasingly scarce and it's reassuring to hear them. But a pair is nesting near Rushbury and I catch a glimpse of a grey wagtail, not seen here before. Spring suddenly breaks out in the May warmth, seemingly dead twigs appear with a green mantle and the unstoppable flood of life bursts through. Somewhere not far away a cuckoo is calling.

Chatting to guests at breakfast my eye catches the flick of a long tail and further investigation reveals a pied wagtail emerging from the neglected nest box. They've finally decided to give it a go. Outside I do my best to persuade them I'm not really watching but it's intriguing how they now approach along the gutter, with a quick dive inside to the chicks. They must surely find it more comfortable in there. The busy pair spend a lot of time running on the ground, rather than flying.

Driving over the hill from Stone Acton the sun glints on something in the fields and it takes a moment to realise it's newly bagged bales of silage glittering like giant black jewels. The wide aspect of Apedale's patchwork landscape is a vista of gold and green, bright yellow oilseed rape in full bloom below the dark ridge of Wenlock Edge, heavy with the leaves of early summer.

Shropshire is blessed with trees, many ancient oaks embellishing the county in hedgerows or standing alone in the corner of fields or left to stride in line across parkland. I often wonder how many drivers appreciate or even notice the avenue of oaks on the way into Craven Arms. Tiny oak seedlings pop up in the pasture, their young red leaves bright among the grass, not yet demolished by grazing mouths. The twenty year old oak Beck planted in the early years is growing well with acorns of its own and a tiny seedling in its

shadow. Freeing them is surprisingly difficult, the long tap root struck from the acorn already reaches far down into the soil. Potting a few is an act of faith, thinking of all those who long ago planted trees for future generations to enjoy, knowing they would never see them mature. More wild flowers are scattered across the bank field, a flush of cuckoo flower — or lady's smock — has sprouted almost over night along with ragged robin, which has never bloomed here before. It seems the cuckoo flower's delicate lilac heads are good in salads and taste like mustard or wasabi — part of the cabbage family. Their presence is a pleasing result of no longer using chemicals on the land.

Cowslips too have come up this time in abundance. We had only a few of this once endangered flower but now there are small nodding crowds, carefully avoided by the mower. But the Welsh poppies, once admired and brought here deliberately, need to be controlled. Their bright yellow flowers bring a splash of colour to the borders especially when paired with purple alliums. But they tend to take over, popping up where they're not wanted. Their seed heads are removed before they can spread.

Not having heard from Dan for several years, it's good to get an email from New England with possible dates for a stay. Especially pleased after Covid as you're never quite sure what might have happened. He arrives with his sister and is back again within two months, this time on a huge bike. He's travelled from his lair in the Alps all through the villages of France, enjoying the freedom of back roads. In the end he comes four times in the year, once with a

Swiss friend, both in full leathers on very large machines. They're staying overnight en route to the Isle of Man for the TT. On this visit I discover he's visited every US state bar one — because he can't get to Hawaii on a motorbike. The frequency of his visits makes me think he's getting tired of life in America and certainly on this trip he has an eye open for a suitable cottage. He says Shropshire is good for the soul.

At breakfast the subject of trains comes up and Dan reminds me of the railway geek he'd met on a previous stay who'd astonished fellow guests with his knowledge of the British railway system. Someone asked about trains north from Church Stretton and this guy was able to tell him all he needed to know in amazing detail.

A few guests are suffering from long Covid including the couple with an Italian Spinone who are part of a research project testing a specific drug. They're forced to cut short their stay and leave a day early because they're expecting it to arrive by special delivery.

An American woman, a potter, provides fascinating company for several days. In her late seventies from an island off the coast of Washington state, she finds around her all the basics for her work. Impressions of fir and other botanicals, twigs, leaves, items of flora, all pressed into damp clay before firing, then stained ready for decoration and glazing.

Meeting her train from the Lake District, we're quickly on the same wavelength. Staying in Windermere, she'd taken a nasty tumble in the road, which broke her nose — tripped on an errant piece of wire. Waiting with her meagre luggage she looks decidedly battered. But she seems captivated by the place, occupying herself with wandering the footpaths, taking in local flora and wild life. She particularly enjoys breakfast, especially the smoked bacon, sayingAmerican bacon was just not the same as our tasty back rashers. Her approach to life, believing with me that interaction with the natural world is vital for humans, as well as her political views, help soften my attitude to America, convincing me they are not all right wing bigots like Trump.

High summer and the heat beats down all day from a copper tinged sky, so oppressive and close it makes each movement an effort. The sinking sun is masked by a young oak tree making it cool enough to eat outside on the Kite terrace with friends from East Anglia. As the evening deepens, the heat drops to a pleasant warmth with the flow of wine and conversation. The last fading rays pale into dusk behind the Wilstone crags. The bats are out, flitting overhead in their search for insects in the fading light. We talk till it's dark and the moon peeps through as a face above the grass and to my wine-soaked eyes it seems to be dancing. Beyond the fence the horses are silhouetted against its light and thunder rumbles in the distance.

Outside at six am with Sprite the Gordon puppy, the sun above Wenlock Edge is a huge crimson ball of fire, directing a strong beam onto the cottage. Even in the freshness of morning the unaccustomed heat is almost unbearable as I wander across the fading grass while a rabbit slips away through the fence.

When the Kite guests come over for breakfast I make my usual enquiry about their welfare. Though smiling now, they had been shocked awake at sunrise by the screech of the fire alarm. They hadn't drawn the blind on the kitchen window and the sun's rays through the glass had struck the alarm in the ceiling. We spend several minutes discussing this phenomenon, surprised at the sheer power of the sun so early in the morning. It has never happened before and highlights the unaccustomed temperature. The blind will be in place tonight.

Lights move across the valley at bedtime, the combine harvester working in the dark to finish the field. In this scorching time the sun displays in splendour at both ends of the day, turning the reflecting windows to gold, while a ghostly moon lingers in the blue of morning.

The heat and the intense blue sky make us more aware of the increased noise of aircraft overhead. The sound of screaming jets and at night a sinister rumbling somewhere in the darkness remind us of what's happening far away in Ukraine.

At the height of the heat wave, as the dogs go out first thing, I'm startled by movement at my feet. There's something in the dogs' water bowl. With them safely out of the way it's revealed as a handsome little frog, whose large eyes peer anxiously upwards. Outside on the gravel, in the dank area by the hedge, I empty the water carefully. The unexpected guest clings for a moment to the edge of the bowl as if reluctant to leave its safety, before hopping away behind the log store.

It must've popped into the boiler room when the door was open, desperate to drink, scenting water inside, then hiding beneath the worktop before diving in. Strange the dogs made no attempt to grab it and surprising to find a frog because there's not much natural water on the farm. They appear from time to time along with the resident toads. Hedgehogs also need water but we've never seen any evidence of them here, only an empty skin in the field. The land maybe too high for them or perhaps they become victims of the increasing number of badgers. The garden supplies plenty of water for birds but it's

easy to forget the other creatures who need it. As I'm refilling the dish on the wall a wasp flies over my shoulder and settles on the rim to sip. I make a mental note to provide more bowls in suitable spots to cater for all needs.

Another morning with six for breakfast, as I'm serving two plates of Beck's Special, they're all clustered at the window. The focus of interest is sparrows again, all enjoying a bathing party on the wall. Their energetic splashing soon empties most of the water from the shallow bath.

A mother and daughter are staying and the subject of the heat wave turns the conversation to climate change. We've always had hot weather in the summer, that's when you expect it, but never at these temperatures and never causing such devastation in many areas of the world. Wickedly destructive fires and ruinous floods which leave millions dead or homeless. It struck an ominous chord when the daughter mentioned what a friend had said to her recently — that her grandchildren might never see snow; never experience the joy of building a snowman, the fun of a snowball fight or speeding downhill on a sledge.

The hottest day of the year brings the highest temperature on record, close on forty degrees, and a flush of butterflies. They fly close to me to feed on the escallonia bush, each tiny proboscis thrust into the heart of the small pink flowers. When the sky clouds over at last we stand outside to feel the relief of the first raindrops. Though we often curse it , there's a deep seated joy in rain, a tenuous delight to feel it cool on bare skin after weeks of heat as it draws out the scents of the earth. To the east a strangely vertical light creates a small stump of rainbow soon drowned by heavy clouds. After the rain we're treated to the best sunset this year, a broad band of crimson light dappling at its height into the grey cloud, breaking up into flecks. Much higher, another band of clear gold sky, with soft pink rays, spreads out from the sun now vanished behind Caradoc.

As the temperature drops September kicks off with wind and grey skies but little rain. The sunshine lingers and dark clouds threaten but come to nothing. Then the evening is shattered by a sudden explosion of torrential rain with thunder banging loud and sheets of lightning. A small camp site has appeared in the valley, two tents and a shepherd's hut and I wonder how they're faring in the downpour.

The long spell of drought has affected the mushroom crop. Rain after dry weather usually triggers a flush but this time only a meagre few appear on the hill.

A swallow flies around in panic on the landing, it probably swooped in via the open front door, left open on warm days to let the outside in. This one circles desperately till it settles panting on the floor. Gently enclosed in my hand and held through the open window it launches with a flourish into the air and is gone. Then it's a young blue tit, frantic till it's caught behind the curtain. It waits a while on the sill, recovering from shock, before flying away.

The faint sound of church bells drifts up from the village in a muffled lament for the late Queen. A shock for the nation as the news spins across the world, expected considering her age but it always seemed she would go on for ever. The bells are muffled each day until the funeral; but for one day only they ring out clear and joyful to mark the accession of a new king.

Early morning and the wires are thick with birds, swallows and house martins from the village. A huge gathering which I hope doesn't mean they're leaving soon. Second broods are still in the stables waiting to fledge but they can't be long now. The different species stick to their own kind on the line. When I attempt counting them, with a dog beside me, most fly off in a mighty flurry, circling for several minutes over and around the house, close to the windows, before settling again. My estimate is two hundred or more. The air is very still, the clouds unmoving, reminiscent of the balloon incident.

A last minute booking turns up a guy who says he's been before but the name doesn't ring a bell. But when he arrives I recognise him as Jim from two years ago and last year when he stayed down the road because we were full. He'd called in then to say hello, catching me at a busy moment. At the time I thought nothing of it but when he extends his stay from day to day it's obvious he's got problems. He seems very down in spirit and enquires about a longer stay, confiding that a deal about his London home in the Covid year had gone badly wrong.

Now he's homeless and out of a job but he has contacts and good friends, or so he says. After a week he decides to move on, leaving me to wonder about his future welfare. Such lost souls appear from time to time and it's impossible not to be concerned.

Much of the massive crop of Bramleys is still on the tree, burnished rosy ripe on the south facing side from long days of heat. The best ones are kept to store and several stay on the table outside waiting to be sliced and frozen. Some have been pecked, others lie on the ground and I puzzle over the culprit until I see a cheeky cock blackbird busy on the table, gobbling greedily, his eye on the window to make sure it's safe.

Blackbirds are a major presence. Two males joust constantly on the grass, up and down and through the border, careless of my presence. Or they're threatening each other on the Chaffinch roof ridge.

They may be young ones from last season, trying their metal, arguing over the last of the apples hidden under fallen leaves. Their behaviour in spring is a great time waster, watching them square up, one emerging from the hedge bottom, scurrying awkwardly to the shelter of the big round bush. Then a second cock approaches, sidling slightly. Like bookends, they stay a couple of feet apart, each mimicking the movements of the other. They shake their bodies slightly in an attempt at intimidation but don't face each other directly. When they appear to think they've done enough, both move forward together, back to the shelter of the hedge.

Perhaps this charade is necessary to maintain territorial rights. Sometimes the males are brown, like the hen birds, and these are bullied by the rest. Two females follow similar tactics marking their territory in the lane.

So many blackbirds about but song thrushes are less common, the richly melodious throstle with its plump speckled breast. A single bird appears sometimes, mainly in autumn. Increased land drainage and ploughing have reduced the number of earthworms and other crucial invertebrate prey on farmland. But a mistle thrush comes more often, usually when berries and crab apples are available, vying with its migrant relatives.

Large gatherings of kites circle in the evening above the hill near Stone Acton, an impressive sight not seen here before. As the days shorten they gather at dusk and roost together; mostly young birds, they are pleasing proof of successful breeding in the county.

Such groups boost the chances of finding food and animal carcasses are often big enough for several birds. Farmers have begun to complain about them, saying they displace the local buzzards, but this is unlikely given the buzzards are much heavier. They seem to co-exist happily together.

A young couple from Surrey book for five nights as part of a long delayed honeymoon. Their wedding was postponed twice because of Covid and the original plan for a couple of weeks somewhere warm and exotic has changed to a month spent exploring parts of the English countryside they've never seen. North Hill popped up on Google maps and they liked the sound of it. Obviously very much in love, they arrive for their second stop as the sun is beginning to drop behind Caradoc with that certain clarity in the sky which sharpens the perception. They stand together on the cottage steps in raptures at the view.

It is beautiful and I never tire of absorbing it but they appear to be totally captivated. I'm trying to tell them there's a bottle of fizz in the fridge and ask what they'd like for breakfast but the young wife keeps repeating: 'What a fantastic view, it's just what we hoped for.'

The plums have ripened early and there's a dish on the sideboard for breakfast but she can hardly sit still for watching the bird antics out in the crabapple tree. I have to name them for her and mention my thrill at spotting a tree creeper a few days before. The flash of white breast feathers made me look twice before I realised what it was, after not seeing one for a few years. The bird book is fetched so she knows what to look for. Their enthusiasm for my home is almost intoxicating as I give them the map ready for a day's walking.

In the early afternoon they're back for a rest but are off again in early evening to walk up and view the sunset from Wilstone Hill. The warm sun keeps me outdoors, lounging on the terrace with a glass of pink wine. The guests are clear on the hill, entwined into one figure, silhouetted against golden light. Before long they're back, leaning breathless at the gate, asking: 'May we join you for a while?'

With two more glasses fetched from the summer house, they sit down to admire a different aspect of the valley, the village appearing so near in the subtle light. We drink a toast, to them and the simple joys of Shropshire. 'You're so lucky to live here,' she says.

'Yes,' I answer slowly. 'I think I am, wouldn't want to be anywhere else.'

It strikes me then how I have become defined by it all. Such attachment to place is maybe not healthy, people often long to move on. But the girl is telling me how they plan to look for a rural home before thinking about a family. Her husband, more reticent, says quietly that their journey so far has already shown them what they really want for the future and that it should be possible in the new world of working from home. Love tinges everything of course but their delight seems to distill the essence of this place. Seeing their happiness makes me understand that despite everything what I want is here, where there is still time to stand and stare.

The swallows have gone. One day they're here, a winged host chattering their plans on the wires. The next the yard is silent. But the Wrekin remains, a brooding presence on the horizon. My roaming eyes come always back to it, tree darkened flanks and patches of light in the day, marked at night by the unwavering red warning on the summit. Whatever the world may do the hills remain. And in spring the swallows will return.

ACKNOWLEDGEMENTS

My thanks for all
the help, advice and infinite patience
offered at all stages of this work
by Fran Beck, Liz Beamish,
Doreen Beattie,
Lyndall Davey, Anita Marsland,
Nikki Rees-Jones and Anne Searle

and of course to
Howard Waters,
whose brilliant drawings have
brought this book to life

About the author

Frances Brand lives in Shropshire among the glorious countryside of the Marches where ravens can fly quickly over the border into Wales.

Frances is a former journalist who changed career when the internet was hitting regional papers; she began a new writing career and opened the doors of her hilltop home to paying guests.

Love of the landscape and the natural world in all its beauty and harshness forms the backdrop to her work, providing both inspiration and characters.

Latterly she was editor of a farming newspaper, working closely with farmers and others involved in agriculture. She knows at first hand the problems and vicissitudes of farming in the 21st-century in a claustrophobic rural society, as depicted in her first novel *Thorns*.

The elevated location of her small farm was also key to the theme of a second novel, *Adam's Ark*, which imagined the impact on the landscape and community of extreme flooding caused by global warming.

Milton Keynes UK
Ingram Content Group UK Ltd.
UKHW040319291024
450297UK00012B/62